RELIGION
What Is It?

RELIGION
What Is It?

William Calloley Tremmel
University of South Florida

HOLT, RINEHART AND WINSTON
New York   Chicago   San Francisco   Atlanta
Dallas   Montreal   Toronto   London   Sydney

Library of Congress Cataloging in Publication Data

Tremmel, William C
  Religion. What is it?

  Bibliography: p. 251
  Includes index.
  1. Religion. I. Title.
BL48.T7   200′.1   75-38955

ISBN 0-03-015551-7

Part of the poem "Vestigia" is reprinted by special permission of the Bliss Carman Trust, The University of New Brunswick, Canada.

6 7 8 9 0   065   9 8 7 6 5 4 3 2 1

This book is dedicated to my teacher
William Henry Bernhardt, who aimed
me in this direction, and to my wife
Opal Mitchell "Mike" Tremmel, who
has accompanied me the full distance.

Foreword

The aim of this book is to introduce students to the phenomenon of *Religion. What is it?* A number of basic questions are asked: (1) Why does man* do religion? What is it about him which makes him the "religious animal"? (2) What does he do when he does religion? What are the procedures and techniques employed in doing religion? (3) What are some of the central concepts which emerge and guide the beliefs and actions of religion? And (4) What human benefits are available in religious life and experience?

To get at the answers to such questions, I have employed basically a method of functional analysis, which I have found in my own introductory courses to have considerable explanatory power.

This functional procedure also lends itself to viewing religion not only from a single faith system but from the perspectives of any number of world religions. Such viewing fosters an appreciation of the richness of non-Western religions, and, at the same time, while distancing the student from his Western religious traditions, gives him a new perspective from which to view his own more familiar traditions.

The book is primarily a functional outline of the phenomenon of religion, with a number of pertinent examples for each topic ana-

* This author takes no responsibility for sexist usage allegedly inherent in the English language. When he uses the terms "man" and "he" to refer to *homo sapiens*, he does so simply in the ancient and accepted manner of speaking the *mother* tongue.

lyzed. Breadth and depth, beyond what is possible in a relatively brief and primarily introductory work such as this, can be achieved by using other readings, such as those recommended for each chapter in the bibliography at the end of the book. Also, the structure of the book is flexible enough for an instructor to concentrate time and attention on one part or another of the five parts into which the book is divided, if he so chooses.

A special effort has been made to write this book so that it can be read by students just beginning a serious study of religion and, at the same time, is more than just a cursory excursion through what is actually a highly disciplined subject matter, as well as a profoundly significant human phenomenon. The hope is that it will serve students as a comprehensible and meaningful guide to an understanding of what religion is, and was, and apparently always will be.

Tampa, Florida   WILLIAM CALLOLEY TREMMEL
December 1975

Contents

x   CONTENTS

Program

This book is concerned with the not so simple question, What is religion? and attempts to answer this question by presenting a functional description of why men do religion, what they do when they do religion, what benefits they get from doing it, and what happens to them when they do it.

We shall define religion functionally, that is, according to the proper service it performs in the life and self-fulfillment of man. This is different from attempting to define religion within the scope of one of the modern sciences of human behavior (anthropology, sociology, psychology), although each of these disciplines will be useful to us in determining how religion functions. Also, a functional definition of religion steps away from giving a sectarian definition of religion in which one specific religion is claimed to be the "true religion," a procedure that inevitably identifies all other religions as not true religions, and, therefore, actually not religions at all. Particularly those of us who are Westerners (Jews, Christians, Muslims), by taking a functional approach, can avoid the temptation of defining religion as something God is doing, rather than something man is doing, and thus avoid the trap of religious provincialism. If we were, for example, to take—as we often do—a Christian posture and begin by defining religion as the activity of God in his creation of the world and mankind, and the holy history of Israel, and the soteriology of Christ's life, ministry, death, and resurrection, we would exclude from serious consideration the religious life of a vast number of people who are not Christians, but who consider themselves to be quite religious. Even if we became more ecumenical and acknowledge as religion, albeit religion in error, all those other systems that endorse a God who is providentially and actively concerned with seeing men attain a heavenly future and avoid perdition, we would extend the class of religion, but not much. Jews and Muslims would join the ranks of religious men, but Hindus of the Jnana Marga variety, Theravada Buddhists, Zen Buddhists, Taoists, most primitives, and many others would still be excluded. To define religion God-centeredly or theocentrically amounts to defining it in terms of a Western type (theistic/personalistic) God, which is not what God is to a vast number of people, both now and in the past. Theocentric definitions are too provincial for the phenomenon of religion. An investigation of religion as a human phenomenon must endorse equally the beliefs, behaviors, and experience of all religious people, not just some religious people.

A functional approach appears to be a better option. This approach makes it possible to deal with all religions (the whole phenomenon of religion) because it deals not with what a particular God is doing in a special religion, but with what men in all religions are doing for themselves as they behave in ways called religious. (Also, as we shall see, the anthropocentric approach makes accommodations for all sorts of God concepts.)

This is the direction we shall take in an attempt to understand religion as a human phenomenon. We shall do this by performing an exposition of the several parts of the following proposition:

I. RELIGION IS THE WAY A PERSON (OR GROUP OF PERSONS) BEHAVES IN AN EFFORT TO DEAL ADEQUATELY WITH THOSE ASPECTS OF HUMAN EXISTENCE WHICH ARE HORRENDOUS AND NONMANIPULABLE;

II. DOING SO BY THE EMPLOYMENT OF VARIOUS INTELLECTUAL, RITUAL, AND MORAL TECHNIQUES;

III. AND DOING SO FROM THE CONVICTION THAT THERE IS AT THE CENTER OF HUMAN EXPERIENCE, AND EVEN OF ALL LIFE, A BEING OR PROCESS (A DIVINE REALITY) IN WHICH AND THROUGH WHICH A PERSON (OR COMMUNITY OF PERSONS) CAN TRANSCEND THE LIFE-NEGATING TRAUMAS OF HUMAN EXISTENCE, CAN OVERCOME THE SENSE OF FINITUDE.

IV. WITH ALL THIS, RELIGION STILL TURNS OUT TO BE NOT SIMPLY A METHOD OF DEALING WITH RELIGIOUS PROBLEMS, BUT IS ITSELF AN EXPERIENCE OF GREAT SATISFACTION AND IMMENSE PERSONAL WORTH. RELIGION IS NOT ONLY SOMETHING FOR PEOPLE (FUNCTIONAL), BUT IS SOMETHING TO PEOPLE (AN EXPERIENCE, EVEN AN ECSTASY).[1]

---

[1] Parts I and II of this proposition are reformulations of the functional definition of religion given by William H. Bernhardt in his *Functional Philosophy of Religion,* where he states that "religious behavior is a complex form of individual and group behavior whereby persons are prepared intellectually and emotionally to meet the nonmanipulable aspects of existence positively by means of a reinterpretation of the total situation and with the use of various techniques." (Denver: Criterion Press, © 1958, p. 157).

part 1

speculations on the origins of religion

And God stepped out on space
And he looked around and said:
I'm lonely—
I'll make me a man.

James Weldon Johnson

one

Origins of Religion: Primitive

Religion is as old as man. Possibly as long ago as a half million years, it was being practiced by Paleolithic men in the burial of the dead, in fertility rites, and in hunting magic. Twenty-five thousand years ago in Europe those marvelously formed humans, now called Cro-Magnon, were not only performing funeral ceremonies, and fertility rites, and hunting magic but were executing with marvelous skill religious murals on the walls and ceilings of their caves, as well as molding and carving religious figures in clay and bone. Ten thousand years ago men were exerting enormous effort to hew out tombs in large stones, and to erect menhirs and dolmens and cromlechs,[1] all of which undoubtedly had religious importance for the persons involved. With the rise of the civilizations in Egypt, Mesopotamia, Iran, India, and China, religion continued apace as a central concern of mankind. And in spite of woeful cries to the contrary, religion is alive and well in the world today. It is safe to say that where you find humans, you will find religion, both now and always.

With so much religion everywhere, one might expect that the question "What is religion?" would be easy to answer. And in one sense it is easy to answer. Indeed, from the number of answers given, one might suspect *too* easy, which means, in fact, not easy at

---

[1] *Menhir:* single, tall upright stone; *dolmen:* two or more upright stones set apart and capped by a horizontal slab of stone; *cromlech:* prehistoric monuments consisting of monoliths encircling a mound.

all. In sampling some of the answers, we find the brilliant modern philosopher Alfred North Whitehead declaring religion to be "what an individual does with his own solitariness." The equally brilliant eighteenth-century philosopher Immanuel Kant tells us that it is "the recognition of our duties as divine commands." The innovative German theologian Friedrich Schleiermacher, a generation after Kant, discerns "the common element of religion," to be "the consciousness of ourselves as absolutely dependent." The late Paul Tillich, among the very best of modern theologians, identifies religion as man's Ultimate Concern. Someone, perhaps not so intellectually formidable but exercising an equal right to answer the question, has said that religion ain't doing nobody no harm, leastwise not intentionally, and anyway not very often. As we know, multitudes claim that religion is surrendering in faith to the Lord Jesus Christ, and multitudes more claim it is the surrender of ego to the oblivion of Nirvana. This book too, here and now, will give a succinct answer to the question of religion, and declare it to be *Man's Conquest of Finitude*. But the obvious thing about these several answers is that they all need tremendous amounts of "unpacking." Whatever is wrapped up in these parcels is only partly apparent from the shape of the package. About any one of them, much more needs to be revealed. We must look for a description and explanation considerably more detailed than can be accomplished in any capsule comment, no matter how insightful it might be. To do this we have, from the broad field of contemporary religious studies, a number of options: (1) We can try to answer the question, What is religion? by discovering how it first arose in the life of prehistoric man. (2) We can look for the answer in the nature of man. What is it about the psyche of man that makes him the religious animal? (3) We can try to answer the question by seeing it as an experience "inflicted" on man from an outside source—from a "God out there." (4) We can try to answer the question by observing how it actually functions in the life of man.

It is obvious that the first three options (primitive origins, psychic origins, divine origins) are similar in that they all look for the answers genetically. Religion is to be understood through its origins. Option number four is different. Here the effort is to explain religion not in terms of its origins but in terms of how it operates in the lives of men, that is, in terms of human needs (both emotional and intellectual) and the answers given in religion to satisfy those needs. This book will pursue the last option and try to define religion according to what it does, not simply how it begins, but the valuable data and insights of the other options will not be excluded. Indeed, the data of origins are crucial to any real grasp of function. So, we shall proceed immediately in this introduction to consider some of the pertinent and interesting data available from the studies that have been made about the genesis of religion.

PRIMITIVE ORIGINS[2]

In getting at the question, What is religion? a number of anthropologists and sociologists began, in the second half of the nineteenth century, to zero in on the religion of primitive people. They studied both the artifacts of prehistoric men and the societies of living primitives. A number of observations were made and theories proposed which, although sometimes rejected by later students and almost always revised by them, continue to be important ideas in the study of religion.

Animism   First is the idea that religion somehow "personalizes" the great forces of nature and endows ordinary things with spiritual qualities. Religion sacralizes the secular. F. Max Müller,[3] sometimes called the father of the science of religion, proposed that religion originated when primitive men mistook natural objects and events as "acting subjects," and then proceeded to give these subjects personal names. For example, prehistoric man might look upon the wind as alive, even as men were alive, and sometimes the wind was "happy" and sometimes it was "angry," even as men were happy and angry. The wind had human characteristics. Being like a human, the wind had a name, or perhaps several names. When

[2] The term "primitive" is used in this book not in a pejorative sense. Primitive religions are not "bad religions" or even wrongheaded religions. They are, rather, earlier religions, primordial religions. They are the religions of preliterate people and differ from "high" religions (which we shall subsequently call consummate religions) only in style, not in function. In other words, primitive or primordial religions do for preliterate people just what high, or advanced, or consummate religions do for literate people, and often much more directly and effectively.

[3] F. Max Müller, *Essays in Comparative Mythology*, 1856.

happy, its name was, perhaps, "The Tree Whistler." When angry its name was, perhaps, "The Big Howler." Müller contended that religion began when men rationalized the forces of nature and gave those forces feelings, emotions, passions, thoughts, and names. Men still sometimes humanize and personalize nonhuman things and events. No man with a tiller of his own ever thinks of his boat as "it" nor doubts that "she" is as emotional and capricious and self-willed as any real woman ever was. Annually we characterize the passing year as an old man, and the new year as a diapered infant. The biological environment in springtime is a mother. And "fog comes in on little cat feet" (Carl Sandburg). Whether or not Müller was right that religion actually originated from prehistoric man's endowing natural phenomena with human characteristics and names does not alter the fact that religious people even yet often "rationalize" the world and endow its processes with living spiritual agents—with Gods and/or God.

Another anthropologist, Sir Edward B. Tylor,[4] also believed that religion began when man erroneously read manlikeness into nature. Tylor believed that this came about when prehistoric man first began to rationalize his experience of life and death, and his experience of persons appearing in his dreams and visions. Primitive man came to realize that there was a difference between physical things and spiritual things—between bodies and souls. There was obviously something in living things which went out of them when they died. That something was not like a stick or a stone, which could be touched and held, but was like smoke or breath. When that something, that breath, that soul, departed the body permanently, the body never lived again. But that something might leave the body only temporarily, as when it went adventuring in dreams but was back in the morning. Furthermore, even when the soul departed the body permanently only the body was dead, not the soul, as was evident in the fact that sometimes the souls of the dead came back in dreams and visions. They could be seen and heard, and they looked like, or almost like, the body they formerly inhabited. They were ethereal duplicates—ghosts.

Tylor correctly observed that once men grasped the idea that

---

[4] Edward B. Tylor, *Religion in Primitive Culture* (New York: Harper & Row, 1958; first published, 1871).

human life was composed of two parts (physical and spiritual), it was but a short step to spiritualizing not only human life but all life, and even as Müller had contended, all sorts of nonliving things. The animation seen in humans and nonhumans was caused by souls. The world was full of souls—full of Gods.

This widespread primitive belief that all sorts of inanimate objects as well as living creatures have souls, or spirits, is called animism (from *anima:* breath or soul). Animism is by many scholars no longer held to be the earliest form of religion, the genesis of religion, as Tylor thought; but the fact remains that religion, old and new, primitive and modern, has not discarded the notion that humans are composite beings, both physical and spiritual, and that the soul animates and survives, and that, if not always in nature itself, there is behind nature, causing and animating it, something spiritual called by such names as Brahman or Heaven or Tao or God.

Mana   In both Müller's and Tylor's contentions, religion began when primitive men "rationalized" some of their experiences. It was a "logical inference" drawn from experiences. But other students of primitive anthropology believe that religion came before theology, before rational explanation. It was prelogical. Religion predated logical inferences and arose originally simply as the emotions of awe and fear *felt* by prehistoric man as he confronted "the powers" in his world. Such men did not live in a "universe," in a world where order has been discerned in, or imposed upon, nature. They lived in a world where "out there" were wildness and destruction and chaos and perpetual danger. They lived in a world where everything devoured everything else—where only the fit survived, and even the fit eventually fell to be devoured by scavengers and rot. They lived amid powers, and they responded to the powers, propitiating, avoiding, using those powers in any way they possibly, pragmatically could.

In 1891 Bishop Codrington[5] reacted against the idea that religion had begun in logical speculations about the character of man and nature. From Codrington's encounter with the religious expres-

---

[5] R. H. Codrington, *The Melanesians* (New York: Dover, 1972; first published, 1891).

sions of living primitives—people of the Melanesian Archipelago—
he concluded that religion originated prelogically in man's response
to the fact of impersonal power in his world. The Melanesians had a
word for this power—mana.[6] *Mana,* Codrington found, was a word
for the power or the powers that made things special: the power in
hurricanes and storms, in charismatic men, in seductive women, in
great artists and warriors, in medicine men and prophets—in all
marvelous and awesome things. Mana was not a living spirit, was
not good or bad, was not friendly or unfriendly. It was just power—
sheer, special power. Codrington observed that mana was not something that men "concluded" about nature, but something they
simply encountered in special circumstances.

Concurring with Codrington, Professor R. R. Marett, in 1900,
published a widely read and influential article entitled, "Preanimistic Religion." In that article he forcefully contended that religion
predated rational speculations about man and nature. It began in
the sense of awe felt by early man as he experienced the impersonal
powers that he encountered everywhere in his world—those powers
causing things to be, sometimes intriguing, sometimes terrifying,
usually dangerous, often desirable, and always awesome. Not in-
ferred souls or assigned names, but experienced power, Marett held
(as did Codrington), was the genesis of religion.

Whether or not mana was the genesis of religion and the "father" of the Gods may be argued (as some ethnologists are inclined
to do), but the fact is that mana, differently named and extremely
theologized, remains a central dynamic[7] of religion. When, Paul
Tillich speaks of the Power of Being, or Being Itself, or the Ground
of Being, and a Hindu philosopher speaks of Brahman, one might
seriously ask, "How, except in sophistication, does their God behind
the Gods differ from mana?"

The Prelogical Character   It is important to take special notice
of the prelogical, prerational aspect of religious phenomena. Man
acts before he thinks. He is alive before he is rational. He is, as the
existentialists (Sartre) tells us, in existence before his essence (his
humanness) is accomplished. Thinking and reasoning come after

---

[6] Later it was observed that primitive people all around the world had their
own equivalent terms for such power.

[7] Manaism is also called dynamism.

experience or, at least, concurrent with experience—and this is so not only where individual humans are concerned, but it must have been so in the emergence of mankind. Let us enter a fictitious time machine for a few moments and be transported back in time a half-million years or so, to a primeval forest somewhere on the Continent of Europe, perhaps in what is now called France or Spain. We see a man or near man, fleeing from some enemy. Our man stumbles. Where he falls there is, quite by accident, a broken tree branch of hand-size diameter and about three feet long. He seizes it, turns and bashes in the head of his attacker. Having slain his enemy, he looks at the club and thinks "That's a good thing for bashing heads."

This simple little fictitious account makes a fundamental point, not only about the genesis of weaponry, but about the genesis of religion. Observe: the man did not think to himself, "That tree branch over there will make a good weapon," and then picked it up and used it. He picked it up first, used it, and then thought about it. He was in the condition of weaponry, before he comprehended weaponry.

On another day, with his trusty club in hand, our man went forth to bash a bear for dinner, or anything else he could find. He guessed that the bear might be in the rocks where the bear caves were. The rocks were beyond the swamp. He did not like the swamp. It was full of powers—full of frightening and dangerous "things." Not things like bears or wolves, but things you could not really see. Things that suddenly opened their mouths and sucked you in. Things that got inside you and made fire in your gut; things weird, demonic, unseen. He would prefer to avoid the swamp. But it was a long way around the swamp, and only a little way through it. As he hesitated, he observed that he had come to the edge of the swamp at a point he had never been before, at a place where there was a most fantastic tree, very old, very gnarled and wind-bent, but very strong, very powerful, full of mightiness. He sensed that it was a *special tree*. A tree afraid of nothing. A tree stronger than the swamp things. He did not think such things exactly; he felt them along his spine. Coming closer to the tree he saw a place on the trunk where the bark had been rubbed smooth by passing animals, perhaps. He touched the smooth place. It was good to touch, to slide his hand over. Somehow it made him feel strong—like the tree. After a short time spent gazing at the tree and touching it, he continued his journey through the swamp to the other side, without mishap, unassailed by the things. And on the other side he had good luck. He did not even have to fight a bear. He found and bashed a ram instead. After that he crossed the swamp many times, but always first he went to the place of The Tree and touched the smooth spot. At first he did not think of why he sought The Tree, he just did so. Later, maybe, he started to think about it, but only after The Tree had, in fact, become a thing of "religion," and his performance a "religious act."

Our primitive man, or near man, was in the "condition of religion" (as well as the "condition of weaponry") before he ever comprehended it, before he rationalized it. Primitive people *happened* into religion before they ever happened to understand it. Primordial man was terrified by lightning, stricken with diseases, and devastated by death before he began to comprehend these extraordinary powers and began to give them names and explanations, and to devise ways to deal with them in some hopeful, spiritual fashion. Later we shall begin to doubt the implication here that religious behavior occurs before religious thinking, but at the moment we will let it stand.

Magic   One method that primitive man used (and uses) to deal with "the powers" in his world is called magic. Magic is the direct control of nature by the employment of supernatural/extranatural power. It is ubiquitous in primitive religion and not unknown in "civilized" religions, even the religions of modern, scientific cultures. There is obviously some kind of affinity between magic and religion, so it seems reasonable to ask how they are alike and different, and how they are related to each other.

The distinguished Scottish classicist and anthropologist Sir James George Frazer (1854–1941) who, in his multivolumed work, *The Golden Bough,* did pioneering work on the nature of magic and religion, concluded that magic (being the simpler form) was the forerunner of religion. The basic difference between magic and religion, he observed, was in the attitude and expectation of the persons using each. In magic it was believed and expected that desired results could be accomplished by a direct manipulation of the environment through the direct employment of supernatural or extranatural techniques. Men, (usually special men—magicians or shamans) who were privy to the supernatural techniques for controlling the powers of nature, could control and/or coerce those powers to accomplish desired human ends. Thus, Frazer (and Tylor before him) held that magic was for primitive man a form of science. Like science, magic understood the laws governing nature and directly manipulated those laws for human benefit. This, Frazer held, was different from religion. Religion did not attempt directly to control the powers of nature; rather, it made an appeal to those powers or, more correctly, to the supernatural agents that controlled those powers. Frazer believed that religion developed when primitive men (1) grew dissatisfied with the accomplishments of magic, and (2) when they advanced in their thinking to the point where they began to conceive of their world animistically, as being dominated by spirits in nature (animism) and, to some extent, by the souls of departed humans (ancestors). They began to perform rites intended to propitiate the Gods, not coerce them. They began to behave in ways that amounted to worship and genuine religion. Magic continued, but religion moved to center-stage. It became the dominant actor in the drama of life and death in a menacing world.

Frazer's theories that magic preceded religion and that it was the primitive man's substitute for science and technology were seriously challenged by other students of primitive life. It was pointed out that there was no evidence that magic came first, or that religion evolved when magic failed. Primitive people did both magic and religion, and they did so often in the same magico-religious rite. The primitives often propitiated and coerced in the same breath, so to speak. Indeed, Wilhelm Schmidt tried to reverse Frazer's contention and argued that the religion of primitive men began in the experience and worship of a high God, and that only later did their religion devolve into the religious beliefs and practices called animism, ancestor worship, and magic. But Schmidt's position, although evidence supported his high God theory in primitive religion, has been generally less acceptable than Frazer's. Probably the most reasonable position to take for the moment is that both magic and religion should be viewed as two associated ways in which primitive men saw themselves and their world and tried to cope.

That magic was primitive man's science was also challenged. Bronislaw Malinowski, reporting on the religion of the Trobriand Islanders, made a special point of the fact that Trobrianders employed both magic and natural technology (science) in their programs for food getting and health, and that they never mistook the one for the other. When it was time to build a canoe for deep-sea fishing, or to plant a garden, or to medicate for a simple ailment, they did so "scientifically," that is, by rules and procedures based on natural law and technological know-how. When, however, they wanted to infuse their boats and farm plots with extranatural powers, or deal with serious illnesses, they suspended their technology for the performance of magic. Protection from bad storms at sea, from droughts and insect infestations, and from deadly maladies (none of which were understood or directly controllable by their normal technology) demanded different, more potent forms of belief and action. Those beliefs and actions were not scientific (dealing with natural laws), but supernaturalistic (dealing with the supernatural powers in and behind nature). Science and technology dealt with natural law; for example, boat design and structure, seed planting and cultivation, simple medical remedies. Magic dealt with the supernatural. One was not the other, and Malinowski's Trobrianders never mistook the one for the other, or used the one for the other, or identified the one with the other.

Frazer's distinction between magic and religion as direct and indirect methods of effecting change in the life and world of man invites further consideration. He points out that magic was used to alter natural situations by the direct, man-manipulated employment of special "lawful" powers. In this it has a real affinity with science and technology. In science the laws are viewed as natural, in magic as supernatural, but in both cases *man* is the direct agent controlling the change. Religion operates indirectly, appealing to the gods to change things, which, unlike in magic and scientific technology, men cannot change by their own manipulation of law and power.

Observe, however, that the important "human" thing occurring here is not some nice distinction between methodologies but the fact that desired changes are being made, or are believed to be being made. This is the real and basic affinity between magic and religion. Things that cannot be altered naturally can be altered supernaturally. Rather than trying to distinguish between magic and religion as separate systems somehow intimately interrelated, or to do so on some kind of scientific ground, we should perhaps consider magic and religion from a metatechnological viewpoint. *Metatechnology*[8] is a term that stands for all human attempts to

8 See William Henry Bernhardt, *A Functional Philosophy of Religion* (Denver: Criterion Press, 1958), p. 42.

introduce extranatural or supernatural powers into natural processes. Metatechnology is not science or even technology, but the attempt to go beyond (meta-) science and technology to employ, directly or indirectly, higher power. Setting aside the notion that magic is one thing and religion another, we here propose that religion is a complex form of human behavior in which there is metatechnology, which is sometimes employed directly, as in magic and exorcism, and sometimes indirectly, as in praying for divine intervention. For this second form of metatechnology we shall employ the term *rogation*, from the Latin word *rogare*, which means "to beseech." We shall return to the subject of metatechnology later. For now we shall make only one more observation about the question of magic and religion. The real difference between them is to be seen not in the fact that they are separate systems but in the fact that magic is limited to effecting environmental changes (is completely metatechnological), whereas religion is not so limited. Religion not only beseeches to get things changed, but exults and glories in what is. It is also doxological—giving praise to God. Religion not only tries to control the world and change external circumstances but also tries to heal the inner man, to unify the community, to redeem the times, and to be thankful.

In our attempt at a succinct definition of religion we proposed that religion is a man's conquest of finitude. We will now further propose that this conquest is accomplished by the dual-polar modes of exorcism and ecstasy. Religion is a form of human behavior in which persons (1) exorcise the demonic elements of life (its finitudes) on the one hand and (2) experience the divine elements of life (the transcendence of finitude) on the other hand. Metatechnology, including magic, sorcery, witchcraft, and all forms of miraculous intervention in natural process, belong to the exorcistic pole, whereas such things as soul healing, spiritual unity, redemption, worship, mystical awareness, belong to the ecstatic pole.

two

Other Origins

SOCIOLOGICAL ORIGINS

Much of what we have said so far, especially with reference to religion as emerging from man's reading of his own emotions into nature (Müller), or from misreading dream persons as being disembodied souls (Tylor), or from magic as a technique for coercing nature (Frazer), seems to base religion in primitive man's faulty thinking. Religion arose out of human illusion. But the eminent sociologist Émile Durkheim (1858–1917) flatly rejects such a notion. In his impressive work entitled *The Elementary Forms of Religious Life*, he declares:

> Our entire study rests upon this postulate that the unanimous sentiment of the believers of all time [that there is an order of reality different from the order of reality commonly experienced in ordinary things] cannot be purely illusory . . . these religious beliefs rest upon a specific experience whose demonstrative value is, in one sense, not one bit inferior to that of scientific experiments, though different from them.[1]

The basis for religion, according to Durkheim, was society. Religious beliefs and practices had their origins in social forces. It was society itself that first aroused the experience of divinity in the minds of its individual members. From the forces of society in

[1] Émile Durkheim, *The Elementary Forms of Religious Life* (London: Allen and Unwin, 1957), p. 417.

controlling its individual members arose the notion of superior power and inversely the notion of personal dependence. The moral authority of society over its members engendered a sense of sacred demand controlling each individual life. Society dominated individual members in spiritual ways effecting attitudes of reverence and submission and veneration. It was to the society that one must turn to find nurture and self-meaning. And all of this led to the feeling that there were forces and "active causes from which [man] gets the characteristic attributes of his nature, and which, as benevolent powers, assist him, protect him, and assure him a privileged fate."[2]

Society established religious attitudes, sentiments, and concepts which in turn rewarded society by effecting cohesiveness in the system and by giving sustenance and courage to society's human participants. It was religion that sacralized certain structures within the sociocultural system and thus endowed that system with cohesiveness and spiritual power. It was religion that constrained people and curbed antisocial passions, often with the threat of divine punishment. On the other hand, it was religion that assisted individual persons in finding themselves and fulfilling themselves within the confines, protection, warmth, and nurture of an essential communal life.

There is no doubt that society is basic to human life. Humans cannot begin to exist or survive, or even become "human," as George Mead has made so emphatically evident, except in a structure of sociality. There is, also, no doubt that religion is affected by (in Durkheim's terms, produced by), and affects, the social structure. Society informs religion. The religious expression is always connected with the language, science, and mores of the social culture where it resides. On the other hand, religion sanctifies society. It idealizes the social system and makes it, or some important part of it, more than ordinary, makes it sacred.

With Durkheim one views religion as a sociogenetic phenomenon—a phenomenon produced by society or social forces—which is different from seeing it as arising in animism or manaism or magic. This perspective does not dispense with the insights we have observed in the work of the anthropologists of religion. It simply adds to them, and clues us to the possibility of viewing religion from still other perspectives for other possible insights.

[2] Ibid., p. 212.

PSYCHOGENETIC ORIGINS

One fruitful perspective is the view of religion which sees it as a psychogenetic phenomenon. William James (1842–1910), a pioneer thinker in the field of modern psychology of religion, held that all of our knowledge of ourselves and our world begins in our own experience, in consciousness. Sigmund Freud (1856–1939), of psychoanalytic fame, insisted that we are what we have experienced. And Edmund Husserl (1859–1938) created a method of philosophical analysis called Phenomenology which purports to lay bare the very essence of experience—our unadulterated consciousness. In each case—in James' radical empiricism, Freud's psychoanalyzed personality, and Husserl's transcendental ego (i.e., the source of consciousness)—religion appeared as a primary datum.

James found religion to be a psychically healthy response which loosened the "strenuous mood" in man and set him on the highroad to dynamic, unconquerable, spiritual living. James informed us that religion was a primary value in man's inner nature, for it released "every sort of energy and endurance, of courage and capacity for handling life's evils."[3] Indeed, James argued that if there were no other grounds for believing in God, "Man would postulate one simply as a pretext for living hard, and getting out of existence its keenest possibilities of zest."[4] In the conclusions of his touchstone work entitled *The Varieties of Religious Experience*, James included these desirable characteristics as among the primary characteristics of religious life:

> . . . prayer or inner communion is a process wherein work is really done, and spiritual energy flows in and produces effects, psychological or material, within the phenomenal world . . .
> A new zest which adds itself as a gift of life, and takes the form either of lyrical enchantment or of appeal to earnestness and heroism . . .
> An assurance of safety and a temper of peace, and, in relation to others, a preponderance of loving affection.[5]

[3] William James, "The Moral Philosopher and the Moral Life," *Essays in Pragmatism*, ed. Alburey Castell (New York: Hafner, 1951), p. 86.
[4] Ibid.
[5] William James, *Varieties of Religious Experience* (New York: Random House, Modern Library, 1961; first published in 1902), p. 475.

Freud, like James, believed that religion was an effective element in man's psychical life, but unlike James, Freud saw it as anything but healthy and desirable. Religion, Freud held, was a sign of man's inability to face life in any genuine fashion. Religion was the product of man's emotional immaturity. It was a surrogate for facing reality. It was the way that adults, by employing disguised childhood mechanisms, sought to deal with the threatening conditions of their everyday living. Freud wanted people to "grow up" and get over the need for religion: which was, in its basic psychic origins, simply "wish fulfillment."

Concerning religion, Freud addressed himself primarily to the religions of the West, especially Judaism and Christianity, and he saw them as unfortunate answers to immature man's psychotic needs. He said:

> . . . a store of ideas is created, both from man's need to make his helplessness tolerable and built up from the material of memories of the helplessness of his own childhood and the childhood of the human race. . . . Everything that happens in this world is an expression of the intentions of an intelligence superior to us, which in the end, though its ways and byways are difficult to follow, orders everything for the best. . . . Over each of us there watches a benevolent Providence which is only seemingly stern. . . . Death itself is not extinction, is not a return to inorganic lifelessness, but the beginning of a new kind of existence. . . . In the end all good is rewarded and all evil punished, if not actually in this form of life then in the later existences that begin after death. In this way all the terrors, the sufferings and the hardships of life are destined to be obliterated. . . .
>
> These, which are given out as teachings, are not precipitates of experience or end-results of thinking: they are illusions, fulfillments of the oldest, strongest and most urgent wishes of mankind.[6]

James' ambition was to have men have religion, Freud's was to have them get over it. In both cases they saw religion as arising out of the psychic needs of man as man.

Both James and Freud made judgments about the psychogenetic origins of religion. Husserl would have them, and us, refrain from such judgments. The question in phenomenology is not, "Is

[6] Sigmund Freud, *The Future of an Illusion* (Garden City, N.Y.: Doubleday, Anchor Books, 1964), pp. 25–27, 47. For a carefully considered answer to Freud see Charles Hartshorne and William Reece, *Philosophers Speak of God* (Chicago: University of Chicago Press, 1963, © 1953), pp. 478–486.

the religious experience good or bad, healthy or psychotic, or even is it about anything 'real', but simply, what is it for anything to be an instance of religion?" When one pursues religion in this fashion, it becomes increasingly obvious that when the consciousness is laid bare (either by phenomenological analysis or by mystical contemplation) it is found that religion is simply there—an innate part of human nature. For example, as an instance of religion we can look at the religious experience called "salvation." Peter Kostenbaum[7] points out phenomenologically that the instance of salvation is situated within the condition of man's fundamental consciousness. Salvation is an experience of anticipation pointing beyond ordinary human consciousness. "Man's condition is to reach for some perfection, some otherness, some solution to this yearning, that leads him to a region beyond his personal ago."[8] The center of his being reaches outward to some external reality. His nature is to transcend himself. The ultimate symbol for such outreach is the word God. So, in Jean-Paul Sartre's apt phrase, "Man's project is God." This outreach, this passion to transcend, this God project, this religiousness, is not because it is good for him (James) or bad for him (Freud), but because it is his nature, his condition, his consciousness.

Another illustration of religion as the condition of human consciousness can be seen in the phenomenological discovery of the inner core of consciousness, or as Husserl called it, The Transcendental Ego. This Ego is the consciousness of consciousness: our center, our soul, which experiences our experiences. As expressed in mysticism (which is pure phenomenological experience) the soul "has close affinity and may be considered as even identical with the Transcendental Realm or the totality of Being."[9] Which is to say, also, that human consciousness possesses a direct consciousness that behind all "things" there is essential "is-ness"—that is, a necessary ground of being; that is, God.

However accurate are the judgments of James and Freud, or however adequate the method of phenomenological analysis, the

[7] See Peter Kostenbaum, "Religion in the Tradition of Phenomenology," *Religion in Philosophical and Cultural Perspective*, ed. J. C. Feaver and W. Horsz (New York: Van Nostrand Reinhold, 1967), pp. 174–214.

[8] Ibid., p. 181.

[9] Ibid., p. 191.

insight of importance remains: religion is based in and arises from the psychic nature of man. Man is by nature the religious animal—the only religious animal.

THEOCENTRIC ORIGINS

Thus far we have noted theories on the origin of religion which are anthropocentric, that is, arising out of human origins. But one might shift to the opposite pole and consider religion as a god-imposed phenomenon. Religion begins not with man but with God.

In 1898 Andrew Lang published a book, *The Making of Religion*, which, he believed, "exhibits religion as probably beginning in some kind of Theism, which is then superseded, in some degree, or even corrupted, by Animism in all its varieties."[10]

Wilhelm Schmidt also proposed, in 1912, that the most primitive of contemporary people (for example, the Pygmies of Africa) have beliefs and practices that indicate that man's earliest form of religious expression was the worship of a high being—an original monotheism. Today, the respected history of religion scholar, Mircea Eliade, holds that the most primitive of people do have a belief in a supreme being, but that this high God does not play an important role in the religious life of the people who affirm it.

Such observations may suggest to us not only that the idea of God is very old in the history of man, but that it may be that God and not man is the genesis of religion—that is, religion is an experience "inflicted" on man from an outside source—from a God "out there."

One can speculate that this imposition of religion from without is primarily a rational affair, or that it is primarily an existential encounter. The French philosopher René Descartes (1596–1650) proposed the former; the German theologian Rudolph Otto (1869–1936), the latter.

In his "Third Meditation," Descartes made an argument on the epistemological grounds that our knowledge of God's existence is innate, given in the human mind. The idea of God could not be in our minds if God had not put it there. Descartes made this claim by

[10] Andrew Lang's 1898 edition was reprinted by AMS Press, New York, in 1968.

reaffirming an old Aristotelian axiom that a cause must have as much reality (actuality) as the thing it causes. You cannot, so to speak, have more water in your bucket than you had in the well. There is no free lunch. You cannot get something from nothing. In his own words Descartes put it thus:

> It is obvious . . . that there must be at least as much reality in the total efficient cause as in its effect, for whence can the effect derive its reality, if not from its cause. . . .
>
> And from this it follows, not only that something cannot be derived from nothing, but also that the more perfect—that is to say, that which contains in itself more reality—cannot be a consequent of the less perfect.[11]

Man has in his mind the idea of an infinitely perfect being, "an infinite substance, external, immutable, independent, omniscient, omnipotent"[12] God. But nowhere in man or in his world is there anything absolutely perfect that could cause man to have such an idea. Yet man has the idea—an idea that as an effect must have come from a cause equal to, or greater than itself. Therefore, it must have come from God, the absolutely perfect being. It must have been imposed upon the human mind from out there somewhere. And it follows, then, that (1) God exists, and (2) that our knowledge of God's existence is not something that man has invented, or found in his world, but is something God-given.

Like Anselm before him, Descartes demonstrates the reality of the "philosopher's God": the God of cognition, the God of thinking, which is to say, the fascinating God of speculation; but hardly the God of a shaman, or of Abraham, or Gautama, or Jesus, or anyone else who stands in awe and wonder, in fear and trembling, before the incalculable mysteries of life and death, before the horrendous nonmanipulables of human existence. The philosopher's God seems a bit cerebral to be the source of religion. If religion is of theocentric origins, it appears that one must look elsewhere (outside the operations of philosophical speculation) for evidence. And this Rudolph Otto does.

In looking at the primitive origin of religion, and the sociogenetic and psychogenetic origins, we have seen religion interpreted

---

[11] René Descartes, *Meditations on First Philosophy* (Indianapolis: Bobbs-Merrill, 1960), p. 39.

[12] Ibid., p. 43.

as arising totally within the human condition: religion as anthropo-centric. But Otto rejects this. Religion is, he believes, not something men invent but something given to them, revealed to them, but not, as with Descartes, as primarily a rational affair. It goes far beyond reasoning; it is predominantly a *feeling* that is aroused by the impact of a sense of holiness that sweeps over us and evokes an awareness of our createdness, and of the existence of a *Holy Other*.

There is an experience of awesomeness and dread, of wondrousness and spiritual excitement, which arises in man as he encounters a quality of overpowering mystery and might that comes to him from "out there." Otto calls this experience the "*numinous* state of mind," and it is evoked by a de facto numinous reality outside of man. In primitive people we see this numinous state reflected in their dread of demons. In ourselves we can sometimes feel something like it when we shudder at a ghost story, or when our flesh creeps at a howl or hysterical laughter coming to us out of the night. But it can be infinitely more than fear and creepiness. This mysterious and tremendous feeling can also come sweeping into us

> like a gentle tide, pervading the mind with a tranquil mood of deepest worship. . . . It may burst in a sudden eruption from the depths of the soul with spasms and convulsions, or lead to the strangest excitements, to intoxicated frenzy, to transport, and to ecstasy. It has its wild demonic forms and can sink to an almost grisly horror and shuddering . . . again it may be developed into something beautiful and pure and glorious. It may become a hushed, trembling and speechless humility of the creature in the presence of—whom or what? In the presence of that which is *Mystery* inexpressible and above all creatures.[13]

We have thus far accumulated a number of insightful observations about religion and religious behavior. We have observed:

1. the proposal that religion began when men mistakenly read their own emotions into nature (Müller),
2. and mistakenly concluded from their dream life that the world was full of souls (Tylor).
3. We observed the primitives' awareness and religious response to màna power (Codrington),

[13] Rudolph Otto, *The Idea of the Holy*, trans. J. W. Harvey (London: Oxford University Press, 1924), pp. 12–13.

4. and Frazer's observation about the place of magic in primitive life.
5. We observed the proposal that religion is simply society writ large (Durkheim),
6. and the proposal that it is the inner psychological dynamic in adventuresome living (James),
7. and that it is a sickness to be cured as soon as possible (Freud).
8. We observed the phenomenological analysis which sees religion as an innate aspect of the human condition,
9. and the proposal that it is (a) an intellectual and (b) an emotional response to a divine reality self-disclosing itself to man.
10. And running through all of these observations we can discern that religion functions especially for people in their personal distresses by giving them transcendence and even infinite assurances in the face of immediate, traumatic circumstances. Religon gives men something to hang on to when their lives go devastatingly awry. It is with this cumulated insight that we shall be preoccupied for the remainder of this book.

Of the several disciplines cited above—anthropology, ethnology, sociology, psychology, phenomenology, philosophy—this book has closest affinity with the discipline of psychology. It takes seriously the psychic nature of man as the basic drive and source of religious need and passion. It sees the successful functioning of religion as an affair of courage, self-fulfillment, and inner psychic-spiritual power. At the same time it is not a psychology of religion. Rather, it is an analysis of the functioning of religion as it operates in the human scene. It observes what men do when they do religion; it discerns the human reasons for their doing religion; and it comments on various values that people get from doing religion. This book appropriates data and insights from the several sciences of religion—anthropology, sociology, psychology. But it also makes extensive use of purely religious data—theology, religious philosophy, myth and ritual, religious and moral philosophy.

Basically we shall answer three questions: (1) *Why* do people do religion? What kinds of human problems demand religious answers? (2) To get answers to their religious problems, *how* do people go about doing religion? What do they do to solve their religious problems? And (3) *what* happens to people when they do religion successfully?

part II

a functional definition

Saturday's Child has far to go . . .

Anonymous

three

The Religious Animal

Apparently man is the only animal that does religion. This makes him a special animal: the religion-doing animal.[1] Of course he is, also, the only animal that does quite a number of things—philosophy, science, retail merchandising, plumbing—but for our purposes his specialty in religion will suffice. First, we want to know why he does religion. What motivates him to this kind of thinking and doing. We suspect that the answer is somewhere in the statement, He does this because he has a special kind of mind. But precisely what kind of mind? With Aristotle we might say, "a rational mind," and that is certainly part of it, but not all of it. Man does think about religion. He tries to be reasonable in his faith. But there is something more visceral than reason in man's urge to do religion. That something lies in the fact that he has the kind of mind that presents him with a vivid and immediate awareness of *him*self. He not only has a cool, problem-solving (rational) mind, but he has, also, a disturbing (self-conscious) mind which tells him *that* he is and *where* he is. And

[1] To say that man is the religious "animal" does not imply that he is not a very special being. It does not decry the contention that he is made just a little less than perfect, a little less than angels (a Jewish-Christian claim) and crowned with glory and honor. Indeed, all religions, no matter how they malign man's present condition, hold finally that man is infinitely worthful and capable of direct communion with divinity. When we say that man is the religious animal, we are saying that he is not *just* an animal. He is an animal of special qualities and qualifications.

knowing that he is and where he is, is disturbing, even horrendous, because it informs him accurately that he is living in a *self* defeating world. The self (that is, any person) is disturbed because once he is old enough to have much sense, he gets the sense of the true situation into which he has been born. He is involved, even trapped, in a world, in a human environmental condition that sooner or later defeats and annihilates all selfhood. Put simply, this is to say that nobody ever gets out of life alive, and nobody ever gets out of life even a small part of what he wants; and man is the one animal who really knows this. He knows that things are not as good for him as they should be, or perhaps even could be. He thinks about himself, and thinking about himself is bad for happiness, or if not happiness, bad for tranquility. And he thinks about himself not necessarily because he wants to think about himself but because he has to. He has to think, if he wants to survive, because he is the animal most deficient in DNA knowledge. Humans are deficient in the instinctive responses sufficient to the essential life support acts, which are genetically built into other animals. The only alternative to genetically established support responses is thinking. The human animal, far more than any other animal, has to learn how to keep himself alive. He has to think about himself in his world or he will not make it. The basic problem of human life, which sets mankind on the path of *homo sapiens* instead of *homo naturalis*, is that he is born short on instinctive "know-how."

THE NONPROGRAMMED ANIMAL

To say that man is the animal who is deficient in DNA knowledge, short on instinctive "know-how," is to say that he is the nonprogrammed animal: the one whose life and meaning depend not upon simple maturity but upon instructed maturity. He cannot just grow up and be himself (wise man); he must grow up instructed, educated. The Existentialist philosophers are on target when (according to Sartre's account[2]) they observe that man is the only animal whose existence precedes his essence. The essential nature of other animals is instructed, programmed, built into the genetic structure.

---

[2] Jean-Paul Sartre, "Existentialism Is a Humanism," *Existentialism from Dostoevsky to Sartre*, ed. Walter Kaufmann (Cleveland: World Publishing, Meridian Books, 1965), pp. 287–311.

Man's is not. A duck is always a duck. He is born that way. He can never be anything but a duck, and exactly that kind of duck. All of the instructions, even the migratory route, are put down in the beginning of his time. But this is not the case with man. It is true that at birth, even at conception, there is an instructed part laid down in man: his physical existence. His body begins, and the instructions for its physical maturity are all there; but not his humanity, not his mind, not his language, not his attitudes, nor loves, nor antipathies, nor sadness, nor religion. All this—and all else that makes him a person, a personality, a human being—is yet to be learned, yet to be created. So, man is different because of the absence of certain instructed regulations in his genetic equipment. As Erich Fromm puts it:

> The first element which differentiates human from animal existence is a negative one: the relative absence in man of instinctive regulation in the processes of adaptation to the surrounding world. . . .
>
> The less complete and fixed the instinctual equipment of animals, the more developed is the brain and therefore the ability to learn. The emergence of man can be defined as occurring at the point in the process of evolution where instinctive adaptation has reached its minimum.[3]

But this deficiency in programming is far from tragic, for it is the deficiency out of which burgeons man's self-consciousness, his memory, his foresight, his language, his reason, and his imagination. Or, as Fromm puts it:

> He emerges with new qualities which differentiate him from the animal: his awareness of himself as a separate entity, his ability to remember the past, to visualize the future, and to denote objects and acts by symbols; his reason to conceive and understand the world; and his imagination through which he reaches far beyond the range of his senses.[4]

All that constitutes man's created humanness is important to his doing religion, but for our purpose here we need to observe only two of his especially human qualities: self-consciousness and imagination.

---

[3] Erich Fromm, *Man for Himself* (New York: Fawcett World Library, 1973), p. 38.
[4] Ibid.

SELF-CONSCIOUSNESS AND IMAGINATION

To say that man is self-conscious is to say that he *sees himself*. He sees himself as involved in a past, a present, and a future. Largely through the mechanism of speech and play,[5] made possible by a distinctive physiological and neurological inheritance, Mr. Jones knows himself to be Mr. Jones. He is an object to himself. He is at the same time both an object and a subject. He may not see himself exactly as others see him, but he definitely sees himself. He sees himself in his own immediate awareness, and he sees himself in his imagination. That is to say, he is a *self*-conscious being, and a being who sees himself as here and now (acting in the present), and sees himself as there and then (acting in the past), and sees himself where he yet may be (acting in the future).

Perhaps other animals have some degree of self-consciousness and imagine themselves in other places doing other things, but if they do, they do not do so very effectively, because generation after generation they go on living in the same old way. If things are imagined differently, changing modes of operation and ways of life ought to occur. But nonhuman animals rarely change their modes and ways. Apparently other animals live in the immediate world, with some memory of the past, but with little thought about, or imagination of, themselves living (or dying) in the future. In this, of course, man is really different. He is extremely aware of the future—tomorrow, next month, next year, retirement, eternity. Indeed, he often seems to be doing more of his living, or trying to, in the future than in the present. Man, especially modern man, endlessly worries and wants for tomorrow. He looks at his immediate world and imagines how it could be different; how, in fact, it will be different tomorrow. Because man possesses the power of self-consciousness and imagination, he wants for himself what is not, and is afraid for himself of what is not. He lives positively and negatively, not only in his actual world, but in his "wished-for" world and in his "afraid-of" world. Positively, he imagines what is not and desires it, sometimes passionately. Negatively, he imagines what is not and fears it, sometimes desperately. This puts him in the condition of estrangement. Wherever he is, indeed in the world

[5] Identified by George Herbert Mead as the basic mechanism in the creation of the human mind.

itself, he feels as if he does not belong. He is constantly aware that things are not to his liking. They never measure up to his expectations, and they never could, because that is the character of the expectations of a self-conscious, imaginative human being. Whoever we are, wherever we are, whatever we have, it is not enough. We want to be more than we are; we want to be somewhere else; we want to have greater possessions. If only I were eleven (the age when some of us were to get our first bicycles), I would be happy and not need anything else ... if only I were twenty-one, through college, had a good job, were married to Susie, were famous, rich, richer. There is no end to it. Even when one rebels and turns against "this rat race," it is the same. The only thing that changes, important as that may be, is the style of doing the self-consciousness and imagination: the style of imagining ourselves as we are not, and where we are not.

NEW WORLDS

Because things are not to his heart's desire, because he can imagine them differently, and wants them so, man always strives to make his life different, and he always has so striven. He builds new worlds for himself. Motivated by his desire for a better life (desires that arise naturally in his self-disturbing mind), man goes to work imaginatively and creates his fantastic, artificial worlds, wherein one finds central plumbing, air conditioning, rapid transit, $E=MC^2$, the Roman Papacy, the Law of Parsimony, the Republican Party, the Pietà, hospitals, faith healing, stereophonic noise, and television commercials to keep him reminded of what he does not have, and to keep him wanting it. What is being said here is that all human enterprises—especially those of significance, such as science, philosophy, religion—arise in human need, in man's awareness of the inadequacies in himself and his world, and work to accomplish human welfare, or what is believed to be human welfare, or, at least, things closer to his heart's desire.

Because the world does not measure up to man's wants and expectations, and because he has the kind of mind to know this, he tries to reform the world with technology and science; he tries to make it reasonable (less mysterious and frightening) with philosophy and theology; and he tries to relate to it adequately or transcend it successfully with religious beliefs, devotions, and commitments. Religion, so regarded, is the way one believes and behaves in his effort to overcome and transcend the existential estrangement, the horrendous, nonmanipulable aspects of human existence, the sense of finitude—which is to say, the *human condition*.

THE HUMAN CONDITION

Special consideration should be given this phrase, "the human condition," for it lies at the base of man's religious motivations. The human condition is the condition of estrangement. Just below the surface of tranquilizers and other superficial distractions, it is the condition of man to feel estranged from his world and in disharmony with his own life. He is a part of nature and at the same time divorced from nature. This dichotomy, as we observed, occurs because man, unlike other animals, knows his destiny in nature. Man is caught in an impossible split: being subject to nature and transcendent to nature. Possessing a body that wants to stay alive, he possesses at the same time a mind that informs him that his body's wish is doomed. As an innocent part of nature, his heart beats as if it would never stop, but his mind knows better. Other animals find their fulfillment in simply repeating the patterns of their species, but man is not so fulfilled. Evicted from innocence (from instinctive almost thoughtless existence even as he experienced it prenatally), he is doomed to work forever at a problem he cannot possibly solve. As Fromm puts it, "having lost paradise, the unity with nature, he has become the eternal wanderer (Odysseus, Oedipus, Abraham, Faust),"[6] endlessly searching to restore a unity between himself and the rest of nature which was irreparably ruptured on the day of his birth. In an attempt to repair the rupture, Fromm tells us, man first constructs all-inclusive world hypotheses, that is, world views within which he can answer the question of where he stands in the midst of life and what he ought to do. But, Fromm explains, such thought systems are not adequate. If man were only a thinking animal, a mind, that would be sufficient; but man is also endowed with a body. Thus he must respond not only

[6] Fromm, *Man for Himself*, p. 50.

by thinking, but also with his feelings and actions. "He has to strive for the experience of unity and oneness in all spheres of his being in order to find a new equilibrium. Hence any satisfying system of orientation implies not only intellectual elements but also elements of feeling and sense to be realized in action in all fields of human endeavor. Devotion to an aim, or an idea, or a power transcending man such as God, is an expression of this need for completeness in the process of living."[7]

Doing Religion   Fromm goes on to point out that these systems of orientation, these world views, vary depending upon the culture in which they happen, but they are nevertheless all concerned with the same thing: giving man a framework of meaning in which to find his own personal meaning. They are, in fact, reinterpretations of the world (theologies) developed so that the horrendousness of life may be mitigated, or perhaps even denied. For example, one might say, with the Hindu: This is only an illusory world (maya); search behind the appearances of it for the real world. Or one might say, with the Christians: This is only a preliminary world, a testing place for eternity; beyond is Heaven, or, if you are not careful, Hell. Fromm admits that he would like to call such orientation systems religions or religious systems, but because some of these systems are not theistic, he gets hung up on the provincialism of a theocentric definition, and backs away saying: "For lack of a better word I therefore call such systems 'frames of orientation and devotion'."[8] It is our intention not to back away, because constructing such frames of orientation and devotion is exactly what men do when they do religion, whether or not they do it with reference to a theistic/personalistic God.

Horrendous and Nonmanipulable   We have asserted that religious behavior is a complex response to those aspects of human existence which are horrendous and nonmanipulable. By "horrendous" we mean to convey the sense, not simply of fright and frightening things, but of the deeper-seated dread that arises in the face of those things that threaten to destroy basic human values, to destroy essential life-styles and even life itself. Religious responses

[7] Ibid., p. 55.
[8] Ibid., p. 56.

are not evoked at horror movies—although a person may be half scared to death by them—or by walking through a graveyard at night, or by hearing an eerie sound coming through the fog, but by circumstances that put in peril the life and meaning of the person involved. An example of this kind of horrendousness is the dread that accompanies death. Death is not only a universal problem—everybody has to face it sooner or later—but it is also, except sometimes when given an adequate religious interpretation, a horrendous problem. In its blunt factuality, death terrorizes man. The death of another person, the death of a loved one, one's own death, is horrendous both in fact and contemplation, and it evokes religious responses.

Death is a classic example of the horrendousness of religious problems. But it is not the only one. Living can also be horrendous. Indeed, for many people death is not the most terrible thing a person ever has to face. Much worse for some people is facing life. The fact that some people commit suicide indicates, at least, that for them death is the lesser of two evils. And even among those who do not commit suicide or even contemplate it, there are many persons who find the really difficult problem is not how to die well, but how to live well. Many discover that Thoreau's quiet desperation, or even a screaming desperation, is the really devastating thing in their lives. For those who live past the tender years, the basic tragedy of living may not be in death, but in disillusionment: in the discovery that life must be lived in picayune ways far beneath the expectations of youthful dreams and ambitions. For many sensitive people, the trauma of life, the horrendousness, comes in the lost beauty of life, the lost ecstasy of living, in the dulling of expectancy by the hard facts of mundane existence, in the general loss of youthful ideals before the calculating motion of the years. The real frustration is not that life must end, but that it must be lived in little ways. In any generation there are only a few "stars" of first magnitude, and the lament of St. Paul, "I do not do what I want, but . . . the very things I hate."[9] indicates that even the stars can be profoundly disillusioned. The religious question is not whether to make "a quietus" with the "bare bodkin," but to decide whether life is indeed shattered by the slings and arrows of fortune, by the grunt and sweat of weariness, by the cowardly conscience, sicklied with pale thoughts and terrified of dreamful sleep—or if it need be. Death is

[9] Romans 7:15, Revised Standard Version (RSV).

merely a convenient, everyman illustration of the kind of frustration that evokes religion, the kind of frustration that is religiously horrendous.

Religious problems are horrendous problems. They are also nonmanipulable problems. John O'Hara took the title for one of his novels, *Appointment in Samarra,* from a parable by W. Somerset Maugham in which with startling clarity both the inimical (horrendous) character and the inevitable (nonmanipulable) character of death are exemplified.

> Death speaks: There was a merchant in Bagdad who sent his servant to market to buy provisions and in a little while the servant came back, white and trembling, and said, Master just now when I was in the market-place I was jostled by a woman in the crowd and when I turned I saw it was Death that jostled me. She looked at me and made a threatening gesture; now, lend me your horse, and I will ride away from this city and avoid my fate. I will go to Samarra and there Death will not find me. The merchant lent him his horse, and the servant mounted it, and dug his spurs in its flanks and as fast as the horse could gallop he went. Then the merchant went down to the market-place and he saw me standing in the crowd and he came to me and said, Why did you make a threatening gesture to my servant when you saw him this morning. That was not a threatening gesture, I said, it was only a start of surprise. I was astonished to see him in Bagdad, for I have an appointment with him tonight in Samarra.[10]

The point of this story, so far as we are concerned, is not the overtone of fatalism, not the precision of the appointment, but the final inevitability of such an appointment for all of us, sometime, somewhere, if not today, tomorrow, if not in Samarra, then in Bagdad. Also, there is no denying that when death gestures at us, we are threatened. It is an enemy, and it cannot finally be outflanked. It is horrendous and it is nonmanipulable.

By nonmanipulable we mean circumstances that are beyond direct human control. By religiously significant nonmanipulables, we mean nonmanipulable circumstances that are also horrendous.[11] The phases of the moon, the rising and falling of the tides, the

[10] W. Somerset Maugham, "Sheppey" (Garden City, N. Y.: Doubleday, 1934).

[11] "Nonmanipulable" is an adjective. It has no noun form. However, it is convenient at times to treat it as a noun. We shall do this occasionally, using it to mean a thing that cannot be altered, changed, or reordered by man.

progression of our galaxy toward Andromeda are all nonmanipulables, but they do not evoke religious responses because they do
not threaten human life or essential life-styles. An ocean cannot be
manipulated, but it does not become a religious problem until, in a
storm, it threatens to swamp your boat, and your life along with it.
At that moment the nonmanipulable becomes horrendous and religiously significant.

There are, it appears, two kinds of religiously significant nonmanipulables: first, those *of ignorance,* which are temporary, and
second, those *of condition,* which are permanent.

First, *of ignorance:* this class of religiously significant nonmanipulables includes all those uncontrollable, horrendous circumstances that cannot be manipulated simply because one does not
know how to manipulate them *at the moment.* They are temporarily
nonmanipulable. Take, for example, famine: some people's lives are
threatened by famine, not because famine is nonmanipulable, not
because we do not have the know-how and technological skill to
banish famine, but only because *those* people do not yet have the
know-how and skill. The situation is nonmanipulable for them, but
simply because of ignorance. Again, as with famine, such diseases as
diphtheria, scarlet fever, small pox, poliomyelitis, can be controlled.
Yet in certain places they are not controlled and for the people of
those places they remain religiously significant nonmanipulables.
Again, certain kinds of social ills are nonmanipulables of ignorance.
In many situations where life and life-styles are threatened, we
simply do not know enough to do what should be done, or how to
inform or persuade people to do so even if we did know. Thus the
world is plagued with war, racial prejudice, human deprivations,
crimes, broken homes, broken persons, and ten thousand other social ills, all of which are theoretically solvable, but not immediately
or practicably so.

In the horrendous nonmanipulables of ignorance, religion gets
involved and remains involved until the nonmanipulable is solved
and becomes manipulable; with that, technology replaces religion in
that situation. If this were all there were to it, we could expect that
the kinds of problems that drive men to religion might eventually
all disappear, and religion along with them. Once ignorance was
overcome, through the accomplishments of science and technology
and perhaps some applied social ethics, the need for religion would

end and all men would live happily in a prayerless everafter. But this is not all there is to it. There are certain kinds of religiously significant problems that are apparently permanently nonmanipulable. Such problems we shall designate as nonmanipulables of condition.

Second, *of condition:* This second type of nonmanipulable is characterized by permanence. These are the horrendous circumstances of life that will not go away with a little more know-how. These are the nonmanipulables of the human condition. As long as man is man they will continue to frustrate him and drive him to the "hope" of religion rather than the manipulations of technology. These nonmanipulables have ontological status—that is, they are essential to the nature of man's being man. For example, it appears that no amount of scientific knowledge or technological skill will ever change the basic self-disturbing character of man's self-conscious, imaginative mind, as we noted earlier. The only possibility of ending man's normal condition of estrangement would be to tranquilize him to the point where he would no longer be anything like an authentic man. As long as he is real man he will live forever wanting it better and expecting it worse. To the degree that there are permanent horrendous problems in human existence there are nonmanipulables of condition. The difference is that the "of ignorance" type is manipulable at least in principle, whereas the "of condition" type is not.

What nonmanipulables of condition basically do to man is threaten his being. They threaten him with nonbeing. Nonbeing here means the denial or loss of those conditions that are essential to genuine human life—such things as life itself, a sense of personal worth, an awareness of moral integrity. Paul Tillich, in his insightful little book *The Courage To Be,* identifies these permanent threats to man's being as fate and death, emptiness and meaninglessness, guilt and condemnation. Fate and death threaten man's *ontic* self, that is, his existence as a being. Emptiness and meaninglessness threaten his spiritual self. Guilt and condemnation threaten his moral self. It is the condition of man to be born at a moment in time, at a place in time, and possessing certain genetic equipment. His life is thus set in a definite matrix. This matrix is more or less fixed. Within the boundaries of his time, space, and genetics, man must strive to find or create a meaningful life, for, as we have noted, he cannot live satisfactorily, or with satisfaction, simply performing animal functions. He must somehow fulfill the demands of his human ego. He must effect a sense of personal, individual worth. He must find a way to "belong" in spite of his normal estrangement. He must acquire a spiritual status that makes him worthy of respect, especially self-respect. And this is not easy to do. No matter who he is he will experience times of depression and emptiness; times of quiet desperation. Indeed, just below the surface of all of his activities, the anxiety of emptiness/meaninglessness lurks disquietingly, for, as we noted, estrangement is the natural condition of man, and anxiety is the persistent symptom of that condition. When the sense of emptiness becomes extreme, it slides into the horrendous experience of meaninglessness—a life without purpose or worth, a life worse than death.

Accompanying the anxiety of emptiness/meaninglessness is the equally permanent anxiety of guilt/condemnation. After a while it becomes impossible to go on blaming others for our own faults and failures. We may say that we are "worthless bastards" because of bad toilet training, but we know better. It is not somebody else's fault; it is my fault. I am guilty. I have failed others. I have failed myself. I have failed life. I have failed God. I am responsible and no one else. God help me! When this anxiety of guilt spreads and colors the whole of one's life, the condition of condemnation asserts itself. I am not only guilty, but am condemned. God forgive me. And, of course, during this whole living process, we are dying, and at least part of the time we know it. The condition of "fate" accelerates to the extreme and death happens. To a spiritual nonbeing and a moral nonbeing is added the final nonbeing—the ontic; the nonbeing of the self.

Tillich's threats to being (fate/death, emptiness/meaninglessness, guilt/condemnation) are examples of nonmanipulables of condition. No amount of know-how will change them. Religion is the only answer, for religion is an admission of the worst, and a stance of courage in spite of it. Before the threat of nonbeing, religion gives man *The Courage To Be.*

To the several examples of nonmanipulables of condition given so far, one more might be added. It is the condition of social ignorance. Social ignorance can be viewed partly as a nonmanipulable of ignorance instead of a nonmanipulable of condition. The problems of racial injustice, crime and rehabilitation, poverty and urban blight, and the like, all arise out of social ignorance, and are possible to solution, and are, thereby, nonmanipulables of ignorance. But on a deeper level, social ignorance has a permanent structure, and in its horrendous dimensions must be dealt with as a nonmanipulable of condition. Here we are dealing with the ontology of human societies, and recognizing that ignorance is a permanent feature of the structure (being) of society. It is a sad fact that vast numbers of people always have been ill informed and ignorant and have acted in stupid ways, and apparently they always will. Especially in times of cultural change, the structure of social life is simply too complicated to be understood adequately by most of the people involved. And even if the masses of mankind had the reasoning power to understand all they would need to understand, there is no evidence that they would choose to act reasonably. To be sure, men do make rational choices part of the time, but more of the time, and often in the critical issues of life, they choose willfully, passionately, irrationally. How else are we to account for the mob's concurrence in the crucifixion of Jesus, the lynching of blacks in Alabama, the Nazi holocaust, the years of war in Vietnam, the enormous overkill of modern nuclear armaments, the slums and poverty surrounded by affluence, and the vast number of people living in McLuhan's "Bonanza Land"? The cutting edge of each day, each year, each generation is always running ahead of the institutions, customs, convictions, education, and morality which determine and govern the life of each day, each year, each generation. There is little reason to believe that the masses of mankind will ever be a spearhead for any social progress whatsoever; that their education will ever match the complexities of their times; that enough of them will at any time be wise enough and coolheaded enough to allay the enormous social ills that endlessly spawn in the muck of human ignorance. Like death, social ignorance seems destined to plague man to the end of time.

four

Metatechnology and Metapsychology

When we considered Sir James Frazer's notion of magic and religion, we introduced William Bernhardt's term *metatechnology*, and observed that metatechnology is employed both as magic and as rogation.[1] In magic, man himself manipulates the supernatural powers to effect desired changes in natural processes. But we also saw that man often, perhaps more often, tries to get God or the Gods to intervene and effect the desired changes for him. We are calling this second form of metatechnology, "rogation," from the Latin *rogare*, which means "to beseech." Early in the Christian Church rogations were performed in times of disaster. Those rogations might involve processions, litanies, fasting, penitence, prayers, all beseeching God to alleviate the calamity. An instance of this occurred in A.D. 590 when Pope Gregory the Great ordered a rogation ritual called *litania septiformis* to be performed in an attempt to get divine succor during a pestilence that followed an inundation in Rome. By rogation we shall mean any sacrifice or prayer or other performance, by anybody, which makes appeal for divine intervention to alter the natural conditions; for example, praying for rain, or to be given victory in battle, or to be cured of disease. Rogation is a form of metatechnology different from magic in form, but like magic in intention.

[1] Metatechnology is any attempt to introduce extranatural or supernatural power into natural processes. What man cannot do for himself, he attempts to get the powers (Gods) or *the* power (God) to do for him.

We need, now, to introduce another term into our considerations: *metapsychological,* a term to designate those inner psychological changes which are effected by religious beliefs, actions, and experiences—especially those religious responses which go "beyond" normal, expected, psychological responses. For example, when a martyr faces death serenely, praying for his slayers, or when a person responds to personal tragedy courageously and even serenely *because* he believes that there is in God's Plan reason for his suffering, they are evidencing, not normal psychological responses, but metapsychological responses.

Metapsychological response must be further delineated as (1) self-conscious or intentional and as (2) subconscious or unintentional. As self-conscious, it is intended; as subconscious, it is accidental—a by-product. In self-conscious metapsychology persons do not expect to change "things," but to change themselves. They attempt to go beyond the usual, normal psychological response and establish a courage-to-be-in-spite-of response. In self-conscious metapsychology one turns to religion to find wisdom and courage in order to take whatever happens, which cannot be changed, and to do so with dignity, and even serenity. This is what the biblical Job finally discovered: He was supposed to trust God and accept life, no matter what. It is what the Chinese Taoist does when he chooses to practice *wu-wei,* that is, quiet nonaggressive, nonresisting action. It is the very essence of a commonly spoken prayer: "God grant me the serenity to accept things I cannot change, courage to change things I can, and wisdom to know the difference."[2] This prayer is obviously a self-consciously metatechnological prayer. In it one is asking not for the world to change, but for himself to change. On the other hand, when the President of the United States asked the nation to pray for the safe return of the astronauts in the damaged Apollo 13 spaceship, the concern was obviously metatechnological. The prayers were to get supernatural intervention into a natural process. The prayers were to get God to make *things* right. Whether or not God answered the prayers and assisted in getting the craft back, a lot of people felt better for having done their part. They got some psychological benefits out of the "religious exercise." In a mild way at least, they experienced some subconscious metapsychology.

[2] Reinhold Niebuhr is credited by many as being the author of this prayer.

The second form of metapsychology is subconscious meta-psychology. In this form the religious inner change takes place not so much by request as by accident. It is a sort of by-product of faith; the releasing, as James suggests, of the strenuous, courageous, adventuresome mood as a result of one's religious conviction that the magic works, or that God is on our side. This aspect of meta-psychology will become more obvious as we turn now and ask, How are metatechnology and metapsychology related in religion?

Metatechnology versus Metapsychology   To understand how these two aspects of religion relate to each other, we should first make clear the relationship between technology and metatech-nology. William Bernhardt, in his *A Functional Philosophy of Religion,* establishes the fact that there is a concomitant relation between technology and metatechnology: the more technology one has, the less metatechnology he uses. From an examination of the religious practices of a primitive society, the religious practices of the Romans during the Augustan Age, and the religious practices of some modern Christians, Bernhardt concludes that in the areas of food supply and human health, metatechnology is extensively used in prescientific cultures where good production techniques and medical skills are minimal, and is rarely used by people who have attained advanced technologies in food supply and scientific capacity in medicine.

Professor Malinowski, in his *Magic, Science and Religion,* illustrates the relationship of technology to metatechnology in the culture of the Melanesian primitives of the Trobriand Islands. The Trobrianders use both technology and metatechnology (mostly of the magical type) and they know in each case what they are doing and why. The Trobrianders are, among other things, fishermen. They venture out beyond the safe reef-protected lagoons of their islands into the deep not always pacific waters in search of fish. They do this in outriggers, dugout canoes. With long-established technologies, the boat craftsmen build fine seaworthy boats. They do this in a straightforward technological fashion. As craftsmen they use technology, not metatechnology. But a good sailing craft is not the last word in deep-sea fishing. One needs not only a good boat to ride the waves but also a lucky boat to get through or avoid storms, and to find fish. The sea is big and dangerous, and fish are where you find them. Something more than craftsmanship and smart fishing is involved. This "something" takes special handling, and so along with their technology, the Trobrianders employ metatechnology. Malinowski tells us:

> Canoe building has a long list of spells, to be recited at various stages of the work, at the felling of the trees, at the scooping out of the dugout; and towards the end, at the painting, lashing together and launching.[3]

He reports the same kind of technology/metatechnology in the Trobrianders' farming enterprises. They use farming techniques, but because crop failure means hunger and perhaps starvation, they also employ metatechnology to deal with those aspects of farming which seem to need something more than ordinary know-how. Also, Malinowski reports that the Trobrianders use metatechnology to ward off, or cure serious illnesses. They have no modern medical practices. They do employ some natural remedies for minor afflictions, but in all serious illness they employ metatechnology extensively. What the Trobrianders cannot manipulate technologically, they try to manipulate metatechnologically. They get God, or the Gods, or just plain magic to protect them from horrendous nonmanipulables, to fix it so they can survive, and even prosper.

An obvious question to ask at this point is: Does it work? Do they get it fixed? Is the nonmanipulable really manipulated for them? We can answer by saying that it is obvious what the natives think they are getting. They think they are getting extranatural or supernatural assistance in the face of nonmanipulable aspects in their existence. They believe they are getting control in those areas which are precarious and in which important values are threatened. They use their religion to restore, or preserve, or promote vital values they believe are in danger.

Of course, what they are getting, as seen by an outsider, might be something else altogether. An observing outsider might conclude that the Trobrianders are mistaken. They are not really getting a guaranteed harvest, or a safe and successful fishing voyage, or protection from, or cure of, diseases. They just think they are. But one might also conclude that despite a metatechnological impotence in

---

[3] Malinowski, *Magic, Science and Religion* (New York: Free Press, 1948), pp. 165–66.

their activities, they are getting something else quite valuable: a by-product. Believing in the efficacy of their metatechnological techniques, they are getting an inner surety, a sense of assurance, a fund of courage. They are getting subconscious metapsychological benefits. Through their religious activities, they are going beyond the fear that normally arises at the prospect of famine or drowning or serious illness, and are securing for themselves a courage, a morale, they would not otherwise have. If their world has not really changed, at least they have.

Although we might regard the metatechnological practices of the Trobrianders as being only subjectively beneficial, we may not be willing to be so restrictive when viewing our own metatechnological practices. Surely many of the enlightened, scientifically cultured persons who prayed for the astronauts' return believe that their prayers did assist with more than psychological benefits. If, for example, we ask: Does prayer change *things?* we find voices in the modern world declaring an emphatic *yes.*

Of course, we hear denials also. William Bernhardt voices his denial as follows:

> Historically . . . religious behavior was essentially metatechnological. Persons sought for supernatural or magical aid in their attempts to conserve their values. Present day information leads one to believe that all such metatechnological activities were futile so far as objective results were concerned. . . . At the same time, religious behavior continued despite its metatechnological impotence because it served man in other ways. It had subjective success which more than compensated for its objective failures. . . . Religious behavior, in other words, aided individuals to make subjective adjustments to situations not subject to objective control at the time, and to do so without loss of morale.[4]

The evidence would indicate that Bernhardt writes the "minority opinion" in this case. Prayer for health, for rain, for the security and preservation of tangible, physical values is still widely practiced and ardently defended. It is still something people do when they do religion, and they justify their doing so usually based on two types of arguments: it is reasonable, and it works.

Peter Bertocci argues that it is reasonable. If God is a person,

---

[4] William Bernhardt, *A Functional Philosophy of Religion* (Denver: Criterion Press), p. 157.

as Bertocci believes, and a person whose very essence consists in his concern for increase in value, then it is reasonable to expect that he will take every opportunity to help persons increase values. In his *Introduction to the Philosophy of Religion,* Bertocci argues that the laws of nature are themselves evidences of God's loving concern for man. Without a minimum of physical, biological, and mental laws, the world or communal life could not exist. God shows his care for us through these "impersonal" laws.

But is this all? Does this exhaust God's concern for the individual? Bertocci insists that the answer is definitely, No. God's general providence is just the basis for his special providence. God listens and responds. Within, but not in conflict with the laws necessary for an orderly nature and a communal life, there is no reason, argues Bertocci, why God cannot or would not respond to human invitation and initiate or preserve the existence of some prayed-for essential, human value.

Bertocci is, actually, a rather cautious protagonist for metatechnology. Much more radical and passionate statements are available for those who wish to believe that divine intervention really happens. But the more usual grounds for holding to the effectiveness of metatechnology, for believing that prayer changes things, is not an argument at all. It is an experience. If you want *the word,* ask the man who prayed for rain and got it; ask the man who was healed by faith; ask the man who "felt" the power of God invade his being. For such persons, there is no arguing; there is only affirmation.

That metatechnology actually effects changes in the environment is questionable, but that metapsychology changes people is not questionable. It is a demonstrable fact. People's lives are changed because they believe in the claims and engage in the behaviors of religion. William James, in his essay "The Moral Philosopher and the Moral Life," makes this point with his usual inimitable style. He declares

> that even if there were no metaphysical or traditional grounds for believing in God, men would postulate one simply as a pretext for living hard, and getting out of the game of existence its keenest possibilities of zest. Our attitude towards concrete evils is entirely different in a world where we believe there are none but finite demanders, from what it is in one where we joyously face tragedy for

an infinite demander's sake. Every sort of energy and endurance, of courage and capacity for handling life's evils, is set free in those who have religious faith. For this reason the strenuous type of character will on the battlefield of human history always outwear the easy-going type, and religion will drive irreligion to the wall.[5]

The Trobriander who believes that his boat sails with supernatural luck, sails with confidence, and probably even with more skill. In a storm he is less likely to be incapacitated by a sense of his own helplessness. He can count on more than himself. As James puts it, for those who have faith, "every sort of energy and endurance is set free." Better to sail with that man than with the other kind. What is true of primitives in this regard is not less true of their sophisticated, civilized brothers. Courage, someone has said, is fear that prayed, and for the millions who know from experience what this means, nothing more need be said.

The prayer that Jesus is reported to have prayed in the Garden of Gethsemane appears to have been about half metatechnological and half metapsychological. He prayed for God to change the circumstances and spare his life, but if this would not be done, then in his prayer he resolved to accept God's will. He prayed, first, for the cup to pass him by, and, second, if not pass him by, for the courage to take it, no matter what it was. The cup did not pass. The prayer did not "change things," but, if we can trust the account of how he behaved during those last hours of his life, we may surely conclude that the prayer changed him. The man who was terrified when he went into the Garden (who fell on his face and sweat blood) became a man walking with courage and dignity and transcendence to the top of The Skull, and beyond it into the hearts and lives of countless millions ever since.

RELIGION AND TRANSCENDING HOPE

The courage afforded by religion is not simply grit-the-teeth-and-bear-it courage. It is courage characterized by transcending hope. Jean-Paul Sartre tells us that "man's project is God," which is his paradigm expression for the fact that man's nature—both affective

[5] William James, "The Moral Philosopher and The Moral Life," *Essays in Pragmatism*, ed. Alburey Castell (New York: Hafner, 1951), p. 86.

and cognitive—is to transcend itself, to ride above its human condition, to overcome its finiteness. Man needs to be (or to be with)
God; just a little lower than the angels; born again; Christ-man
rather than Adam-man. Religion does not prepare persons by having them cringe, whimpering before death, or flee to suicide before
the slings and arrows of outrageous fortune. Rooted in horrendous
frustrations, it is nonetheless directed optimistically to the transcending of those frustrations. Religion is not so much a running away as
it is a rising above. In a voice that is not only authentically religious,
but more excitingly so than a prayer for rain, the Prophet Isaiah
sings:

> They that wait upon the Lord
> Shall renew their strength.
> They shall mount up with wings as eagles.
> They shall run and not be weary.
> They shall walk and not faint. (Isaiah 40:31, King James Version.)

If human need is the rootage of religion, great expectations is its
bud, and great aspirations is its flower. On all levels of human need,
religion speaks. When life is trapped in physical needs, when hunger and danger are man's constant companions, his major religious
concerns are also concentrated upon the physical, and on how to
manipulate it to his welfare. He will employ all he knows (technologically, metatechnologically, metapsychologically) to better his
lot. As soon as he succeeds at this, he will discover other needs,
which can be just as important, and just as threatened. As soon as
he gets enough bread, he discovers that bread alone is not enough.
More sophisticated needs (personal, social, intellectual, aesthetic,
moral, spiritual) thrust upon him demandingly. And he will cry out
for the needs of his soul just as ardently as he ever cries out for the
needs of his body.

Spiritual needs create a dimension of religion which can transcend the desperation in which religion has its roots. The nonmanipulable remains. It is still horrendous. The anxiety is still there.
The man who, for example, strives for sainthood is motivated by
anxious need just as surely as the frightened man praying for de-
liverance from wild waves, but the direction of their expectations is
not the same. One man aspires to something; the other man flees
from something. Religion is not fear only; it is fear transcended. It
is characterized by hope quite as much as despair, by courage quite

as much as fear, by laughing quite as much as crying, by living quite as much as dying. Religion not only has the preciseness of need; it also has the scope of aspiration. Alfred North Whitehead, who zeroed in on a narrow target and called religion "what an individual does with his own solitariness,"[6] just as emphatically reversed the narrowness and opened the scope to an infinite breadth.

> Religion is the vision of something which stands beyond, behind, and within, the passing flux of immediate things; something which is real, and yet waiting to be realized; something which is remotely possible, and yet the greatest of present facts; something that gives meaning to all that passes, and yet eludes apprehension; something whose possession is the final good, and yet is beyond all reach; something which is the ultimate ideal, and the hopeless quest.[7]

TOTAL COMMITMENT

Another observation to be made about man's religious behavior concerns the affective and/or intellectual involvement in the religious commitment. Religious behavior, when genuine, is total behavior. It is affective/intellectual behavior. Religion is not an intellectual exercise, on the one hand, nor a noncognitive emotional binge, on the other. It is an amalgam of both. Edna St. Vincent Millay, in her "Interim," tells us: "Not truth, but Faith it is that keeps the world alive." The poem goes on to declare that birds fly because they have "unconscious faith," and fishes swim and the world follows its orderly way because all things basically give themselves in trust. They believe, and the believing is more than just an intellectual nod. It is a complete persuasion. "I not only *know* that this is so, but *feel* it to the marrow of my bones." It involves a believing which is both of reason and of passion. Religious faith is an emotional commitment, a passionate giving of one's self. But it is not just passion. It is passion surrounding a proposition, or a whole system of propositions, which make it, also, an affair of knowledge, of intellect, of truth. It is to certain "truths" that the believer is tenaciously loyal and emotionally committed.

Just as science and philosophy are concerned with the facts of

[6] Alfred North Whitehead, *Religion in the Making* (Cleveland: World Publishing, Meridian Books, 1969; © 1926), p. 16.

[7] Alfred North Whitehead, *Science and the Modern World* (New York: Macmillan, 1944), p. 275.

existence and with true understandings, so is religion. But religion is not only concerned with the controlling facts of science and the clear understanding of philosophy; it is also concerned with establishing the whole person in dynamic, saving relation with the power or powers believed to determine life and destiny—with the God or the Gods. Keenly aware of the frustrations of finitiude, or horrendous nonmanipulables, man turns not just his hands and head to the basic problems of life, but his heart as well. And in this fact (that the heart is involved) religion, at least theoretically, differs sharply from both science and philosophy. Religion is an engagement with life, an existential engagement; science and philosophy try not to be. Science and philosophy are "objective" in their approach to facts and truth and the welfare of man. The scientist and philosopher try to remove themselves, their prejudices, passions, biases, from the experiments and critical examinations. Presumably all is cold and calculated and cautiously reasonable. But religion is not like that. Rather it is willfully emotional and personal. It is concerned not only to know the truth but, in the very act of knowing, to be engaged totally, committed completely, and saved utterly.

Apropros this pretense of objectivity in science (to say nothing of philosophy), Pierre Teilhard de Chardin has this to say:

> In its early naive stage, science, perhaps inevitably would imagine that we could observe things in themselves, as they would behave in our absence. Instinctively physicists and naturalists went to work as though they could look down from a great height upon a world which their consciousness could penetrate without being submitted to it or changing it. They are now beginning to realize that even the most objective of their observations are steeped in the conventions they adopt at the outset and by forms or habits of thought developed in the course of their research; so that, when they reach the end of their analysis they cannot tell with any certainty whether the structure they have made is the essence of the matter they are studying, or the reflection of their own thought. And at the same time they realize that because of the return shock of their discoveries, they are committed body and soul to the network of relationships they thought to cast upon things from the outside: In fact, they are caught in their own net.[8]

[8] Pierre Teilhard de Chardin, *The Phenomenon of Man* (New York: Harper & Row, Torchbooks, 1965), p. 32.

SALVATION

To be saved utterly, this is the destination of the transcending hope and the total commitment of religion. Salvation, also called by other names such as *moksha* in Hinduism and *satori* in Zen Buddhism, is the ultimate religious answer given to the human condition. It represents the final conquest of finitude.

Many times salvation is associated with a place such as Heaven, and it is often anticipated as something yet to come. But a close scrutiny of the existential nature of salvation indicates that it is not essentially identifiable with a place, nor is it necessarily futuristic. Rather it is a condition of being, a kind of consciousness, which may happen in Heaven or some similar place, later on, but may also happen here and now. In Zen Buddhism, it (satori) apparently happens abruptly here and now. Gautama's "enlightenment" also was a "here and now" happening. And the divine possessions reported by shamans (as we shall see in some detail later) happen in the present, wherever the shaman happens to be.

Salvation appears to be an experience in which the "old man" is reborn as a "new man," and the transformation is complete; the whole nature is changed. If this account is accurate, it follows that salvation is not simply a metapsychological affair, in which one self-consciously or subconsciously achieves a new spiritual morale for the facing of horrendous and nonmanipulable circumstances. Rather, salvation seems to be not a limited modification in one's normal psychological responses but a major transformation of one's basic psychic set, that is, of the essential depth structure of one's psychic system. The one who experiences salvation apparently does not become a re-arranged person, but a radically re-formed person. St. Paul describes how it was with him. In his letter to the Galatians he states boldly: "I have been crucified with Christ; it is no longer I who live, but Christ who lives in me" (Gal. 2:20, Revised Standard Version). Similarly Gautama, after his moment of enlightenment, was simply not the same man. As we shall see later when we investigate the Religious Experience in chapter fifteen, primitive religions often claim that the shaman's "helper spirit" actually takes over the body and soul of the entranced shaman, who thereby becomes literally what the possessing spirit is.

In the salvation process a new person is created. "The old psychic set is transcended and transformed into something as radically (qualitatively) different from its old form as a Brillo box is from a

Warhol painting."⁹ Jones is still Jones. He still eats and sleeps, catches colds, works, loves, weeps, laughs, suffers, dies. But there is a difference. He seems to have gone through religious need to the other side and to have found liberation. He is no longer the anxious slave of finite frustration, but seems to have come to a point of view which accepts finite limitation as somehow a minor dimension in the total scheme of things. Ordinary life may be as precious to him as to anyone, and as threatened, but for him it seems not to be the whole of it, or the truly important part of it. He has gotten hold of something, and in getting hold of it has been made different by it.

Simply to say that someone was saved (saved from the Devil, saved from drowning, saved from anything) implies that he was saved *from* something, saved *to* something, and saved *by* something. Thus far we have been saying what, in religious salvation, one is saved to; namely to a new condition of being. One is saved *from* the anxiety (*angst*) of the self-conscious human condition, from the trauma resident in one's vivid awareness of his finitude. Finitude is the core of the problem. Man wants infinity, but he possesses, on his own, only finiteness. In the contradiction between man's projection of himself toward infinity and the fact of his finitude (as demonstrated horrendously by death), we see the paradox of human life—a paradox that makes of the meaning of life, as Albert Camus puts it, an utter absurdity. The meaning of human life demands infinity; the fact of life offers finitude; therefore, for man all is finally absurd. It should be noted that Camus is not lashing out against "things" that are wrong. His absurdity of life does not arise because of an especially absurd age, or because of pain, or poverty, or disease, or war, or any other pernicious things or combination of things. These things are but symptoms of the deeper malady which is, as we observed earlier, a natural condition of human estrangement, which arises from the nonprogrammed (therefore, self-conscious, disturbingly imaginative) nature of the human beings. It arises because man "knows" that his only significant meaning is to be like God. His project, as Sartre puts it, is God. But he is not God. He is not infinite.

Thus Camus concludes that all is absurd. But it is absurd only

⁹ William C. Tremmel, "The Converting Choice," *Journal for the Scientific Study of Religion* (Los Angeles: University of California Press, Spring 1971), pp. 17–25.

for a genuine atheist like Camus, who does not subscribe to the final transcending hope of any religion. With others, the reach for infinity, the project God, is possible, as evidenced in the gigantic doctrines of apocalyptic resurrection of Christianity; of Karma, Reincarnation, and Nirvana in Hinduism and Buddhism; of the cycle of rebirth in the religion of the Trobrianders; of the Day of Yahweh in Judaism.

From the anxiety of finitude, *to* a new infinitely supported life, *by*—what? By religion, in all of its various forms. Release from finitude is the promise made by theologians in all the religions of the world; not always made the same way, but always made. In general the "by" is offered in one or more of three ways: (1) through resignation, (2) through life after death, and (3) through identity with God. We shall examine these ways to salvation more closely in chapter six, as Jobian resignation, as life after death—immortality and resurrection—and as mystical identification.

part III

the techniques of religion

What does the Lord require of you,
But to do justice, and to love mercy,
And walk humbly with your God?

Micah 6:8

five

Theology:
Empirical and Rational,
Witnessing and Story

Our observations thus far have informed us that to deal with certain kinds of problems (horrendous, nonmanipulable problems), men employ religion. We need to observe now just how they do this. We shall examine the techniques of religion—intellectual, ritual, and moral.

THE RELIGIOUS POSIT

As a preliminary observation we should recognize that individual men, in the face of religious problems, do not go out and invent theologies and rituals and moral codes. These techniques of religion are already provided by the religious heritages into which the individuals are born. With rare exceptions, the religions accepted by people are those they find already operating. The most that usually happens are some simple modifications by the child of "the father's religion." The child internalizes, privatizes, individualizes, the posit of religion he has inherited and learned in his father's house and world. He may change some details (even become a Presbyterian instead of a Baptist), but seldom does he change any of the essential features. A person is born Muslim and usually stays that way, or Jewish and stays that way, or primitive and stays that way. The religion one espouses is usually an accident of birth. It comes from the parents by a kind of intellectual osmosis. One's need for religion is human, but the answers to that innate need begin with the postulates and practices of the religion into which one is born, and usually remain there.

THEOLOGY

One of the things that man does when he does religion is think about it. Especially he interprets his human existence in response to his awareness of the human condition. We shall call all such intellectual activity, theology: *logos*, reasoning, thinking, speaking about *theos*, God and religious things.

As stated earlier, according to some scholars (e.g., Schleiermacher and Otto and Marett), religion is based not in thoughts but in feelings. We, also, suggested that our prehistoric man, with his club and tree, was in the experience of weaponry and religion before he thought about it. But the fact is that thinking about religion (doing theology) is so intimately involved in "having religion" that it is probably a mistake to say that one really preceded the other. In his *Systematic Theology*, Paul Tillich makes this point by saying that theology is as old as religion. Thinking pervades all the spiritual activities of man.

> Every myth contains a theological thought which can be, and often is, made explicit. Priestly harmonizations of different myths sometimes disclose profound theological insights. Mystical speculations . . . unite meditative elevation with theological penetrations. Metaphysical speculations . . . unite rational analysis with theological vision. Ethical, legal, and ritual interpretations of divine law create another form of theology. All this is "theo-logy," *logos* of *theos*, a rational interpretation of the religious sustenance of rites, symbols, and myths.[1]

Whenever it occurs, theology is a technique employed to explain and make reasonable, from a religious perspective, the hidden forces that control the destinies of men and the ultimate meaning of human life. Theology tries to explain man to himself in his world. It functions to deterrorize the horrendous nonmanipulables of life and to offer proper ways of dealing with them. "In the night imagining

---

[1] Paul Tillich, *Systematic Theology*, 3 vols., (Chicago: University of Chicago Press, 1951–1963), vol. 1, pp. 15–16.

some fear/how easy is a bush supposed a bear" (*Midsummer Night's Dream*). To overcome the paralysis that accompanies an undefined, terrifying experience, we name it; we explain it, and then, in terms of the name, we get a basis for action. Once the name is given (once the explanation is available), we are prepared to act in some reasonable way: to run if we name it "bear," to offer sacrifice or prayer if we name it God. Subsequently it may be beneficial to get the right name, but initially we need get only *a* name. Theology gives names (descriptions and explanations) to the life of man, especially in the face of the horrendous, nonmanipulable issues of human existence.

It is sometimes difficult to draw a definitive line between myth (stories about what the Gods have done for man) and theology (words about God; rational interpretation of religious things), especially among primitives. Myth seems to be more dramatic and fanciful and theology more systematic and prosaic, but such a distinction is vague and not always accurate. The myths of primitives are often very carefully organized and precisely articulated, and the theologizing of mystics can be quite poetical. Yet myth and theology are sufficiently distinctive that examples can be found which would not be mistaken for each other; for example, the creation of man in the Garden of Eden versus Anselm's ontological argument for the existence of God. (A neglect of mythology at this point is excused in the promise to return to it later in reference to ritual, where it has a functional relationship that can be immediately seen and identified.) For now, we shall consider two unmistakable pieces of theology: both concerned with rationalizing something about a central religious symbol—God. The two theologians happen to be Christians, and they have in mind the Christian God, but the fact is that their arguments have universal significance. What they have to say about God (which is actually nothing especially Christian) applies everywhere, and if their theological arguments are valid and incontrovertible, they are as valid in Tokyo as in Rome. These theologies are two proofs for the existence of God: one by St. Anselm of Canterbury in the eleventh century, and the other by St. Thomas Aquinas in the thirteenth century. Anselm makes his theology on strictly rational grounds; Thomas makes his several arguments on empirical grounds. We shall start with Thomas.

Empirical Theology   It would appear that we know some things because we see, taste, touch, or hear them, that is, we sense them. If one is asked: "Is it raining outside?" he may go out and look about and there discover that the sun is shining and there are no water droplets falling. With this evidence he could declare: "It is not now raining outside." He has a proposition supported by empirical evidence. Evidence here means a structure of experience which informs a critical consciousness concerning the truth or falsity of a proposition. Experience is the basis of empirical knowing.

Empirical theology is that kind of religious knowledge which is grounded in shareable sense experience. It is religious "truth" established and guaranteed by systematic observations of the world around us. In this kind of reasoning (inductive reasoning) one observes and then draws conclusions from his observations. For example, from the observation that men have always died in the past, we conclude that they will continue to die in the present and future. If all the available data support a given proposition, we accept that proposition as true. It is truth based upon empirical evidence. This kind of truth is, of course, rarely absolutely proved because rarely do we have a chance to examine all of the samples involved in the truth claim. For example, although we may conclude from the death of all men in the past that all men in the present and future will die, we cannot be absolutely certain of this—until, of course, they are all dead, including us. It is at least possible that some person of the present or future may not die. Nevertheless, from past examples the evidence supporting the demise of all men is so persuasive that we operate as if it were absolutely proved.

As an example of empirical theology we can look at some of the works of the great thirteenth-century theologian Thomas Aquinas. Thomas studied the philosophy of Aristotle, and he used Aristotle's thought as the basis of his own philosophical thinking. Aristotle had contended that the world coexisted eternally with God. Thomas was concerned with saying that the world, which might have coexisted eternally with God or might have been created *ex nihilo* (from nothing) was in either case not itself self-sufficient. It was contingent upon God in a number of ways for its reality. In trying to demonstrate this dependence, and therefore the necessary existence of God, Thomas performed what amounts to the classical attempt to reason from the world to God. Thomas believed that men could do "natural theology." They could arrive at certain religious truths by thinking about the world as they experienced it. To be sure, there were certain religious truths that man did not have the capacity to discover by his own reasoning; for example, that Jesus Christ was both God and man; that Father, Son, and Spirit constituted a single Godhead. Such truths God had to deliver to man through divine revelation. But there were some religious truths that man could get on his own. Among these truths was the truth of God's existence.

Thomas offered five arguments for God's existence. In each argument he argued that we could not have the kind of world we all experience unless there was a sufficient reason for this world, and for this kind of world; namely a world that is here and a world that demonstrates purposeful activity and accomplishes values. Each of Thomas' arguments was empirically based. Each argument contained at least one premise that was known by experience to be true of the world we live in. From the obvious fact that things move, he argued to a necessary source of all motion—an unmoved mover. From the obvious fact that things are caused, he moved to the necessary source of all causation—a first cause. From the obvious fact of change, he moved to the unchanging necessity that must underlie all change—necessary being. From the obviously intelligible processes of nature, he moved to the need for an ultimate, intelligent planner of all the world's teleological activity.

Probably the most persuasive of Thomas' arguments is the third argument—the one from possibility and necessity, or from the contingency of the world.

> The third way is taken from possibility and necessity and runs thus. We find in nature things which are possible to be and not to be, since they are found to be generated, and to be corrupted. . . . But it is impossible for these always to exist, for that which can not-be at some time is not. Therefore, if everything can not-be, then at one time there was nothing in existence, because that which does not exist begins to exist only through something already existing. Therefore, if at one time nothing was in existence, it would have been impossible for anything to have begun to exist; and thus even now nothing would be in existence—which is absurd. Therefore, not all things are merely possible, but there must be something the existence of which is necessary. . . . This all men speak of as God.[2]

2 *Summa Theologica*, Question 2, Article 3.

Rem B. Edwards, in his *Reason and Religion*, paraphrases Thomas' third argument as follows:

(1) Some contingent things exist.
(2) An extended series of causes on which these contingent things depend also exists.
(3) Either this entire series of causes is contingent, or it is necessary.
(4) The entire series of causes is not necessary.
(5) If the entire series is contingent, then there is a necessary being.
(6) This necessary being is God.

Therefore, there is a necessary being, God.[3]

Even more simply put, Thomas is saying that (1) we experience the world, but (2) we do not experience anything which is absolutely necessary. Everything we experience comes into being and goes out of being. But (3) if this were all there were to it, there would be no world to experience, because there would have been a time when none of these contingent things existed. If there had been such a time, there would be nothing existing now, because "something" (what we experience now) could not come from nothing. Phenomenologically this is a substantial argument, for it basically argues that we experience the world in such a way as to demand a reason for its being. We ask Heidegger's famous question, "Why are there things rather than nothing?" and the only answer seems to be: there must be something not contingent, something essential; there must be, to use Tillich's postulate, a *ground of being*, which is the source of all the beings we see and taste and touch and smell—even the whole cosmos.[4]

---

[3] Rem B. Edwards, *Reason and Religion* (Harcourt Brace Jovanovich, 1972), p. 258.

[4] Thomas' other arguments were (1) There must be a cause for every motion which is going on. The universe is moving. There must be a first cause of the universe: an unmoved mover. (2) For every effect there must be a sufficient cause. The whole universe is an effect. Therefore, there must be a cause for the whole universe: a first, uncaused cause. (4) In order for evaluations to be made (e.g., good, better, best) there must be a supreme value against which measurement can be made. (5) When one finds teleological (intelligent, purposeful) activity, he may be sure there is a directing mind behind the activity. There can be no plan without a planner. The whole universe is teleological. Therefore, there must be behind it "some intelligent being . . . by whom all natural things are directed to their end; and this being we call God."

Thomas was not talking simply about a ground of being. He was talking about a specific kind of God: the personalistic God of theism; a God who both knows and plans, and who causes the world to be, and to be as it is. Yet·Thomas' arguments do not necessarily lead to that conclusion. The sum of his five arguments actually supplies us with several possible conclusions about the ultimate reality. First, we can conclude, with Thomas, that there is a God out there, intelligent and creative, who is the cause, necessity, and teleological director of the world. But, second, we could equally well conclude that the entire series of natural events itself could be the necessary ground of its own being. One does not have to go out of the natural realm to explain motion, or cause, or ground of being. All he has to do is shift his presuppositions from Aristotelian teleology to modern physics, astronomy, and biology, where he will find all the motion, causation, and ground he needs for his entire universe. It is possible to conceive that the entire series of natural events is totally self-sufficient. In an energy-based, oscillating universe, one seems to have all the motion and causation he needs, and as far as intelligent (i.e., intelligible) process is concerned, one need not say it is imposed from the outside. Intelligent process may be nothing more than the way we read the orderliness with which an oscillating universe oscillates and the way that biological life, under evolution's mandates, sustains itself.

To be for God or for nature in this circumstance seems to come down finally to one's metaphysical overview. If he is a theist to begin with, he is "persuaded," with Thomas, that the experienced world is from a supernatural source. If he is a "naturalist," he believes that the experienced world is from itself. And if he is a pantheist or an immanentalist,[5] he agrees with both, partially: the world is its own source and that creative source is what God is—not just an energy system oscillating, but a ground of being of infinite spiritual capacity and worth.

Rational Theology   Besides knowledge from sense experience, there is knowledge established directly from the operation of deductive reasoning: rational knowledge. Reason itself, proceeding formally from established premises, can establish conclusions that

[5] Pantheists identify God with the world; immanentalists identify God with some dominant phase of the world, usually the creative process.

cannot be false. Take, for example, the classic syllogism: All men are mortal. Socrates is a man. Therefore, Socrates is mortal. This syllogism is absolutely valid. No other conclusion can be drawn. Again, if the statement "All the pictures are hanging on the wall" is true, then the statement "None of the pictures are hanging on the wall" is false. Or if the statement "Some of the pictures are not hanging on the wall" is false, then the statement "All the pictures are hanging on the wall" is true. This kind of thinking is very impressive. Unlike empirical reasoning, which may be persuasive but seldom absolute, this formal logical operation appears to be indubitable. To build theology out of this kind of logical operation would be, it would seem, highly desirable.

The classic example of this kind of "highly desirable" theology is an argument made to prove the existence of God by St. Anselm (1033–1109), a Benedictine monk and Archbishop of Canterbury. He presented in rigid rational form what has become known as the Ontological Argument—the argument from the nature of God's perfect being. The same argument was restated by the brilliant, seventeenth-century philosopher-scientist René Descartes. (This is a different argument from the Descartes argument stated in chapter two.) Although Anselm was a true believer who needed no further proof for God's existence than his own faith, he yet desired, so he stated, to establish a "single argument which would require no other for its proof than itself alone; and alone would suffice to demonstrate that God truly exists."[6] Anselm tells us that he struggled desperately to discover this argument, but could not find it, and finally desired only to forget that he had ever sought it. But by that time the problem had become an obsession he could not escape, until "one day, when I was exceedingly weary with resisting its importunity, in the very conflict of my thoughts, the proof of which I had despaired offered itself, so that I eagerly embraced the thought which I was strenuously repelling."[7]

The argument he conceived, he worked out in two forms. The first began with a capsulizing of the Christian concept of God into a formula: God is "a being than which nothing greater can be con-

---

[6] Anselm, *Proslogium*, trans. Sidney Norton Deane, from John A. Mourant, *Readings in the Philosophy of Religion* (New York: Thomas Y. Crowell, 1969), p. 9.

[7] Anselm, *Proslogium*, pp. 9–10.

ceived." By "greater" Anselm meant more perfect. God is the most perfect being that can be conceived. If such a being is to be conceived, then the existence of such a being must also be conceived, for existence would be one of the attributes of absolute perfection. Think of it this way: a person says, "I conceive of a being that contains absolute perfection. This being is the ultimate in perfection. There can be no greater being." A second person asks, "Does the perfect being you conceive have actual existence outside your mind?" The first person replies, "No. This is purely a conceptual being." The second person can then reply, "You have not conceived of a being than which nothing can be greater (more perfect), for I have conceived of a greater being than yours. My being also has the perfection of 'perfect objective existence'." Anselm said it this way:

> if that, than which nothing greater can be conceived, exists in the understanding alone, the very being, than which nothing greater can be conceived, is one, than which a greater can be conceived. But obviously this is impossible. Hence, there is no doubt that there exists a being, than which nothing greater can be conceived, and it exists both in the understanding and in reality.[8]

In the *Proslogium*, Anselm formulated his argument a second time, this time directing his argument not simply to the existence of God but to God's uniquely necessary existence. Here he defined God in such a way that it was impossible to conceive of Him as not existing. To say that the most perfect being is conceivable and at the same time can be conceived as not existing is to deny and affirm something at the same time; namely that God both is and is not "that than which nothing greater can be conceived." In his own words, Anselm states:

> If that, than which nothing greater can be conceived, can be conceived not to exist, it is not then that than which nothing greater can be conceived. But this is an irreconcilable contradiction. There is, then, so truly a being than which nothing greater can be conceived to exist, that it cannot be conceived not to exist.[9]

René Descartes reformulated the ontological argument (Anselm's form one above) in the seventeenth century and attracted

[8] Anselm, *Proslogium*, p. 11.
[9] Anselm, *Proslogium*, p. 11.

wide attention to it. He insisted that existence must be included among the predicates of God just as surely as 180 degrees must be included among the predicates of a triangle. A triangle whose internal angles did not equal two right angles would not be a triangle. Even so, God without the predicate of existence would not be God. In his own words Descartes stated:

> I find it manifest that we can no more separate the existence of God from his essence than we can separate from the essence of a rectilinear triangle the fact that the size of its three angles equal two right angles, or from the idea mountain the idea of a valley. Thus it is no less self-contradictory to conceive of God, a supremely perfect Being, who lacks existence—that is, who lacks some perfection—than it is to conceive of a mountain for which there is no valley.
>
> From the fact alone that I cannot conceive of God except as existing, it follows that existence is inseparable from him, and consequently he does, in truth, exist.[10]

Neither Anselm nor Descartes escaped criticism of their arguments. The monk Guanilo of Marmoutiers immediately argued with Anselm's technique, saying that by using it one could arrive at absurd conclusions. One could, for example, prove the existence of an absolutely perfect island. All one would have to do would be to conceive of an absolutely perfect island, an island than which no greater could be conceived. Such an island, by Anselm's reasoning, would have to exist. But Anselm replied, saying that the element missing in Gaunilo's island refutation was the element of necessity. An island (or any other ordinary object) is part of the contingent world, and can be thought of as contingent, and therefore, as not existing. But this is not true of God. In his second formulation of the Ontological Argument Anselm demonstrated that God could not be conceived of as not existing. Thus Guanilo's argument might be cogent against perfect islands, but not against a perfect God.

It has been widely believed that Immanual Kant devastated the Ontological Argument by showing that there is no necessary connection between the concept or idea of an absolutely perfect being and the objective fact of an absolutely perfect being. But some philosophers—Charles Hartshorne and Norman Malcolm, in particular—point out that Kant missed the mark as Guanilo had

[10] René Descartes, "Fifth Meditation," *Meditations on First Philosophy* (Indianapolis: Bobbs-Merrill, 1960), pp. 63–64.

done. He attacked Anselm's first formulation, but missed the second formulation.

Kant argued that as "an idea" the predicate angularity does belong to a triangle, and the predicate existence does belong to God. As a concept, in each case, the appropriate predicate is necessarily linked to the subject. But, Kant argued, it does not follow from this analytical necessity that these subjects with their predicates actually exist. If there actually is a triangle which is not simply an idea, then its angles will be of a certain character; and if there actually is an infinitely perfect being which is not simply an idea, it will have existence as one of its perfections. "To posit a triangle, and yet to reject its three angles, is self-contradictory," said Kant in his *Critique of Pure Reason,* but, he went on to say, "there is no self-contradiction in rejecting the triangle altogether with its angles. The same holds true of the concept of an absolutely necessary being." Kant was arguing that we can have the *idea* of a triangle, which would have to include all necessary predicates; but the idea might be only an idea. It need not have an objective counterpart anywhere outside the idea. There could conceivably be the idea of a triangle without there being any "real," nonmental triangles. The same is true of God's existence. If we are going to think of an absolutely perfect being, we must think of it as existing, but thinking it exists does not make it exist, except in thought. An idea, Kant pointed out, is not made more perfect by the "objective" existence of what is conceived. External existence does not add anything to the perfection of the idea of God, or any other idea. For example, the idea of a hundred dollars is not made more perfect, or even changed, by the existence of a hundred "real" dollars in one's pocket. The Ontological Argument, Kant insisted, does not prove the "real" existence of God. It only proves that existence is a necessary predicate if one is going to *think* of an absolutely perfect being.

Norman Malcom argues that Anselm's critics, including Kant, have missed the point in supposing that the proposition "God necessarily exists" is equivalent to the proposition "If God exists then he necessarily exists." *If God exists* implies the possibility of contingency. He might not exist. But Anselm's proposition places God in the category of absolute necessity. The whole of his argument is that God is not a contingent being, as Anselm most emphatically informed Monk Guanilo. By the very nature of Anselm's argument, God possesses necessary existence; therefore, to say, as the Kantian attack does, that God necessarily exists, but it is possible he may not exist is to state a contradiction. Indications are that Anselm's deductive theological argument has not been summarily removed from theological contention. His deductive theology survives and even resuscitates.

It might be useful, however, to remember that Anselm did not rest his faith on this argument, or any other argument. He was a "true believer" because of assurance: an assurance that came from an inner esoteric knowing. His Ontological Argument was more an act of reverence than a basis of faith. As Anselm himself put it:

> I do not endeavor, O Lord, to penetrate thy sublimity, for in no wise do I compare my understanding with that; but I long to understand in some degree thy truth, which my heart believes and loves. For I do not seek to understand that I may believe, but I believe in order to understand.[11]

By no means is theology always so precise and philosophical as Thomas and Anselm presented it. Indeed, much more often it is loose in structure, even poetical in form, and it covers the whole range of religious life.

Witnessing   Thus far we have looked at theology as a formal and formidable enterprise, and have split it off from mythology. But theology is not necessarily so philosophically precise, and indeed usually is not so. More often it is in the form of preachments, especially "witnessing" preachments, and "storytelling" preachments, which pertain directly to the mythos.

The launching of the Christian Church illustrates a theology of witnessing. According to the record, the Pentecost Church was presented and supported with empirical arguments that had little to do with philosophy. Early Christian theology was guaranteed on the evidence of miracles, even the miracle of Resurrection. According to the Book of Acts, on the Day of Pentecost, Peter delivered a sermon to the citizens of Jerusalem.

> Listen to these words, men of Israel! Jesus of Nazareth was a man whose divine mission was clearly *shown* to you by the miracles and

---

[11] Anselm, *Proslogium*, p. 10.

signs which God did through him. . . . God raised him from the dead. . . . God has raised this very Jesus from the dead, and we are all *witnesses* to this fact (Acts 2:22, 24, 32, *Good News for Modern Man*, New York: American Bible Society, 1966).

The early Christians were, first, concerned to convince themselves that Jesus was indeed Messiah/Son of God. Their conviction came in the miracles performed by the man himself, and especially the miracle of his return from the dead. Today it is not possible to recover the details of what really happened during the brief public career of Jesus and during the few days and weeks following his death. The Gospels were not written to be accurate histories of the life of Jesus, or even biographies of Jesus. Each was written for theological reasons, and each used the stories and reports of Jesus' activities and sayings to make its particular theological claim.[12] Because the Gospel writers used history rather than recorded it, the details of the Jesus Story are confused and confusing. There are, for example, no fewer than four accounts of what happened at the Resurrection—who saw him, when they saw him, under what conditions. Today only one thing seems absolutely sure. The people who were there were absolutely sure that he had arisen and returned to them. The Christian Church began in an absolute conviction of Resurrection. Resurrection was the final and conclusive eyewitness assurance for the faith and subsequent proclamation of that faith. Such theology continued and continues. The faith is proclaimed because (1) it was witnessed by the ancient ones, and (2) the apostolic witnessing is rewitnessed in the continuing life of the Church.

It should be remembered that in the earliest days of the Christian Church only a handful of people had ever heard of Jesus, and even fewer had been with him. He was practically a nobody, and an executed nobody at that. That handful of believers needed as-

---

[12] Recognizing that it is far too simplified to be more than superficially accurate, the theological claims of the various Gospel writers can be stated so: Mark presented Jesus dramatically as the Messiah, a secret revealed only gradually in the Mark story. Matthew, supporting the Messiah claim, wanted to say in addition that Jesus was also Teacher, Law Giver, a second Moses, and even more than Moses, he was the new Abraham, the fulfillment of Israel. Luke wanted to present him more widely as the savior of mankind. And John, finally, presented him as not just Messiah, nor Law Giver, nor Savior, but as the Word of God, the Logos, even God himself.

surance that their trust in him was solidly based; that he was what he had proclaimed himself to be. The Resurrection was their assurance. Its importance to the first Christians cannot be gainsayed. Thomas was symbolic of their need. He had to *see* the Christ, and *touch* the Christ that he might declare: "My Lord and my God!" Paul voiced the issue in his Letter to the Church in Corinth.

> If Christ has not been raised from the dead then we have nothing to preach, and you have nothing to believe . . . if Christ has not been raised, then your faith is a delusion and you are still lost in your sins (Corinthians I, 15:14, 17, *Good News for Modern Man*).

Today this reliance on witnessed Resurrection seems less critical, or, at least, it is not the only evidence upon which the faith is based. This because today the Christians have, also, a two-thousand-year old tradition to rely upon. Some Christians even go so far as to say that the question of the "physical Resurrection" is not especially important; that even if such a Resurrection took place, it would not necessarily prove that Jesus was Messiah/Son of God. It might have been just a good trick. The Egyptian Osiris reportedly accomplished the same return to life after a violent death. But there is today a tradition-witnessing difference between Osiris and Christ. The Osirian religion is gone. It is Christianity that remains; Christ who towers over the age, not Osiris. Christ's posture in religion is demonstrated not merely by some events in the dim past but by the faith of millions of people who still bear witness to, and stand as evidence of, his divinity.

Story Theology   Not dissimilar to witness theology is the somewhat different style of doing theology which may be called story theology. A story is told which may be *The Story*, or it may be a story that illuminates The Story—The Story being, of course, the God story, the mythos. This kind of theology is especially important to those religions such as Judaism and Christianity which explain themselves by reporting unique and remembered events of the ancient past: an Exodus, a Crucifixion, a spectacular birth, a covenant at Mt. Sinai.

Robert McAfee Brown, in a paper delivered at the annual conference of the American Academy of Religion in 1974, told of his growing friendship, during the Vietnam War years, with Rabbi

Abraham Heschel, and of how he began to notice that every time he asked the rabbi a theological question "he would reply, 'My friend, let me tell you a story.'" This Jewish propensity to make a religious point by telling a story is traditional not only in Heschel's Judaism but also in Brown's Christianity. Jesus told stories. He never made points with rational arguments, even, apparently, when invited to do so. For example, we are told that a lawyer once engaged him in a conversation. "What must one do to inherit eternal life?" the lawyer asked. Jesus gave a quick formal answer which should have fit comfortably into a lawyer's way of thinking. "Keep the law," he said. "Love God, as the law commands, and love your neighbor." But when the lawyer persisted and asked, "Who is my neighbor?" Jesus moved immediately into a theology of storytelling: Once upon a time, "a man went down from Jerusalem to Jericho. . . ." He told a story.

And the Christian Church, in its earliest years, followed Jesus' example. One may be sure that when a missionary went out from Antioch to circuit-ride the newly formed churches in Asia Minor, he was not asked to read a paper on the nature of the Divine Being, or even read from the Bible. He was asked to tell them the Stories of Jesus. And a little later, when Mark, for example, wanted to make theological statements about Jesus (that he was, among other things the Messiah) he did so in a story called the Good News.

In both Judaism and Christianity the vehicle of theological communication has always been narrative. This is true of other world religions as well. Robert Brown states that

> Something of the same sort is going on in Greek thought in the gradual shift from *mythos* to *logos*, as Cornford points out in *From Religion to Philosophy*. . . . Owen Barfield, in *Poetic Diction*, . . . details a similar evolution in literature 'from concrete to abstract thinking.' Even Carlos Castaneda in *The Teachings of Don Juan* first gives a narrative account of his contact with a Yaqui Indian, and only after that turns to what he calls 'A Structural Analysis,' where he systematizes the same story in considerably less than half the space.[13]

It is certainly a fact, as Martin Buber informs us in his *On the Bible,* that the Bible does not present us with theological state-

[13] Robert McAfee Brown, "Story and Theology," *Philosophy of Religion and Theology: 1974* (Tallahassee, Fla.: American Academy of Religion, 1974), p. 56.

ments. "It presents us with a story only, but this story is theology; biblical theology is narrative theology."[14]

In the theology of storytelling, the stories are first told, then retold, and retold again, and collected, and arranged, and reflected upon, and rearranged, and gradually systematized, and given official sanction, and declared scriptural, as we shall see more of in chapter seven.

[14] Martin Buber, *On the Bible* (New York: Schocken, 1968), p. 26.

six

Salvation Theology

Pursuing theology further, we shall pick up the proposal at the end of chapter four and observe several ways in which the question of "being saved" is handled in several different religions. What is man to do? What is he to believe as he faces major life problems, horrendous, nonmanipulable circumstances, his human condition, his finitude? We shall consider several proposals: (1) That he resign himself to the tragedies of life by assuming a kind of reverent, Jobian agnosticism; (2) That all will be made right in a life after death; (3) That one can escape finitude by losing (i.e., finding) himself in union with God. Also, (4) That one might assume a quasi-religious, hopefully philosophical attitude of indifference. We shall now look at these proposals in some detail.

Resignation or Reverent Agnosticism   "It was God's will." In this statement is contained a religious resignation of tremendous metapsychological potency and of far-reaching theological significance. It can mean, as in the Turkish *kismet,* that one's fate is allotted and only a fool kicks against the briars. One can push against the shove, but it is wisdom to know when the pushing is futile, and then simply to accept the shove resignedly. This "fatalism" becomes a theology when one is told (or simply learns) to accept his finitude, and to trust that God will finally make right a human condition which to all appearances is unhappily wrong. *Let God's will be done.* Whatever it is, one is encouraged to resign himself to it as *somehow* a meaningful part of God's inscrutable plan. This is a tremendously potent bit of religious conviction. In the face of a really bad scene (e.g., the tragic, premature, seemingly meaningless death of a loved one) many people accomplish an amazing amount of assurance and spiritual serenity by saying, "I do not know why, but God must know. It is God's will." Shifting the blame trustingly to God puts the dimension of infinity into a tragically finite circumstance and, apparently, empowers the true believer to "walk and not faint."

This theme is played out in grand style in the ancient theological drama-poem called Job. The story line of Job is simple, and apparently much older than the finished dramatic portrayal we currently possess. The simple story is told in Job 1, 2, 42:7–17. It is a brief tale of a shepherd prince named Job who is a man of excellent character and great wealth. God himself is proud of his servant Job, but Satan, who is pictured here, not as the fiend of Hell, but as a member of God's advisory cabinet,[1] suggests that Job is loyal to God only because he is so well treated by God's gracious providence. Let Job suffer enough and he too will turn against God. At Satan's urging, God permits Job to be put to the test. His wealth and family are wiped out. His good health destroyed. He is reduced to poverty and misery. But, according to the ancient tale, Job remains patient and loyal, and finally, the test completed, is restored by God to his former condition of prosperity and happiness.

In the fifth century B.C. an unknown poet-dramatist took the ancient tale and developed it into a theological treatise on human suffering and what should be man's religious response to suffering. This new author kept the story line of the original author. Here too at the behest of Satan, Job was tested to determine his loyalty to God. But now the story was expanded into an assault upon the traditional Hebrew notion that human suffering was to be understood as punishment for breaking God's Laws; an explanation of suffering which the author apparently felt was inadequate. Job suffered in spite of the fact that he was a loyal keeper of the Law. He was a righteous man. He did not deserve to be punished, but he

---

[1] In recent considerations of the figure of Satan in the Old Testament, some scholars are suggesting that the Satan of Job is really a personification of the Hebrew God Yahweh. Satan is actually the dark side of God: God's alter ego: in this instance, God's own doubt about Job. See Rivkah S. Kluger, *Satan in the Old Testament* in reference.

was punished horribly and shatteringly, and no reason was ever given to him to justify his suffering.

In this expanded account, Job carried on a series of arguments with several men who came ostensibly to commiserate with him, but who were, in fact, spokesmen for the old broken covenant answer to human suffering. They argued with Job accusing him of some hidden wickedness that justified his punishment at the hands of God. Job, however, staunchly denied that he deserved such punishment. He further pointed out that the world was full of wicked people who were never punished. In fact, they often prospered. In this second edition of Job, the new author turned the patient Job of the first author into an impatient, angry rebel, who did not accept his lot complacently, but railed against it, even to the point of finally demanding an answer from God himself.

And finally God did answer Job. He answered Job—symbolically enough, out of a whirlwind—and the answer given was a theology of resignation or reverent agnosticism. The author did not simply have God tell Job directly that he should be resigned in the face of things he could not possibly comprehend; namely why God does what he does to men. Rather, the author had God squelch Job with tremendous speeches that clearly place Job (and all mankind) in his proper place.

> Then the Lord answered Job out of the whirlwind:
> Who is this whose ignorant words
> cloud my design in darkness?
> Brace yourself and stand up like a man;
> I will ask questions, and you shall answer.
> Where were you when I laid the earth's foundation?
> Tell me, if you know the answer.
> Who settled its dimensions? Surely you should know.
> Who stretched his measuring-line over it?
> On what do its supporting pillars rest?
> Who watched over the birth of the sea,
> when it burst in flood from the womb—
> when I wrapped it in a blanket of clouds
> and cradled it in fog,
> when I established its bounds,
> fixing its doors and bars in place
> and said, "Thus far shall you come and no further,
> and here your surging waves shall halt."
> In all your life have you ever called up the dawn

> or shown the morning star its place?
> Have you taught it to grasp the fringes of the earth
> and shake the Dog-star from its place;
> to bring up the horizon in relief as clay under a seal,
> until all things stand out like the folds of a cloak,
> when the light of the Dog-star is dimmed
> and the stars of the Navigator's Line go out one by one?
> Have you descended to the springs of the sea
> or walked in the unfathomable deep?
> Have the gates of death been revealed to you?
> Have you ever seen the door-keepers of the palace of
> darkness?
> Have you comprehended the vast expanse of the world?
> Come, tell me all this, if you know (Job 38:1–18).[2]

The essential theological point of the tremendous speeches of God was that the problem of suffering was too great for Job's finite mind. He was asking to know what he could not know, had no business to know. Man's knowledge of finite things was slight; how, then, could Job expect to know the meaning of infinite plans and infinite meanings? Job had asked to know the impossible: to know as God knows, to know what God knows. He had, in fact, made league with the cardinal vice and stumbled at exactly the spot of Adam's transgression. Job, like Adam before him, had reached for the fruit of the ultimate knowledge that he might be like God, knowing good and evil.

The truth of his condition struck Job like a physical blow, and once in the midst of God's tirade he cried out:

> What reply can I give thee, I who carry no weight?
> I put my finger to my lips.
> I have spoken once and now will not answer again;
> twice have I spoken, and I will do so no more.[3]

And then when God's speech was finished, Job spoke in humility and resignation.

> I know that thou canst do all things
> and that no purpose is beyond thee.

[2] *The New English Bible with Apocrypha* (New York: Cambridge University Press, 1971).

[3] Ibid., Job 40: 3–5.

> But I have spoken of great things which I have not
>   understood,
> things too wonderful for me to know.
> I knew of thee then only by report,
> but now I see thee with my own eyes.
> Therefore, I melt away; I repent in dust and ashes.[4]

Now Job realized both his own weakness and God's capacity; his own need and God's concern, and no other knowing was necessary. He did not understand, but he believed. He was sincerely and reverently resigned in his agnosticism. In trust he was saved.

Thus we see that one possible theological answer to suffering and death is the posture of reverent agnosticism. A person cannot know why some things happen, but he can believe that God knows, and that God knows best, and that in the end, in this life or in another life, the one who clings to his faith in God and God's goodness will, as Job in the end, be compensated a hundredfold.

Life After Death—Reincarnation   Of contemporary philosophers, Martin Heidegger is the one who most emphatically defines man's existence as a condition determined by the anticipation of death. "Life," he tells us, "is being-unto-death." Because it is a universal, horrendous nonmanipulable of condition, and the major dilemma confronting human salvation, death gets high priority in all theologies. It gets answered, and the answer most often given is in the form of a reincarnation theology. We quickly associate reincarnation doctrine (or transmigration of souls) with the great Eastern religions (Hinduism, Buddhism), but there are many other religions that deal with the problem of death and life after death in this fashion. Indeed, somewhere Arnold Toynbee has stated that for all our Western skepticism about reincarnation, Christianity is one of the "peculiar religions" which does not teach this doctrine.

To see this kind of theology at work, we shall examine a simple form of reincarnation theory; the form found in the theology of the inhabitants of the Island of Kiriwina, which is one of the islands of the Trobriand Chain, a group of islands north and east of New Guinea. Our information about these people comes from the work of Bronislaw Malinowski. The people of Kiriwina believe that men have souls, which they call baloma. At death the soul, which is

<hr />

[4] Ibid., Job 42: 1–6.

apparently an ethereal duplicate of the human being, that is, a ghost, detaches itself from the body and soon travels to a special island (Tuma) where it enters a spiritual life much like its former physical life. It eats, drinks, socializes, falls in love, gets married. Malinowski's informants told him that the spirit women of Tuma were very beautiful and seductive, and they took special pains to distract the newly arrived male ghost from remembering his earthly wife. They usually succeeded. The ghost-man forgets his old wife and settles down with a new spirit wife. However, Malinowski reports:

> a man may wait for his widow to join him in Tuma, but my informants did not seem inclined to think that many would do this. . . . The spirit, in any case, settles down to a happy existence in Tuma, where he spends another lifetime until he dies again. But this death is . . . not complete annihilation.[5]

At its death on Tuma, the baloma is reborn in a human form back on the island of its former life.[6]

The baloma in its life on Tuma grows old. Its eyes dim, its teeth fall out, its strength fails, until in the last stage the baloma goes down to the sea and sloughs off its skin, much as a snake does. What is left is the waiwaia, that is, the embryo of a new to-be-born child. This embryo is picked up by a baloma woman and carried back to the island of its former habitation and secretly implanted in the womb of a woman, which has been opened by former copulation. Or it may be (a different theological explanation) that the baloma goes to sea, where it is transformed into the waiwaia. Then it either washes ashore, where it is found by a baloma woman, or it drifts to the island of former habitation and seeks on its own an open vaginal passage in one of the girls or women bathing in the sea. Thus life begins over. There is a cycle of life on earth, then the passage over to the cycle of spirit life, and finally the passage back to the cycle of reborn human life: reincarnation.

[5] Malinowski, *Magic, Science and Religion*, p. 135.

[6] Kiriwinians have some interesting ideas about pregnancy and how it relates to the preexisting baloma. They believe that the only function of the male in conception is to open the woman so that the baloma embryo (waiwaia) can have passage into the woman's womb. The waiwaia is a metamorphic stage in the reincarnation process. It is the baloma-ghost prepared to return to life as a human.

With this brief account of Trobriander reincarnation doctrine we can see that primitives can and do have elaborate theological systems. And although much of what they believe may appear to us as theologically naive and scientifically inaccurate, it is not without religious profundity. These people have looked at the succession of life and death and have declared that it constitutes a meaningful order. They have looked at death (at being dead) and have declared that it is neither terrifying nor meaningless. They have transcended finitude, have dealt adequately with the horrendous nonmanipulable of death, and have accomplished a viable salvation theology.

The idea of reincarnation in Trobriand theology differs in one major respect from the more elaborate reincarnation theologies of Hinduism and Buddhism. In the South Pacific theology there is no element of reward and punishment involved in the cycle of death and rebirth. This is not the case in Eastern theologies. In the East, reincarnation means rebirth in accordance with the Law of Karma. Karma is the Law that governs rebirth according to the worthiness of the preceding life. A good man (because of the Karma principle) is rewarded with a better life next time than last time. A bad man gets a worse life. Each passage through life is determined by the character of the person's life in the last passage, until eventually, when perfection has been accomplished and the perfect life lived, no more rebirths are demanded by the Law of Karma, and the soul may pass away into Nirvana—become united with God Brahman.

Life After Death—Immortality and Resurrection   Although these two terms (immortality and resurrection) refer to life after death, they are not identical; in fact, according to some theologians, they are radically different. One is a Greek concept; the other is Hebrew. One (the Greek Platonic one) argues that the soul is by its own nature without beginning and indestructible; the other (the Jewish-Christian) denies this, holding that souls are God-created and could be destroyed by God. Furthermore, the destiny of the soul in Platonic thought is to escape the entrapment of the body and be free. In Jewish and Christian thought its proper destiny is to be reunited with the body (resurrected) that it might once again have a full life. We shall first look at the radical difference between immortality theology and resurrection theology, and then look at how some of the Church Fathers modified Greek thought and dressed immortality in a Christian garb.

In the Ingersol Lectures of 1955, Oscar Cullmann read a scintillating paper that drew the radical difference between immortality and resurrection. This difference he dramatically portrayed by presenting as contrasting illustrations the death scenes of Socrates of Athens and Jesus of Nazareth.

In Plato's dialogue entitled *Phaedo* we have an account of the serene and noble death of Socrates. That ugly-bodied, most beautiful of men had been condemned to die by an angry and vindictive city. The charges brought against him had been vague but adequately deadly: association with traitorous people, corruption of the youth, denial of the Gods, radicalism. Tried and convicted, he had been in prison for two months awaiting execution. Now the time had come.

Phaedo tells his friend Echecrates how it was. Throughout the day a number of Socrates' friends, including Phaedo, had been with him in the cell. The old man had wanted to talk about death and immortality, and so his young friends and disciples had once again followed with fascination the marvelous thinking of the great teacher. He had led them to understand that death was a friend, a great liberator, for it freed the soul from the confines and restrictions of the body. While one was alive his soul was really imprisoned in a body that was essentially alien to it. Only with death could the soul go free. And it must go free for it could not be destroyed. The soul was indestructible—immortal. With such "theology" to support him, Socrates welcomed the coming of the end of the day, and with it the end of his days.

Phaedo told Echecrates how as the sunset hour arrived, the jailer came in and tearfully apologized to Socrates for the act that he had to perform, and how Socrates was so impressed by the man's distress, and commented upon what a kind and friendly man he was. Throughout the day Phaedo said, they had all managed to hide their distress at what was happening there, but seeing the jailer and hearing Socrates praise the man, and knowing that the time could not be put off much longer, they began to break down. Phaedo confessed that he found himself weeping openly, until Socrates reprimanded them, telling them that he had sent the women away to avoid such a scene, for he believed that a man should die in peace. Socrates then said they should get on with it. But Crito, who was also there, begged him to wait a while for it really was not late and that many condemned people put it off to the very last minute. Socrates said that he could understand how others might want to put it off as long as possible, but it would not be right for him to put it off, for "I do not think that I should gain anything by drinking the poison a little later; I should be sparing and saving a life which is already gone; I could only laugh at myself for this. Please then do as I say, and not refuse me." So Crito called for the jailer to return with the poison, and Socrates drank it. He went on talking for a while, until the poison began to take effect. Then he lay down and covered his face for a while. Towards the end he uncovered his face and said, "Crito, I owe a cock to Asclepius, will you remember to pay the debt? The debt shall be paid, said Crito; is there anything else? There was no answer. . . . Such was the end . . . of our friend, whom I may truly call the wisest and justest and best of all men whom I have ever known."[7]

So died the sage of Athens, quietly, serenely, securely, supported by a philosophical-theological conviction that the human soul is indestructible—is literally and absolutely immortal. Because it is not a material substance as is the body, it is, by its own nature, imperishable. The very simplicity (noncompoundedness) of the soul makes it necessarily permanent. Furthermore, the soul (the pure reason of man) has no real affinity with the body that encases it. The body is its prison. Only with the death of the body can this prison be opened and the immortal soul be freed. So believing, Socrates goes to his death not wanting to avoid it, or even put it off a little longer.

Not so with Jesus. When death came at him it seemed more like a fiend from Hell. Alone in the Garden he faced it as a terrifying catastrophe. The records tell us that "he sweat blood." Why? Why the difference? Surely Jesus was as courageous a man as Socrates. He, like Socrates, deliberately chose the path that led to his own execution. He was not afraid of the men who would kill him. He had faced dangerous men many times. Surely it was not just the thought of the pain that would come. He could have fled from the

[7] "Phaedo, The Death of Socrates," from *The Republic and Other Works by Plato*, trans. B. Jowett (Garden City, N.Y.: Doubleday, 1960), pp. 551–552.

Garden, escaped into the Judean hills, avoided the agony of cruci-fixion. No, it must have been something else that he feared. *It was death itself that he feared.* Death was not his friend, not his liber-ator. Death did not come blessedly to free his immortal soul. Death came to annihilate him. Death was his enemy, because death was God's enemy.

In his Ingersol Lectures, Cullmann put these two death scenes side by side to indicate how differently two different theological positions present the concept of life after death. From his published lectures we read:

> I have put the death of Socrates and the death of Jesus side by side. For nothing shows better the radical difference between the Greek doctrine of the immortality of the soul and the Christian doctrine of the resurrection. Because Jesus underwent death in all its horror, not only in his body, but also in his soul . . . and as he is regarded by the first Christians as the mediator of salvation, he must indeed be the very one who in his death conquers death itself. He cannot obtain the victory by simply living on as an immortal soul, by funda-mentally *not* dying. He can conquer death only by actually dying, by betaking himself of the sphere of "nothingness," of abandonment by God. When one wishes to overcome someone else, one must enter his territory. . . .
>
> Furthermore, if life is to issue out of so genuine a death as this, a new divine act of creation is necessary. And this act of creation calls back to life not just a part of the man, but the whole man—all that God has created and death has annihilated. For Socrates and Plato no act of creation is necessary. For the body is indeed bad and should not live. And that part which is to live on, the soul, does not die at all.
>
> If we want to understand the Christian faith in the resurrection, we must completely disregard the Greek thought that the material, the bodily, the corporeal is bad and *must* be destroyed, so that the death of the body could not be in any sense a destruction of the true life. For Christian (and Jewish) thinking, the death of the body is *also* destruction of the God-created life. No distinction is made: even the life of our body is true life; death is the destruction of *all* life created by God. Therefore, it is death and not the body which must be conquered by the resurrection.[8]

[8] Oscar Cullmann, "Immortality of the Soul or Resurrection of the Dead," reprinted in *Immortality and Resurrection*, ed. Krister Stendahl (New York: Macmillan, 1965), pp. 18–19.

According to Cullmann, Christians (and Jews), when acting out of their own religious tradition and not out of Platonic philosophy, reject the immortality doctrine in favor of the more radical doctrine of re-creation or resurrection. When a person is dead, he is dead! Totally. Only as God re-creates him does he live again. To die is to be annihilated. To live again is to be resurrected, and, according to John's Revelation, resurrected only at the end of time.

Cullmann's comparison is highly illustrative of the "philosophical" difference between the concept of immortality and the concept of resurrection. It may also be an accurate description of Jesus' own theological position and the theological position of the very first Christians. It is for a fact an accurate observation of biblical theology on the subject. But for all this, it is unquestionable that traditional Christian theology does endorse a doctrine of immortality, as well as a doctrine of resurrection. Quite early the influence of Socrates' student Plato was felt, and Christian theologians made accommodations for immortality as well as resurrection in Christian belief. To them, in the interval between death and resurrection, the soul had an independent life of its own—an immortality. But in their theories of immortality, the early Christian theologians departed from Platonic theory in one important aspect. They did not endorse the idea that the soul was immortal by its own indestructible nature. Whatever immortality the soul possessed, it possessed as a gift from God. God created it, and he could destroy it. Justin Martyr, Irenaeus, Tatian, Theophilus, Arnobus, Lactanius—all held that the soul lived because God willed it so, and would cease to live if that became God's pleasure. Tertullian and Origen have been "accused" of holding that the soul was immortal by its own nature, but this is doubtful. Tertullian apparently meant that the soul could not be killed by men, while Origen apparently meant that souls created by God would not be destroyed by him. Even Augustine, who used Platonic arguments to prove the soul's immortal nature, nevertheless stated that although

the soul of man is, according to a peculiar sense of its own (secundum quendam modum suum), immortal, it is not absolutely immortal as God is.[9]

[9] *Epistolae.*

The theologians had ample philosophical support in Greek philosophy for the doctrine of immortality, but they found little support for resurrection theology in Greek philosophy, except as they could interpret transmigration of souls as analogous to resurrection theology. Resurrection was not a Greek idea. In Christian theology it comes from Judaism.

Apparently neither resurrection, nor any other serious theology of life after death, was a part of the religious tradition of the early Hebrews. Early biblical literature was so silent on the subject that some scholars have held that the idea of life after death was not a part of early Hebrew beliefs. This however, was probably not the case. Probably, as did other Semitic people, the early Hebrews believed that the soul (*nephesh*) or spirit (*ruach*) did survive physical death. The place of this survival was called Sheol. In Sheol the shade or ghost of the departed person existed probably in a state resembling sleep. As some Hebrews picturesquely put it: the soul of the departed slumbered on the bosom of Abraham. Sheol was clearly not a place of reward or punishment. In neither the writings ascribed to Moses nor the writings of the Prophets was Sheol presented as similar in any way to the later ideas of Heaven or Hell. Nor did the idea of resurrection have an important place in early Hebrew thought. In fact, Hebraism was predominantly concerned with this life, and especially the prosperity and future of God's Chosen People—the nation of Israel. Those ancient people seemed to have been perfectly satisfied simply to assign the dead to Abraham's bosom.

At the same time, as early as the eighth-century prophets, there were in ancient Hebrew thought the seeds of the eschatologies that were to be elaborated by later Pharisees and early Christians. First, there was the idea of the Day of Yahweh. The Hebrews came to believe that there would come a day when God would come and rescue his nation from its enemies and punish those enemies—the oppressive Gentile nations. This idea was eventually modified (beginning especially with the Prophet Amos) to include a punishment for all of God's enemies, wicked Hebrews as well as the Gentile oppressors. Amos prophesied that the Day of Yahweh would be a terrible day of judgment for all wicked men. Second, there was in ancient Hebrew thought the idea of rehabilitation of the Hebrew nation, that is, a kind of national "resurrection," at the end of time. If the nation was to be reconstructed, would not one expect Abraham to be there, and Isaac and Jacob, and Moses? Was it not reasonable to expect that some of the righteous dead in Sheol, the heroes of the past, would also be reconstructed; would be resurrected in new bodies? And if heroes, why not all good men, even everybody?

These ideas developed rapidly and impressively after the time of the Babylonian Captivity. In 586 B.C. the Hebrews (Southern Judean Hebrews) were overrun by Nebuchadnezzar of Babylon, and the major Hebrew families were carried into slavery. In Babylon they lived first under Babylonian rule and then, after Cyrus of Persia conquered the lands of the Babylonians, under Persian rule. The contact with Persia was especially important to Hebrew thought. In Babylon the Jews (a term that came to be applied to the Hebrews during the Captivity) were tremendously influenced by (1) the idea of God struggling with a great supernatural enemy (including and especially the Zoroastrian Evil Spirit, Angra Mainyu, also called Satan), and (2) the idea of a place under the earth where evil souls were punished as they deserved because of the wickedness of their lives on earth.

At this time, or shortly thereafter, a new type of literature began to emerge in Jewish culture: the apocalypse, of which Daniel in the Old Testament and later Revelation in the New Testament are fine examples. Concerning this type of literature, Dr. Martin Rist informs us that

> Apocalypticism is the belief that this present evil and corrupt world, now under the control of Satan, will soon be ended and destroyed, along with Satan and his demonic and human agents, by the direct intervention of God, heretofore transcendent; who thereupon will establish a new and perfect age and a new and perfect world, both under his immediate control, in which the righteous from among the living and the resurrected dead will enjoy a blessed, righteous existence without end.[10]

As we can see from this quotation, an apocalypse is an eschatology, that is, an account of the end of time. In both postcaptivity Judaism and early Christianity the end of time would involve (1) a resurrection of all the dead, (2) a universal judgment, (3) destruction or

[10] Martin Rist, *Daniel and Revelation*, a monograph (Nashville, Tenn.: Abingdon, 1947), p. 3.

punishment for all the wicked, and (4) blessed, eternal existence for the righteous.

In late Palestinian Judaism and in early Christianity the idea of Hell for the wicked souls developed. Apparently the idea of a place of flaming punishment came from the Hebrew Gehenna. Gehenna was a valley west of Jerusalem where the Hebrews burned the refuse of the city and also the bodies of executed criminals. It was a place where in earlier times the Assyrian God Molech had been worshipped, and where human sacrifices had been thrown to the flames of Molech. In eschatology, Gehenna became a place of punishment for sinners and was located, not in the Jerusalem garbage dump, but under the earth.

Although the Jews did eventually develop a theology of life after death, this concept never became a central theme of Judaism. Judaism remained (and remains) true to its early biblical teachings. It was a religion of God, and God's chosen people. It was a religion not of life-after-death salvation, but of moral righteousness, and of national salvation. Jews may or may not believe in their own personal survival after death, but to the degree that they are Jews they hold firmly to the keeping of God's holy law, and to the ultimate triumph and fulfillment of Israel as the Kingdom of God. It was Christianity that took personal resurrection and immortality into the center of its religion and made life after death the great goal and expectation of religion. In Christianity the soul of man, through repentance of sin, faith, and the grace of God made possible in the redemptive action of Christ's death on the cross, could be translated from its separate (fallen) condition into a supernatural condition wherein it would enjoy immortal life resurrected in a spiritual body, and living eternally with God. All of the Hebrew nationalistic elements had been expunged. The Kingdom of God for Christians was not of this world (John 18:36). The Christian concern and expectation were not to live in a righteous kingdom but to live in the unutterable joy that would be known when one lived in the direct and immediate presence of God in Heaven: when one lived in the Beatific Vision.

Identity or Union with God (i.e., with the Infinite)   In this kind of theology one is to overcome his finiteness by being or becoming infinite. It is held that the nature of man (or the potential nature of

man) is such that it is possible for a human soul to become identified with the infinite reality of God: for a person to become, more
or less, what God is. We shall examine two forms of this kind of
theology—one from ancient Egypt, the other from modern India.

Five thousand years ago in Egypt men strove to become God
Osiris. Osiris was a soter God—a savior God. He was a Man-God
who was killed and resurrected and who after his resurrection left
the world of men and went to the world of the immortals (to
Khenti-Amenti), where he became judge of the dead and ruler of
the blessed immortals. A human being could go to the world of the
immortals if he had in this life become like the God—if he had, in
fact, become Osiris. This was not easy to do. To become Osiris, a
man or woman must first be initiated into the cult of the God, and
must be clean of hand and pure of heart. The essence of such a
person must have been transmuted into the divinity of Osiris by
eating and drinking the sacred eucharist (the bread and wine which
were the body and blood of Osiris). There were other prerequisites
also (e.g., proper funeral including embalming, proper prayers said
by official priests), but the point of importance for our consideration was that the person became the God. Person and infinity were
united.

St. Paul, in the Christian tradition, seemed to have had a similar notion in mind when he wrote in the Galatians' letter that
through faith one comes into union with Christ. Paul bore witness
to this by saying of himself: "I have been put to death with Christ
on his cross, so that it is no longer I who live, but it is Christ who
lives in me" (Gal. 2:19b–20a, *Good News for Modern Man*, New
York: American Bible Society, 1966). In more extreme forms
(namely true mysticism) the participant believes that he can solve
the problem of finitude either (1) by having his soul absorbed into
the Godhead, or (2) by discovering (becoming absolutely convinced) that his soul is in fact already infinite: is already what God
is.

In Hinduism, salvation is also conceived of as a human-divine
unity, but in Hinduism man does not become divine; he already is
divine, even from the beginning. The problem is that man is ignorant of this fact. He believes that he is a being living among
beings—a thing among things. But this is illusion, error, sin. There
is only one reality: God Brahman, and salvation comes to man

when he knows this finally even in the very marrow of his bones.

Although Hinduism is finally a world-transcending system, it is not characterized by gloom or pessimism. It does not condemn a joyous living in this world, but only, finally, proclaims that ultimate joyousness is in something other than the things man usually pursues. With patient wisdom, Hinduism recognizes that men naturally and therefore legitimately seek a number of goals in life. They seek pleasure (*kama*), and power (*artha*), and moral integrity (*dharma*), and eventually in the course of many rebirths, salvation (*moksha*). No religion is more sensitive to the natural needs of man, nor more generous in endorsing a satisfaction of human needs and desires. It recognizes that all men naturally desire pleasure, and this is not decried. Instead, it is identified as one of the four proper goals of living. Men should seek pleasure. Of course, hedonism, like anything else, demands good sense. One cannot just eat, drink, and be merry, or he may wish tomorrow that he had died. But as long as the basic rules of intelligent indulgence and proper morality are followed, one is free in Hinduism to seek all manner of pleasure. If pleasure is what one desires, let him not suppress the desire. Fulfill it as richly as possible. Hinduism promotes pleasure, and then waits. It waits for that time when the pleasure seeker will recognize that pleasure, no matter how extensive, is not the final answer to a fulfilled and joyous life. When one begins to recognize this fact, he is instructed by the Hindu religious philosophers (and all Hindu philosophers are religious philosophers) to try a second proper goal of life. Let him try for success. Success in the form of wealth, fame, and power is endorsed as perfectly natural and worthy of serious concern. There have been many wealthy men who were good men. Be a wealthy man, and a good man at the same time. There is nothing wrong with that. But, alas, as with pleasure, the wealthy and the powerful will eventually lament, "Surely there is more to life than just this." At this point, Hinduism will suggest that one try a new approach. Instead of pursuing selfish pleasure and power and wealth, turn outward altruistically toward others. Turn from self-centered living and begin to live for the welfare of others. Get married. Become a father and responsible householder. Become concerned with the community life and the needs of mankind. Such a life can be good, rich, rewarding. Perhaps good enough to satisfy one to the end of his days—this time around. But, alas, even this kind of living is not truly enough, and this fact will become apparent either in this life or in some future reincarnation. It does bring praise from peers and self-respect from self, but in the end it does not satisfy the deepest and most demanding desire of man: to be part of what is infinite and unchanging, and eternally beatific and beautiful. There comes a time when nothing in the world, as the world appears to us phenomenally, is enough. It is not that the world is necessarily bad. Indeed, much of it is good, exciting, wonderful; but eventually the question will be asked: "Is this really all there is to it?"

And this is the moment that religion, especially the Hindu religion, awaits. This is the moment it has been coaxing since it first proposed that there were proper goals in life. Now at last Hinduism can speak its piece: "No, this is not all there is to it, for beyond pleasure and success and even duty there is a *beyond* that is not out in the world somewhere, but in the depths of your own being. For within you there is a self, a soul, the *Atman,* which is the very stuff of God. It is infinite, absolute, complete. Center your life in this Atman, and you will never again seek to satisfy a need, for all needs will be satisfied automatically. All finite things will cease to interest you, for you will know that you are not finite, not limited, not restrained. You are free. You are complete. You are God. Your soul, your spirit, is not different from or separated from the soul and spirit of God Brahman. In essential nature, you and God are one.

This is the message of the final goal: union with God. But between the message and the accomplishment of union, there is an arduous discipline. Hinduism, which is a family of religions rather than a single theological system, offers three orthodox disciplines toward the ultimate union with God, which is called Nirvana. The discipline chosen will be largely determined by the kind of person (intellectually, psychologically, emotionally) the searcher is. We shall look at the discipline called the Way of Knowledge (*Jnana Yoga*) because it illustrates the point we are trying to make: namely salvation through identification with God.[11]

11 The other two ways are (1) the way of works (*Karma Yoga*) and (2) the way of devotion (*Bhakti Yoga*). The former is primarily a way of ritual, especially domestic ritual. It is followed by the majority of Hindus who hopefully carry out rites and ceremonies and religious duties in order to advance themselves in merit. Many hope that they can gain sufficient merit to pass at death into one of the heavens of afterlife, or to be reborn on a higher spiritual

For persons of strong intellectual powers, Hinduism offers a path to God through diligently acquired knowledge. Here the proposition is that salvation (the fourth and final goal of life) comes through a complete aesthe-noetic (through the senses and the mind) identification with the ground of being, God Brahman. This is accomplished through a rigorous discipline of philosophical investigation and introspection. What is sought is the ability truly to see the difference between the surface self (the personality) which stands in the forefront of our being, and the basic and real self (the Atman) which lies at the base of both personality and the physical self.

The searcher after final truth must (1) become acquainted with the philosophy that argues that unknown to the surface self there is at the center of the human being a spirit or soul that is actually the source of being itself—which is what Brahman is. The proposal is that the real person (the Atman) and God (the Brahman) are not different beings. They are the same being. This hypothesis must be thoroughly examined in a critical, philosophical manner; and then (2) it must be thought about in prolonged and intensive reflection until the hypothesis is transformed from a mere concept in the mind to a momentous reality in the convictions. Thoroughly understood, it is finally thoroughly endorsed. The end sought is an overwhelming awareness that whereas "I" seem to live in "my" personality, there is a deeper, more basic Self, which is actually the source of personality. Personality is really only the actor's mask through which the deeper spirit speaks. To the degree that one thinks of "myself" as a personality, separate and independent, he is mistaking the mask for the actor. The task of religious meditation is to correct this error. "Turning his awareness inward [the yogi] must pierce and dissolve the innumerable layers of the manifest personality until, all strata of the mask at length cut

and intellectual plain that they might in the next reincarnation achieve union with God Brahman through the higher religious way—the way of knowledge (*Jnana Yoga*). Many other Hindus, also not capable of the intellectual demands of the way of knowledge, concentrate their religious life in devotion to one or another of the multitude of gods and goddesses in the Hindu pantheon, from whom they expect to get aid and comfort in the trials of life. But neither of these ways compares in prestige or importance or finality with the way of knowledge (*Jnana Yoga*). This way offers final and complete salvation: unity with God Brahman.

through, he arrives finally at the autonomous and strangely unconcerned actor who stands beneath."[12]

If the searcher can eventually establish a lively awareness of the true Self underlying all personal selves, all phenomenal personality, he will be ready for the next (3) crucial step. He must now shift his self-identity from the phenomenal, passing, personality level of his being to the deep, permanent, spiritual level. To do this he will meditate in prolonged and intense concentration upon the proposal that the Atman (which he now knows) is his true identity. This will not be easy. It is an exacting art. One is almost wholly self-identified in his body and personality. He is now to dissolve that identity and see himself in a completely different dimension of reality. He is to see himself as *in* but not *of* his body and phenomenal self. He is, indeed, to see himself as being what God is and separated from God's total being only as a drop of sea spray may be separated from the sea itself in the brief time between the wave striking the rock and the droplet falling back into the water. When the believer can say, with total belief, in absolute intellectual and emotional conviction: "Tat Tvam asi" (that thou art), he has become the *true* believer, the emancipated believer. He is at one with God. He is saved.[13]

[12] Huston Smith, *The Religions of Man* (New York: Harper & Row, Perennial Library, 1965), p. 43.

[13] In each of the ways of religion the word *Yoga* appears. Yoga means union: union with God through works or devotion or knowledge. Yoga is also a discipline of behavior which fosters union with divine reality. It is especially important as one of the physical disciplines in the way of knowledge. Yoga is a technique of meditation and concentration which assists in the final accomplishment of the experience of release from error, liberation from ignorance, and absorption into Brahman (*samadhi*), which is the ultimate salvation in Hinduism. The technique became highly refined in the hands of Patanjali, a second-century B.C. yogi. The Raja Yoga of Patanjali has eight steps:

1. *Yama:* the five desire-killing vows. Here one vows to abstain from harming living things, from deceit, stealing, unchastity, and from acquisitiveness.

2. *Niyama:* observance of self-disciplinary rules of cleanliness, calm, mortification, study, and prayer.

3. *Asana:* proper posture, especially the lotus posture.

4. *Pranayama:* regulation of breathing, whereby one gradually comes to control all of the rhythmic processes of his physical being.

5. *Pratyahara:* control of all physical sensation through which the outside world is shut out of consciousness.

Before leaving this consideration of salvation theology as union with God, we should make one more observation. It is different from the theologies of reincarnation, resurrection, and immortality in that it does not propose that one must wait for death for salvation to occur. Salvation is promised immediately. It is not only a Beatific Vision, the direct knowledge of God, later, but the Beatific Vision now. Salvation for Osirians and Paul and Hindu mystics and others is not simply a future reward but an immediate experience.

Studied Philosophical Indifference   Many people attempt to have a sort of nontheology of death and salvation (to be indifferent) by trying never to talk about or even think about such things, which is a good trick if you can do it. A different attempt is to try to establish, by talking and thinking, a philosophy of indifference, which is also a good trick if you can do it. Epicurus of Samos and Athens, who in the fourth century B.C. founded a school of philosophy which became known as Epicureanism, made this move. Epicurus wanted people to be happy, to live rich untroubled lives. He observed that some of the things that upset people and filled them with unease, and even dread, were fear of God (that he would punish) and fear of death (when the punishment would happen). In his letter to Menoeceus, he tried to allay both of these fears. God, he said, was not concerned to punish man. God was blessed and attended to his own blessedness. From that quarter man had nothing to fear. And man had nothing to fear from death either. One need not fear death, not because death was blessed, but because death was nothing. It could not harm one. In his letter Epicurus counseled:

> Become accustomed to the belief that death is nothing to us. For all good and evil consist in sensations, but death is the deprivation of sensation. And therefore a right understanding that death is nothing to us makes the mortality of life enjoyable, not because it

---

6. *Dharana:* concentration in which the mind focalizes upon one single object of thought until all other consciousness disappears.

7. *Dhyana:* meditation in which all of the above disciplines are in full operation.

8. *Samadhi:* the last step in which the mind, emptied of all content and no longer aware of either object or subject, is absorbed into the divine reality—into God.

adds to it an infinite span of time, but because it takes away the craving for immortality. For there is nothing terrible in life for the man who has truly comprehended that there is nothing terrible in not living. . . . So death, the most terrible of ills, is nothing to us, since so long as we exist death is not with us; but when death comes, then we do not exist. It does not concern either the living or the dead, since for the former it is not, and the latter are no more.[14]

We will never know whether Menoeceus found Epicurus' theology of indifference adequate. If he did, he was among the few of literate mankind who accomplished the feat. Many more of us, it would appear, are incapable of such studied indifference. We are more like Hamlet—unable to avoid wrestling with the dread:

> . . . the dread of something after death—
> The undiscovered country, from whose bourn
> No traveler returns—puzzles the will,
> And makes us rather bear those ills we know
> Than fly to others that we know not of?
> Thus conscience does make cowards of us all,
> And thus the native hue of resolution
> Is sicklied o'er with the pale cast of thought . . .
> *Hamlet*, III, 1, 78–85

The Theological Accomplishment   Theology tries to give us assurance that what we want to believe and need to believe is true. If a person is to work out his salvation from something, by something, to something, he needs to know the "truth" about the *from,* the *by,* and the *to.* For faith to function adequately, or even be accepted, it must be true, or at least be believed to be true. If the statements, the dogmas, of the faith are not believed they lose all their force. David Elton Trueblood once speculated on how effective the Covenant of Mount Sinai would have been if the Hebrews had been told, or had come to believe, that God did not really give those Commandments to Moses; Moses just made them up. They would have been the same Commandments, but how commanding would they have been? That religious truths are difficult to understand, or are hidden, or are even irrational, may not violate the religious consciousness, but to be told that the religious truths are not true

---

[14] Epicurus, "Epicurus to Menoeceus", *Ethics*, ed. Oliver A. Johnson (New York: Holt, Rinehart and Winston, 1974).

and that this is not important is unacceptable in the extreme. It is difficult to see how people could accept what they knew to be fallacious religious doctrines just because they found that those doctrines were religiously helpful. They might support pragmatic truths for someone else, saying, for example: "The Trobrianders' religion is a fine religion for Trobrianders. Of course, it isn't true, but it works for them." But would anyone embrace the Trobriander religion for himself so long as he believed it was only operationally true, but not "really" true? Religion is not simply a pragmatic affair. Beliefs are not held just because they work. They are held because they work, and *because they are true*. Much of the business of theology is to say so, and to say how so.

seven

Revelation and
Scripture

Our quotation from Anselm at the end of chapter five ("I do not seek to understand that I may believe, but I believe in order to understand") suggests that theology does not begin from zero and start explaining God and religious things, but rather begins with some kind of revealed knowledge. As Paul Tillich points out in the first pages of his first volume on *Systematic Theology*, there is a theological circle in which the theologian stands to do his theology. His work is rooted in and circumscribed by a "mystical a priori." A theologian works from, and within, a fund of "revealed" knowledge. Theological speculations may in sophistication become universal in application, as did the cosmological and ontological arguments of Anselm and Thomas, but the work begins in a given revelation and does not intentionally desert or violate that revelation. We shall now look at two forms of revealed religious knowledge which may be classified as general revelation and special revelation.

GENERAL REVELATION

We have already noted that Thomas Aquinas believed that knowledge of God and religious things was disclosed to man partly from nature itself when man employed his human reason to discover such knowledge. John Calvin similarly declared that God had conspired "so to manifest his perfections in the whole structure of the universe, and daily place himself in our view, that we cannot open our eyes without being compelled to behold him."[1] The Hebrew writer of the 19th Psalm announced that: "The heavens declare the glory of God; and the firmament showeth his handiwork." William Carruth was saying the same thing in his "Each In His Own Tongue."

> A haze on the far horizon,
>   The infinite tender sky,
> The rich ripe tint of the corn-fields,
>   The wild geese sailing high.
> And all over the upland and lowland
>   The charm of the golden rod,
> Some of us call it autumn,
>   Others call it God.[2]

This form of revelation is called general revelation or natural theology. The endorsers of this position obviously believe that man has the ability to discover religious knowledge on his own. To do this would appear to be a highly respectable and beneficial pursuit, but it is not, for all that, universally endorsed.

Rejection   General revelation was emphatically rejected by the important Hindu philosopher Sankara (788–820 A.D.) Grounding his thought in such Upanishadic statements as the following:

> Now, one should know that Nature is illusion
> And that Mighty Lord is the illusion-maker.

Sankara argued his case from a nondualistic world view. In final reality he held there was only God Brahman. The world did not have a separate existence. People did not have separate existences. They just seemed to. They lived in illusion (*Maya*). By illusion, Sankara meant, in a sense, what the great Western philosopher Immanuel Kant meant when he called the world we experience an "appearance." Kant's position was that men do not experience or conceptualize the world as it really is, but only as it appears to be. The thing-in-itself is beyond thought. This apposition between Kant's phenomenal and noumenal world was matched by Sankara's world of Maya and world of God Brahman. Sankara insisted that the

---

[1] John Calvin, *Institutes of the Christian Religion* (Grand Rapids, Michigan: Eerdmans, 1953), Book 1, Chapter 5, p. 51.

[2] William Carruth, *Each In His Own Tongue and Other Poems* (New York: G. P. Putnam's Sons).

human who relied on his senses for knowledge was doomed to live in ignorance (*aviyda:* nonknowledge). To live in ignorance was to exist only in a low form of "pragmatic truth," and be unsaved. Only when one broke out of Maya, and in deep insight attained the revelation that his separate self was not really separate but the same as the divine self, did he attain true knowledge, and with it salvation.

Some early Christians also rejected general revelation, not because the world was an illusion, but because it was utterly evil. Early in Christian history the gnostic Christians, in their acceptance of a radical dualism between spirit and flesh, earth and heaven, nature and the supernatural, rejected out-of-hand any thought that God could be discerned any place in the natural world. Not even Christ could be viewed as a natural man. He only *looked* like a natural man. He was, they claimed, God incognito, who only appeared to be born and appeared to live and appeared to suffer and appeared to die.

This attitude of rejection is still to be found in some Christian theology. Those modern Christians who emphasize the "Fall of Man" often mean by it that there is a vast abyss separating finite, feeble man from the infinite, absolute God. God can be known only as he discloses himself in some form of special revelation.

SPECIAL REVELATION

Besides general revelation there is a much narrower idea about how one can get God words and God talk. It is special revelation: revelation in which, through special religious means, God and ultimate truths are made known to man. God speaks, either in a literal or metaphorical sense, and the one who hears God informs others of what God has said, or what message God wants conveyed. A person becomes convinced by hearing a voice or by having an "enlightenment" occur within his consciousness, that he is in special communication with divine reality. God, reportedly, spoke literally to Moses, but to Gautama Buddha, apparently, the revelation of ultimate truth came as a sudden insight. However it comes, the prophet seems always constrained to share the revelation. He speaks out to his community, even when, as is often the case, the community would prefer not to hear. But he is heard and sooner or later taken seriously by a constituency. Sometimes the constituency begins very small, even only one person as with Muhammad's wife Khadija, who believed the Prophet's revelations even before he was really sure himself. Eventually the constituency grows, and the members not only listen to the prophet, but tell others about the message which the prophet has gotten from the Divine. In due course the prophet's words are written down and become scripture.

REVELATION AND SCRIPTURE

Scripture is not the revelation itself but the reporting of the revelation, and a reporting that has received the authority not simply of the prophet but of a community. By first preserving and then stamping with its official endorsement, the believing community establishes a scripture. For example, the Jewish Bible is not simply the words of prophets; rather it is a set of special prophetic statements, and a written account of God's mighty acts in the history of Israel, and a collection of wise sayings and celebration hymns and revered stories *that were preserved* by the Jewish community and eventually *given official, canonical status* by a council of rabbis who met in the town of Jamnia about the year A.D. 90. Revelation is born in a moment of divine-human encounter, but scripture is made more laboriously by savants and true believers.

New Scripture and the Scripture Idea   Some of the sacred scriptures of the world's living religions are very old. Parts of the Hebrew Bible go back 3000 years, and some of the Hindu Vedas go back probably 4000 years. But not all sacred scripture is ancient. For example, in Iran, in 1844, a certain Mīrzā Alī Muhammud began to call himself Bāb-ud-Dīn (Gate of Faith) and to proclaim that his mission was to prepare the way for one who would come to complete God's work of perfection on earth. Bāb-ud-Dīn declared that his writings were revelations equal to the *Qur'ān*. This put him afoul of the Muslim authorities and he was executed as a heretic and disturber of the peace. But his religious movement did not end. His followers were called after him Bābis, and the religion he fostered became known as Bahā'i. One of Bāb-ud-Dīn's youthful followers took the name Bahā'u'llāh (Glory of God) and ten years later announced that he was the one who was to come. His writings too became regarded as sacred scripture; among them is the Kitáb-iígán (The Book of Certitude), which was revealed to Bahá'u'lláh in 1862, in two days and nights.

In the same century, a few years earlier (1832), a revelation occurred in the United States. One Joseph Smith of Manchester, New York, found in a stone box on a hillside the record of some people who had lived anciently (from 2200 B.C. to A.D. 421) in the Americas. They too, as people of Palestine, were witnesses "that Jesus is the Christ, the Eternal God." The record Joseph Smith found was engraved on gold plates. He was permitted "by the gift and power of God" to translate and copy what came to be known as *The Book of Mormon*, which in the Church of the Latter-Day Saints is accepted, along with the Christian Old and New Testaments, as a divine revelation and holy scripture.

There is nothing to foreclose the writing of new sacred scripture, for a sacred scripture is, after all, simply a written document that has been accepted by some religious body as a document that reveals the truth about God and/or what God has done or plans to do for man, and/or expects man to do.

A sacred scripture is, first of all, an idea. The word *scripture* in its universal meaning denotes, first, not a set of documents, but an idea about the character of certain documents. It denotes the idea that the word of God, divine truth, ultimate reality, is to be discerned in certain written documents; that religious truth has been, one way or another, transcribed into written form. This is the Bible Idea, or more correctly, the Scripture Idea.

In the religions of the Near Eastern world,[3] the Scripture Idea appears to have developed first in the early decades of the seventh century B.C. In II Kings, in the Hebrew Bible, we are told that in the eighteenth year of the reign of King Josiah a book was discovered in the Temple which declared in written form the relationship between God and Israel, and the will of God for the Hebrew people. With this book, now identified as the Book of Deuteronomy, the Hebrews came to a new conception of how one could discern the way and the will of God for man. Prior to that time they had relied upon living voices (prophets and prophetesses), or upon various forms of divination, to get God's word on any matter. Now they had a God's book, and with it the idea that would expand their

[3] Judaism, Christianity, Islam, and Zoroastrianism.

one book into a whole library of God's books: *tá biblía* (the books), the Bible.

SCRIPTURE: EAST AND WEST

All of the great religions of the world have their own sacred writings. And they are all considered as somehow "inspired." They are all believed to contain revelations of ultimate reality. But, in general, Eastern scriptures are different from Western scriptures in that they arise in, and inform, a different conception of the way of the world. The Western religions are often referred to as "historical religions." In this reference "historical" means seeing the world in time, moving from a specific beginning to a definite ending. The world is seen as beginning in the innocence of Eden and moving toward its final fulfillment in a Divine Kingdom. Eastern religions, instead of being historical in this sense, are cyclical. Their world does not begin and move forward to a perfect fulfillment, but returns upon itself again and again, forever. For example, in Hinduism, developing after the Hindus had established themselves in the Ganges Valley and between 700 and 300 B.C., and recorded especially in their holy writings called *Upanishads,* there developed the doctrine of a cyclic destruction and re-creation of the world. At the end of every *kalpa* (period of created being) the world dissolves. All the souls in the universe depart from their bodies and enter a state of slumbering suspension. After a period of "nothingness," called *pralaya,* the world comes into being again and the quiescent souls take up new embodiments in plants, animals, men, gods, and demons. The holy Vedas (primal scriptures) are recomposed and another *kalpa* proceeds to its inevitable end.

Against this kind of world view the Hindus see their lives, religion, and scriptures differently from those who see the world as beginning, moving forward through time, and finally ending permanently in a utopian condition. Westerners have a God of history: a God involved in and concerned with history; a providential God. Easterners, although their Gods often involved themselves in the lives of men, do not conceive of the world as an "historical event" under the providential aegis of the great high God. Yahweh watches and responds; but not Brahman, or Tao, or Heaven. Brahman, undisturbed, receives into his own being for the remainder of the kalpa any soul who finds the secret of salvation. Tao lends strength and fullness to any person who discerns the true way. Heaven's harmony reigns upon man and nation when propriety is maintained. But none of these great Gods are like the Westerner's Yahweh who broods and agonizes when his people turn away from his laws and ordinances, and rejoices with all his angels when even one sinner repents.

Against such metaphysical differences, one might expect that the attitudes of Easterners toward scripture would be different from the attitudes of Westerners, and that the scriptures themselves would be quite different. And, in general, this is how it is. Perhaps the best way to characterize the differences of both attitudes and writings is to say that the attitudes and scriptures of Eastern religions are more meditative and philosophical, whereas the attitudes and scriptures of Western religions are more matter-of-fact and historical. There is, to be sure, vision literature in the Western scriptures—for example, Ezekiel, Daniel, Revelation—but it is markedly concerned with the history and destiny of man in a perfect world to come. And there is poetry, and there are passages suitable to meditation, but not anything like, for example, the ten books of 1028 hymns to be found in the Hindu *Rig-Veda*. Perhaps the most obvious difference between the character of Eastern and Western scripture is to be seen in their concerns for philosophical speculation. The fact is that there is little philosophical speculation in the Western scriptures. It is surprising to discover that nowhere in the Hebrew-Christian scriptures are there any philosophical discussions on either the existence of God, or God's ultimate nature. God is simply accepted as some kind of powerful, supreme, personal being, and the scriptures go on from there. Not so in the East. Throughout the voluminous 200 books called *Upanishads* in Hinduism there is an almost endless search for the existence of, and nature of, Divine Being. Farther East in China, the basic scripture of the Taoist faith, the *Tao Te Ching*, is a subtly written philosophical search for the place and meaning of God in the realm of actuality and/or being.

The differences are real between East and West, and one might almost agree with Kipling that never the twain shall meet. But actually, concerning a point we made at the beginning of this chapter, East and West do meet; in both Eastern and Western religion, theology is rooted in a fund of "revealed" knowledge. In China, the Taoist philosophers begin with the subtle philosophy of the *Tao*

Te Ching. It is from there that they explain their world and themselves, and derive their principles for salvation and morality, and even for doing their art. In India, the Hindu theologians (even those who wrote the *Upanishads*) went back to the basic fund of original revelation, to the primal Vedic scriptures, even as Western theologians, who are as widely different as Maimonides and Richard Rubenstein or Anselm and Thomas Altizer, go back to their revelation sources before attempting their flights of theology.

LIVING SCRIPTURE WORLDWIDE

Jewish Scriptures   The Bible of the Jews is composed of thirty-nine books or writings, generally known as the Old Testament by Christians, but to Jews—properly—simply, the Bible. These books are usually divided by Jews into three groups.

1. The Torah or Law: Genesis, Exodus, Leviticus, Numbers, and Deuteronomy.
2. Nebiim or The Prophets: Joshua, Judges, I Samuel, II Samuel, I Kings, II Kings, Isaiah, Jeremiah, Ezekiel, Hosea, Joel, Amos, Obadiah, Jonah, Micah, Nahum, Habakkuk, Zephaniah, Haggai, Zachariah, Malachi.
3. Kethubim or Sacred Writings: Psalms, Proverbs, Job, Song of Solomon, Ruth, Lamentations, Ecclesiastes, Esther, Daniel, Ezra, Nehemiah, I Chronicles, II Chronicles.

All of these books were originally composed in Hebrew, except for approximately half of Daniel, parts of Ezra, and a verse in Jeremiah. These sections were written in Aramaic.

There are other documents read by the Jews and held to be of special religious value (at least approximating scripture): the Talmud. Between the year A.D. 70 and the end of the fifth century, Jewish scholars in Jamnia (Jabneh), Galilee, and Babylonia compiled and organized a tremendous mass of rabbinical teachings. First the *Mishna* (instruction), which was largely rabbinical interpretations of Torah (the Law), and, second, the *Gemara* (completion), which was largely commentary on the Mishna. These two works taken together are called Talmud (teachings). They are a record of the rabbis' teachings about the law (*Halakah*) and the rabbis' teachings about historical matters, moral rules, and general religious instructions (*Haggadah*). The Talmud is divided into thirty-six books or tractates, containing some two and a half million words.

Besides the Bible and the later Talmud there are several writings that were considered scriptures by some Jews, especially in Alexandria. These writings are today called Apocrypha (hidden writings). The Apocrypha consists of fifteen writings: some whole books, some additions to existing biblical books. The earliest, Tobit, a short novel teaching Jewish morality, was written about 200 B.C. The latest Baruch, a composite book attributed to the secretary of Jeremiah and combining prophetic statements and wise sayings, was written about 100 B.C. The apocryphal writings were included in many early Hebrew Bible manuscripts, but many rabbis doubted that they should be.

A decision concerning which books of the many books available belonged properly in the Bible was made by the rabbis in the Council of Jamnia about A.D. 90. The canon of the Bible for orthodox Judaism was declared to be the thirty-nine books mentioned above. The additional apocryphal writings were excluded. This canon of biblical books is today called the Masoretic Text, but it did not everywhere replace the more expanded text which included the apocryphal writings. This was especially the case with the Greek translation of the Hebrew Bible, called the Septuagint.

The Septuagint   Beginning in the third century B.C. the Jews of Alexandria in Egypt made a translation of the Hebrew Bible into the Greek language. That translation included most of the writings that are now called the Apocrypha. The translation was called the Septuagint for the seventy (or seventy-two) scholars to whom legend attributed the translation. In the middle years of the first century A.D., this was the Bible that was most available (and usable because it was in Greek) to the Gentiles who began to join the reform movement that was destined to become the Christian Church.

In the fifth century A.D., when St. Jerome translated the Bible into the Latin language, he included in it several of the apocryphal writings found in the Septuagint. The remainder of these apocryphal writings came into the official Catholic Bible (the Vulgate) from other old Latin translations. They remain in the Catholic Old Testament to this day.

But in the sixteenth century, the Protestant reformers chose to restrict the Old Testament to the Hebrew canon established at the Council of Jamnia. With some exceptions, the Protestants continued to regard the remaining books of the Septuagint as worthy to be read, and included them in a separate portion of the Bible, either between the Testaments or at the end of the Bible, calling them The Apocrypha, which was a name first given to these books by St. Jerome.

The New Testament   Originally the Bible Idea among Christians was limited to the Greek Septuagint translation of the Jewish Bible. Christian writings were produced, but were not identified as scripture. Then in A.D. 140 a gnostic Christian (one Marcion of Sinope), desiring to divorce Christianity from its theological connections with Judaism, proposed setting aside the Jewish Bible as a spurious scripture and putting in its place some Christian writings; namely the Gospel of Luke, and the Letters of Paul.

Marcion's gnostic theology and rejection of the Jewish Bible was unacceptable to the orthodox Christians, but apparently his idea of a new Christian scripture was something else. Within a very short time the authorities of the orthodox Church were busy identifying the writings that were to be regarded as new scripture for the Christians.

By the end of the century the idea of collecting Christian writings and identifying them as scripture had spread throughout the entire Church. Irenaeus of Lyons, Theophilus of Antioch, Tertullian of North Africa, Clement and Origen of Alexandria—all moved vigorously to select and promote Christian scripture. The various authorities did not always see eye to eye on all the books to be included in the canon, or excluded from it, but they all agreed that the Gospels Mark, Matthew, Luke, and John, and Paul's letters should be included. And apparently the title New Testament had arisen as the name for the collection. Melito, Bishop of Sardis (c. 180), wrote a letter (preserved by Eusebius) which made specific reference to the "books of the Old Testament." This would imply recognition of a New Testament.

Thanks to Marcion's heretical efforts, the Bible Idea had been established for a Christian scripture. Now all that remained was the Church's final decision on what belonged in that scripture. This took some doing. However, gradually, over the years, agreement was reached, and in his famous Festal letter, Athanasius of Alexandria, in the latter half of the fourth century, listed as New Testament exactly the twenty-seven books now accepted, and about them he remarked: "These are the springs of salvation so that the thirsty may be filled with the utterance within them. In these alone is proclaimed the good news of the teaching of true religion. Let no one add to them or remove aught from them." In 397 the Third Council of Carthage ordered that only canonical writings were to be read in church under the title of divine scripture. A New Testament had been finally, securely established.

Islamic Scripture   Islam also endorses the Jewish scripture as sacred, and the Christian New Testament as well. These scriptures represent earlier prophetic revelations from God to man. However, Muhammad was God's Prophet (and the last of the prophets) sent to correct distortions in the earlier prophesies and to give man one final and magnificent scripture: the *Qur'ān,* or *Koran.* The *Qur'ān* is to all true Muslims a book of absolute truth, because it is the word of God himself. It is the last and final revelation from God, revealed completely and perfectly to Muhammad.

Shortly after the death of Muhammad, A.D. 632, Ābu Bakr, who took command of the movement, supervised the collecting and writing of the revelations that had come to Muhammad. A dozen years later, Othman, third caliph, made an additional study of the revelations and prepared an authentic version. The *Qur'ān* as it was finally arranged consists of 114 suras, or chapters. The first sura is a short prayer. The remaining 113 chapters are arranged in the order of their length. The first has 286 verses, and the last has only three verses.

Zoroastrian Scriptures   Another living religion of Near Eastern (Persian/Iranian) origin is Zoroastrianism. The religion founded by Zarathustra (Zoroaster) in the seventh century B.C. survives today largely in India among a people called Parsees (i.e., Persians). There are about 125,000 Parsees, most of them in Bombay and the surrounding area.

Many of the ideas found both in the Old and New Testament stem directly from Zoroastrianism, although the religion itself is not mentioned anywhere in the Hebrew-Christian scriptures. Many of the kings of Persia mentioned in the Old Testament were Zoroastrians; for example, Cyrus, Artaxerxes, Ahasuerus, Darius. The Magi, wise men from the East who came to the birth of Jesus, were Zoroastrian priests. Satan, as described in the extra-canonical writings of the Hebrews and in the New Testament, was a concept that first appeared in Zoroastrian thought, as was the elaborate scheme of angels and demons, the idea of a savior, the doctrine of resurrection and final judgment, and the conception of a future life to be lived in Paradise. These ideas, and others, taught by Zarathustra and his followers, became incorporated into the sacred scriptures of the Zoroastrians called *Avesta* or Knowledge.

The *Avesta* consists of four main groups of writings. The *Yasna* deals with worship and sacrifice and contains the seventeen *Gathas* or Psalms, and is composed largely of prayers, confessions, invocations, exhortations, and praise, combined in many literary forms. The *Visperat* is a collection of invocations to all the Gods. The *Vendidad* is a priestly code which deals with various religious, ritualistic, and civil matters. The *Yashts* is a collection of religious poetry and hymns. Another book, the *Khorda-Avesta*, or Little Avesta, is sometimes included as part of the Avesta. The *Khorda-Avesta* is a handbook of litanies and prayers for daily worship and prayer.

Hindu Scriptures   The Vedas or Books of Knowledge had their origin sometime between 2000 B.C. and 1000 B.C. and form the basis of all Hinduism. There are four Vedas: The *Rig-Veda*, or Veda of Verses; the *Yajur Veda*, or Veda of Sacred Formulas; the *Sama Veda*, or Veda of Chants; and the *Atharva Veda*, or Veda of Charms. During the next 750 years after the writing of these scriptures, Hinduism underwent several major changes. Each change produced a new scripture based upon the original Vedas, but different from them. Between 1000 B.C. and 800 B.C., a strong priestly organization developed in Hinduism. Scriptures called the *Brahmanas* developed from this period. Following the priestly period, between 800 B.C. and 600 B.C., from a period of extensive philosophical interest came the *Upanishads*, or books of philosophic discussion. A strong legal emphasis in Hinduism around 250 B.C., produced the *Laws of Manu*, or code of Hindu law. At the beginning of the common/Christian era a dramatic poem of great beauty and high moral precepts emerged from the Hindu religion: the *Bhagavad Gita*, Song of the Blessed Lord. These books constitute the sacred books of Hinduism, but there are two additional epic poems that have great influence upon popular Hinduism: the *Mahabharata* and the *Ramayana*.

Buddhist Scriptures   Another religion that developed in India, but was destined to have its lasting strength not in India but in China, Japan, and South East Asia, was Buddhism. Buddhism was founded by Gautama who lived from 563 to 483 B.C. The scriptures of this first great international religion were the *Tripitaka*, or Three Baskets. The first Basket is the *Vinaya Pitaka*, or Monastic Rules. It contains the many rules imposed upon those who enter the orders of high-class Buddhists. The second Basket is the *Sutta Pitaka*, or Discourses. This scripture is of special importance because the principal voice heard in it is that of the Buddha himself. Also in it is contained the very important moral treatise, the *Dhammapada*, or Verses on the Law. The third Basket is the *Abhidharma Pitaka*, or the Metaphysical Basket. It is a detailed explanation of Buddhist doctrines and of Buddhist psychology.

Two other scriptures that developed in India were (1) the *Agamas*, or precepts of the Jainist religion, which was founded in India by Mahavira, who lived from 599 B.C. to 527 B.C. and (2) the *Granth*, which is the sacred scripture of Sikhism, a religion founded in the fifteenth century A.D. in the province of Punjab by Nanak.

Far Eastern Scripture   In the Far East, in China, there are scriptures for the two indigenous religions: for Taoism and for Confucianism. The scripture of the Taoists is the *Tao Te Ching*, or Treatise of the Tao and its Power. This scripture was traditionally credited to the founder of the Taoist religion, Lao-tzu, who lived between 604 B.C. and 531 B.C., but as it stands today the *Tao Te Ching* is hardly the product of one mind, although it may be basically so. Interpolations and repeated editings have altered the original form. Most of the present version comes from the fourth century B.C. It is a book, difficult to translate, of about five thousand Chinese characters. It is concerned with the nature of God Tao (the Way of Reality), and with the ethics of quietism, nonaggression, and nonmeddlesome action which are appropriate to the Tao.

The scripture of the other indigenous Chinese religion, Confucianism, consists of the Five Classics and the Four Books. Included in the Classics are the *Shu Ching*, or Book of History; the *Shih Ching*, or Book of Poetry; the *I Ching*, or Book of Changes;

the *Li Chi*, or Book of Rites; and the *Ch'un Ch'iu*, or Spring and Autumn Annals. Some authorities add a Sixth Classic, the *Hsiao Ching*, or Book of Filial Piety. The Four Books are the *Ta Hsio*, or Great Learning; the *Chung Yung*, or Doctrine of the Mean; the *Lun Yü*, or Analects of Confucius; and the *Meng-tze*, or Works of Mencius.

In Japan two of the sacred scriptures of the Shinto religion are *Ko-ji-ki*, or records of Ancient Matters, and *Nihon-gi*, or Chronicles of Japan. *Ko-ji-ki* tells the story of the age of the Gods before men existed on earth. *Nihon*-gi tells of the creation of Japan and of the rule of the Emperors. There is a third sacred document of Shinto called the *Yengi-shiki*, or Institutes of the Period of Yengi. This book dates from about the tenth century A.D., and is a collection of prayers. A fourth scripture of Shinto is *Manyo-shiu*, or Collection of Ten Thousand Leaves. It is an anthology of 4496 poems dating from the fifth to eighth centuries A.D.

INTERPRETING SCRIPTURE

Established scripture is, of course, passed from generation to generation for hundreds and thousands of years. Thus the world in which the scriptures were first presented, communicated, preserved and made official, becomes archaic and obsolete. This necessitates a transposition of the scriptural messages for a new cultural scene. Interpretation is necessary. For a scripture to be a "living scripture," it must make direct contact with the thought patterns and life-styles of the contemporary day. This is the work of the preachers, the rabbis, the gurus, and the other "professionals" of any given faith system. The fact is that interpretation becomes necessary almost as soon as the prophet passes from the scene. When he is no longer available to explain what he has prophesied, it is necessary to consider not only his words but what he meant by his words. If Jesus said, "He who has seen me has seen the Father," but Jesus is no longer around to explain his oblique remark, someone else, when queried on the statement, will surely say: "He meant so-and-so." Another "authority" when asked the same question may give a different *interpretation*.

Scriptural interpretation is necessary, and everybody who takes scripture seriously interprets. Even if he says: "I take it literally," he has not escaped, because "literally" is also an interpretation. We shall look, briefly, at three possible approaches to scriptural interpretation which can be employed by contemporary persons who are especially concerned with the Judaeo-Christian scriptures. These approaches might be called: (1) the stenographic interpretation, (2) the insight interpretation, and (3) the existential-encounter interpretation.

The Stenographic Interpretation   In "stenographic" interpretation, the knowledge of God and/or religious things as recorded in the scripture are taken literally. It is held that, one way or another, God communicated special information to a human "stenographer," who in turn faithfully transcribed the "words of God" into the languages of man. In the Book of Exodus, for example, we read that God delivered to Moses to be set before the Hebrew people all of his commandments and ordinances. God spoke to Moses, and dutifully, exactly, Moses repeated God's words to the Hebrew people. Again, at the beginning of Isaiah's ministry we read that the Prophet cried out: "Hear, O heavens, and give ear, O earth, for Yahweh hath spoken." The writer of the Book of Revelation leaves no doubt about the source and character of his message. In the beginning paragraph he defines his book as

> the Revelation of Jesus Christ, which God gave him to show unto his servants, even the things which must shortly come to pass; and he sent and signified it by his angel unto his servant John; who bore witness to the Word of God, and of the testimony of Jesus Christ, even all the things that he saw. (Rev. 1:1–2, American Standard Version)

In this kind of revelation God is seen as using a human agent to write what God is literally thinking or saying or showing to his chosen vessel of transmission. This kind of claim is not, of course, limited to the Hebrew-Christian scriptures. The same claim is made for Joseph Smith and the Book of Mormon, for Muhammad and the *Qur'ān*, and for others.

The strength of this position is that the beliefs and creeds of one's religious sect can be quickly and effectively evaluated against an established criteria; namely the criteria of what the scripture says. For example, the Jews' claim to be the "chosen people" can be readily evaluated and defended by referring to appropriate passages of scripture. The Christians' claim that Jesus was born of a virgin and arose from the dead can be "proved" by referring to those scripture passages which claim so. The Muslims have a precise criteria for their claim that Muhammad was the Prophet of God Allah. The *Qur'ān* says so. What the scripture says is the strength of this position.

Interestingly, it is also one of the weaknesses of the position, because what the scriptures say is not always all that clear and distinct. For example, the account of Jesus' last Passover meal and the institution of the Lord's Supper is sufficiently imprecise for Catholics to claim absolutely one thing (the bread and wine used are actually the body and blood of Christ) and Protestants to claim absolutely the opposite. Again, to Roman Catholics there is no proposition in the Bible more clear and distinct than Jesus' endorsement of Peter (in Matthew 16:18), and therewith of all the Bishops of Rome as heads of Christ's Church on earth. There are very few Protestants, if any, who are not unalterably sure that Jesus' conversation with Peter that day meant nothing of the kind.

Another weakness is to be seen not in how biblical propositions are interpreted, but in what they state in one place which seem to be contradicted by what they say elsewhere in the same scripture. For example, in the Gospel of Matthew the Holy Family flees from Palestine to Egypt on the night of Jesus' birth, so it would appear; but in the Gospel of Luke they remain in Palestine, and forty days later Joseph and Mary present Jesus in the Jerusalem Temple. There are two different accounts of the death of Judas Iscariot (in Matthew 17:5 and Acts 1:18), and four different accounts of what happened at the tomb on Resurrection Day: who saw what, when, under what circumstances? Read the four separate accounts in the four Gospels and you will never know for sure. Again, how did the animals go into the Ark—two by two, or seven by two? What is the order of creation of the world, man, animals, woman, as stated in Genesis Chapter 1 and in Genesis Chapter 2?

Any attempt to take the Judaeo-Christian scriptures literally, as unerrantly and precisely true, is fraught with difficulty.

Insight Interpretation   A second approach is the insight theory. From this view scripture is held to be a highly significant accomplishment in man's quest for divine truths and spiritual sustenance, but it is not a literal message from God to man. Rather it is a witnessing of people who had a genius for religion (the Jews) much as the Greeks had a genius for philosophy, the Romans for practical politics, and modern Westerners for scientific technology. The scripture is not a stenographic, propositional self-disclosure of God to man, but is a fallible interpretation of God's disclosure as seen and recorded by certain ancient men. As this is the case, the scripture contains both deep insights into the nature of Divine Being, and a great deal of ancient, mythological nonsense. The problem that confronts the modern reader is to separate the true religious insights from the mythology in which these insights are presented.

The work of Rudolph Bultmann, possibly the foremost contemporary New Testament scholar, can be seen in this reference. Bultmann points out the obvious fact that the Hebrew-Christian Bible was written for a different age—a prescientific age; for a world where miracles were expected and accepted as common occurrences in daily life; a world where heaven was straight up and hell straight down (i.e., a simple three-storied world); where evil demons invaded human bodies with illness, and were exorcised by faith healers and miracle workers. It was a world where people believed that all sorts of supernatural things could happen at any time, and so (or so it seemed) all sorts of supernatural things happened. The Bible was written in that world and in that fashion. Its language was prescientific. Bultmann proposes that this mythological style be deleted. The Bible must be "demythologized." Why? Not to get rid of the Bible. Not to demean or deny the biblical revelation, but to free it, because, so Bultmann would have us believe, the self-disclosure of God to man is there, even if now obscured by the mythological language used in presenting it. The Bible should not be confused with science. It is not a book of facts about the world. The writers were devoid of anything that even approaches our modern scientific information—astronomical, biological, medical, social, psychological; but what they did know, or have, Bultmann would insist, was a revelation from God—a religious message for mankind. That message, Bultmann believes, is freed and made visible for modern men when the mythology of a prescientific age is cleared away.

Opponents of this insight position say that it imposes a criterion upon the scripture which is not proper. Science and modern thought are taken as correctives for the Bible. The Bible is treated as if it were just another ancient manuscript. But, they claim, it is not just another ancient book, and one does not have a right to delete from it anything that does not fit into modern "mythology." Either take the Bible for what it purports to be (the Word of God) or reject it, but do not mutilate it. Again, this position is criticized in the fact that what the kerygma (the true message) behind the myth is said to be is often, if not always, just what the "liberal" theologian has been looking for.

Existential Encounter   A third point of view in special revelation is that of existential encounter. It is possible not to take the scriptures in a literal sense; yet, not regard them as simply human insight into the nature of Divine Being. One can take the scriptures to be meditation documents for encounter with God. They are writings, but they can become more than just writings. As writings they can be seen as the product of fallible men who have witnessed to their own encounter with God. On this literal level, the scriptures are fascinating and inspiring in that they show how passionately certain ancient people believed in, and recorded their encounters with God. On another level, the level of scriptural criticism, the scientific level, it is important to know everything that can be known about the text: who wrote its various parts, for what purpose, at what place, at what time, according to what conceptions of the natural world. Such information will help keep one from falling into the superstitions of credulous people who believe that everything in the scriptures was divinely revealed and faithfully recorded, including, maybe, even the punctuation. But having said this much, it can still be insisted that nothing basic has been said about true religion, or the true purpose of the scriptures. True religion is not a set of propositions, or even a supply of insights, but a living engagement. The scriptures are instruments, not *in which* the self-disclosure of God is to be found, but *through which* the self-disclosure of God occurs. God does not speak in his scriptures to the heads of men, but through his scriptures to the hearts of men.

From this point of view, revelation is not regarded as practical information about God for the purpose of "saving souls." Nor, as in the insight theory, is it handled in a way intended to make it adaptable and relevant to the twentieth century. Rather, from the position of existential encounter, revelation is an experience in which a person encounters the mystery of God, and finds it to be energizing, cleansing, renewing, authenticating. The mystery of God is not un-raveled, but it is unveiled. The *I Am* of God is directly experienced, and although the experience is ineffable, it is nonetheless con-vincing.

The weakness of the position is, first, in the fact that being private and ineffable it is hard to explain to any person who has not experienced it. It cannot be taught. There is no catechism for it. To know it one must experience it. A second weakness is that being extremely subjective there is no way to evaluate it objectively. There are no criteria by which the experience of "revelation by engagement" can be criticized and judged.

eight

Ritual

In doing religion, men reinterpret their world so that its devastating aspects are seen in a more meaningful and hopeful light. They establish a religious view of the world. In keeping with this view they proceed to act appropriately so that they may be correctly related to the power or powers that control their lives and destinies. One form of appropriate behavior is called ritual. Ritual is a dramatic portrayal of the "truths" of religion—of a particular religion—and is often done as the reenactment of a special event in the past when God (or the Gods) acted in behalf of man. The Catholic Mass, for example, is the reenactment of Christ's sacrificial death on the Cross. Passover is a dramatic reliving of the story of the Hebrew Exodus from ancient Egypt—a sojourn which each year each Jewish family makes with Moses.

Origins of Ritual   Religious ritual is reverent, stylized behavior performed in acknowledgment of "the sacred." Primitive people especially have a keen awareness that certain places, persons, things, and even rituals themselves, are sacred, and therefore an attitude of carefulness and respect must be taken toward them. The idea of the Sacred, or of the Holy, as we saw in Otto, is an awareness of the mysterious, powerful, fascinating, numinous "out there," toward which one must, for his own good, be cautiously respectful. No one, and especially no primitive person, deals with this power casually or carelessly. Moses took off his shoes because the ground whereon he stood was holy ground. The voice from the throne in

John's Revelation (19:5) instructed all men who *feared* God to praise him. In the presence of sacredness there is anxiety. In this anxiety there is need to act, and to act properly: to appease the Holy, or to praise it, or at least to acknowledge it. Upon entering a Catholic church, one crosses oneself with holy water. On the door of a little Protestant church at the foot of the mountains of Colorado there is a sign that reads: "Compose yourself. No one entering a house ignores him who dwells in it. This is the house of God." In each case, one does something appropriate lest the sacred be profaned.

Rituals, of course, are not performed only by individual persons, as he crosses himself or composes himself. They are more importantly performed by communities of persons for the purpose of community acknowledgment of the sacred, and for community benefits expected from the sacred by such recognition, and to remind the community of the basis and authority for its spiritual and moral life. In many religions there are special rites[1] to bring prosperity and good health to the community: to make the soil productive, the cattle fertile, the fishing successful. There are other rites performed regularly to celebrate God (or the Gods), ancient heroes, saints, seasons, a kairotic moment in history (see chapter twelve), or to make sacrificial offerings to the divine being. Other rites celebrate special events in community life: the birth of a child, the maturing of the child (rites of passage), the marriage of two who are no longer children, and the end cycle of the individual's life in community (funerary).

Myth   Closely associated with ritual is the narration that accompanies the ritual—the myth. The word "myth" comes from the Greek word *mythos,* which means speech, words, story, legend. Religious myths identify the meaning of the ritual by reciting the story of the origin of the ritual in the action of some primordial event of God or hero. For example, in the rite of Holy Communion as practiced in the United Methodist Church, one finds the follow-

---

[1] The terms *rite* and *ritual* are closely related and often interchanged in usage. Thus we hear of the rite of matrimony and the ritual of matrimony. More technically a rite is the prescribed form for a ceremony, while a ritual is a collection or book of rites; for example, the ritual of Holy Week in the Christian tradition is composed of the several rites (ceremonies) performed during that week—the rites for Palm Sunday, Holy Thursday, Good Friday, Easter.

ing combination of instruction (rubric) and myth. *The people shall kneel or bow; the minister, facing the Lord's Table, shall say:*

> . . . in the same night that he was betrayed, he took bread [*here the minister may take the bread in his hands*] and when he had given thanks, he broke it, and gave it to his disciples saying, Take, eat; this is my body which is given for you; do this in remembrance of me . . . (The Ritual for Holy Communion in *The Methodist Hymnal*)

This service is a performance of reverent behavior—a ritual. The accompanying narration tells the story of the origin of the ritual. It is the myth. The myth is not in the instructions of how to perform the ritual (the people shall kneel . . . the minister may . . .), but in the description of the origins and foundations of the ritual. Lord Ragland made the same point in his essay "Myth and Ritual." He pointed out two accounts of animal sacrifice recorded in the Book of Leviticus. First, Leviticus 9:8–11 (*The New English Bible*, New York: Cambridge University Press, 1971), the myth:

> So Aaron came near to the altar and slaughtered the calf, which was his sin-offering. The sons of Aaron presented the blood to him and he dipped his finger in the blood and put it on the horns of the altar. The rest of the blood he poured out at the base of the altar. Part of the sin-offering, the fat, the kidneys, and the long lobe of the liver, he burnt in the altar as the Lord had commanded Moses.

Second, Leviticus 17:6, a rubric:

> The priest shall fling the blood against the altar of the Lord at the entrance of the Tent of the Presence, and burn the fat as a soothing odor to the Lord.

Ragland points out that "those two descriptions are of the same rite, whereas the latter is in the form of a simple instruction, the former is a myth, that is to say an account of the rite told as a narrative of what somebody once did."[2]

Myths, apparently, can become unlatched from their appropriate rituals and continue independent careers of their own either as fairy tales, or folktales, or legends. Also, apparently, although perhaps less successfully, rituals too can continue even after their original meaning and/or mythic narration has become unhinged. One

---

[2] Lord Ragland, "Myth and Ritual," *Myth: a Symposium*, ed. T. A. Sebeok (Bloomington Ind.: Indiana University Press, 1965), p. 122.

knocks on wood, throws pinches of salt over his shoulder, places an evergreen tree at the topping out of a new, tall building, with no memory of, or narration of, the meaning or authority for such action. From such examples it appears that when religious rituals lose their original meaning (their mythos) they either cease to exist or become trivial.

Anthropologists still debate which came first, the ritual or the myth. Which preceded the other, the reverent performance or an articulated account of the ancient divine action that prompted the reverent performance? Prehistoric facts seem too far away to justify one claim or the other. But the facts discernible in living primitive societies indicate the likelihood that neither necessarily came first, and that both rest upon a prior belief system—upon religious dogmas already declared and accepted by the tribe. It might be, as Annamarie de Waal Malefijt proposes, that "myth and ritual are related not because they ... complement and reinforce each other, but because both are based on dogma."[3] That is, both rest upon a prior belief system. Believing something about themselves and their world, men behaved reverently, and authenticated their reverent behavior by identifying it within their theology—their general patterns of social and religious beliefs. Such a suggestion puts not only ritual and myth as primordial forms of religious behavior, but puts theology at the beginning also. Theology, *logos* of *theos*, words about God, is not to be dismissed—as some modern scholars have done—as some kind of intellectual straitjacket imposed upon the "feeling" of religion long after religion emerged from the emotions of man and flowered in rituals and myths. Rather, it is to think that men believed and spoke their beliefs to themselves from the very beginning, and in terms of their "belief-words," they did their religion. They made religious dramas (rituals), and those dramas narrated the action of the divine powers in establishing (and reestablishing) the life, customs, institutions, beliefs, and dogmas of their community life. It may be that before our prehistoric man (of chapter one) went to the swamp and found his Tree, he already lived in a system of beliefs about the powers of his world—a belief system that structured his life and community into a world of ordinary and superordinary things. He was not simply an

---

[3] A. de Waal Malefijt, *Religion and Culture* (New York: Macmillan, 1968), p. 186.

animal reacting to an environment, but a man who had begun to "make sense" of his social system, to make sense of his mundane environment, and to make sense of the tremendous, mysterious, fascinating, numinous world of sacred things. It may be that he was already in a condition of theology, into which his Tree Ritual fit comfortably. A ritual which he would one night at the campfire be challenged to defend and would do so by searching his theologized soul for a vision of how long before at the dawn of time when the Old One walked the earth, he came to the swamp and finding it loathsome and dangerous made the Tree and put it there for Man to see and touch and be made strong for the evils of the swamp.

In spite of certain scholarly claims to the contrary, we have no evidence for thinking that prehistoric men were not thinking men, who had theologies that informed their lives and structured their religious rituals. As we saw, Paul Tillich held that theology "is as old as religion. Thinking pervades all the spiritual activities of man." Indeed, is not mythical narration itself theology—words about God? E. O. James in his *Myth and Ritual in the Ancient Near East* points out that

> even the native tribes of Australia, though they have no recorded history, have traditions which presuppose a very definite continuity with the past when inexorable laws, customs and organizations were given to their tribal ancestors in the . . . Dream-time of long ago, when the culture heroes lived on earth and determined the existing structure of society. . . . Thus, history, in the sense of the course of significant events, is an integral part of the tribal tradition in terms of the myth and ritual which preserve the network of social relations and the state of tribal equilibrium and stability.[4]

Malinowski, in his "Myth in Primitive Psychology," makes the same point when he states that among primitive people myth/ritual conveys much more than is contained in the story being dramatized. The myth/ritual drama fits into a larger structure of belief which the primitive person has learned in the context of his tribal life. "In other words, it is the context of his social life, it is the gradual realization by the native of how everything which he is told to do has its precedent and pattern in bygone times, which brings home

[4] E. O. James, *Myth and Ritual in the Ancient Near East* (New York: Barnes and Noble, N.D., earlier publication, London: Thames and Hudson, 1958), pp. 18–19.

to him the full account and the full meaning of his myths of origin."[5]

In this regard, Joseph Campbell identifies the myth-ritual-theology configuration as a vitally functioning meaning system which (1) creates in man a sense of awe before those powers and circumstances that lie outside his control; (2) enables him better to understand the natural world order around him; (3) gives him a framework in which he can see his society as coherent and meaningful; and (4) gives him a way of understanding his own inner life.[6]

KINDS OF RITUALS

The major rituals of society and cultus are stylized human behavior depicting symbolically and dramatically the authority for socially acceptable and/or socially demanded values. There are secular rituals for various social purposes; religious rituals for various religious purposes; and "quasi" rituals, mixing both secular and religious elements.

Secular Rituals   It was November 22, 1963; the time was 2:38 P.M. (CST); the place, Love Field outside Dallas, Texas. In the rear compartment of Air Force One was a casket holding the body of the 35th President of the United States. Forward in the gold upholstered conference room, in the presence of Mrs. John F. Kennedy and twenty-six other persons, a diminutive woman, Sarah Hughes, District Judge, read from the Constitution of the United States, and Lyndon B. Johnson, holding a Bible in his left hand, his right hand raised, repeated after her the last thirty-five words of Article II, Section 1. And so the torch was passed; the fallen reins of government gathered up. John Kennedy had been dead ninety-eight minutes. Three minutes later President Johnson issued the first order of the 36th President of the United States: "Now, let's get airborne." The Government had been reasserted in proper Constitutional form in a ritual: "I do solemnly swear that I will faithfully execute the

---

[5] Malinowski, *Magic, Science, and Religion* (New York: Free Press, 1948), p. 93.

[6] See Joseph Campbell, *The Masks of God: Occidental Mythology* (New York: Viking, 1964), pp. 518–523.

office of the President of the United States, and will to the best of my ability preserve, protect and defend the Constitution of the United States. So help me God."

On other, more happy days, the Inauguration of the President and the Oath have occurred in more elaborate pageantry. But elaborateness is not the point. The point is that to assert the meaning of the nation in the mind of its citizens, to give solidarity to the diversity which is the United States, rituals are performed. The ritual of Inauguration is real and vital and alive. It literally makes a man *the* President; and more—it makes him *our* President. And it was given to us by our great cultural heroes—the Founding Fathers. When they inaugurated the first President, he too in the presence of the Fathers said: "I do solemnly swear . . ."

The celebration of the Fourth of July and of Thanksgiving Day are rituals of the same secular social stripe. Each in its ritualized form authorizes and solidifies the society with an aura of ancient purpose reborn.

Such rituals are predominantly secular in nature. Presidents do close the Oath with the words "So help me God," but their main concern is not to get supernatural assistance but rather to make a "reverent noise" at an auspicious time. Interesting is the fact that these religious words are not "Constitutional." They do not appear in Article II as part of the prescribed oath. Thanksgiving Day purports to be more religious in intent; its religiousness, however, does not appear to run very deep—not much deeper, it would appear, than table grace. And the Fourth of July makes no religious pretense at all.

There is an argument which would disavow what is here called "sectarian rituals." Robert Bellah argues that there is a "Civil Religion in America" composed of the various official statements and rites performed by the Government of the United States, including the statements of belief in God affirmed in the Constitution; on the coinage of the realm; in the declarations of the Founding Fathers; in the "religious" celebrations of Memorial Day, Thanksgiving Day, and the Fourth of July; and in the occasional prayers of the President for some divine favor for the nation.

However, we shall here contend that what Bellah calls a Civil Religion is not a religion so much as the religious authenticating and celebrating of the nation. Using the Judaeo-Christian heritages (heavily interpreted as Deistic and/or Protestant), the national story and symbols (the mythology) are given a religious aura. But this is hardly a religion. A real religion deals with the transcending of finitude. It addresses the nonmanipulable and horrendous circumstances of personal life and meaning. It is a salvation affair. That "Civil Religion" affects real religion is obvious, as real religion obviously affects the civil performance, but the appropriation of some religious symbols and rituals, and even some religious attitudes, does not transform the body politic into a functioning religion. One may dress a chimpanzee in a child's clothes, but the act does not create a child.[7]

"Quasi" Rites   Some rituals seem to be "somewhat" secular and at the same time "somewhat" religious. They have a secular purpose but are also obviously and essentially based in things sacred: for example, the socially vital, theologically based "rites of passage" of primitive people. In the Inaugural ritual we have a mechanism for passing political authority from one person to another. In many places the same kind of function is performed to signify, authorize, and make real the passing of a person from childhood to adulthood. Such rituals are called "rites of passage."

For example, in the Lake Eyre country of southeastern Australia there is a tribe of people called Dieri. Whenever a Dieri boy or girl reaches puberty, rites of passage are performed to transform the boy into a man and the girl into a woman. In the case of males the rites have a prelude which consists of a ceremonious knocking out of the boy's two front teeth with a wooden chisel, and a service of circumcision and naming. At a later time and without warning the boy is led out of the camp by some older men. They surround him and tell him to

> close his eyes. One of the old men then binds the arm of another old man tightly with a string, and with a sharp piece of flint lances the vein about an inch from the elbow, causing a stream of blood to fall over the young man until he is covered with it, and the old man is becoming exhausted. Another man takes his place, and so

[7] For more on this question see Robert Bellah, "Civil Religion in America," with commentaries by D. W. Bragan, Lee Pfeffer, John Witney, and Phillip Hammond, *The Religious Situation*, 1968, ed. Donald R. Cutler (Boston: Beacon Press, 1968), pp. 331–393.

on until the young man becomes quite stiff from the quantity of blood adhering to him.[8]

In this way the spirit and wisdom of the old men transform the boy into a man by making him of one blood with them. Next the blood-covered boy is gashed on the neck and back to make scars—a lasting evidence of his initiation into manhood. At the completion of this rite, he is given a bull-roarer: a paddle-shaped slab of wood with a long string attached. The bull-roarer when whirled around the head creates a mysterious noise, which the boy and the women-folk had often heard before, but never understood. But the bull-roarer is not to be regarded as a simple trick to frighten women and children. It is believed to have supernatural power and to speak to all living things. It is the symbol and voice of the Mura-muras (the ancient tribal heroes) who first gave the tribe its sacred laws, traditions, and rituals. The boy, now become man, is never to show the bull-roarer to any woman, or tell her about it.

Finally, the initiate is sent alone into the bush where he is to remain until his wounds have healed and he has rehearsed many times the lessons he has heard during this long ritual of initiation. And he has heard many things during this time, for throughout the entire ritual there had been a narration recited by the older men, who carefully explained the supernatural origin of each rite performed. Their recitation began with a retelling of the tribal myths in regard to the ritual being performed. The boy was admonished in his tribal duties. The totemic rules and relationships were defined with exactness. The tribal morality thus comes to each member of the community with the full weight of religious sanctions behind it.

Another "quasi" ritual which can lean either toward the secular side or the religious side is the marriage rite—a rite that can be effectively performed by a judge, a justice of the peace, a sea captain, a Jewish rabbi, a Greek Orthodox priest; that can take place in a courtroom, a courtyard, a swimming pool, a chapel, a temple, or a cathedral; that can be accompanied by a matron of honor, bridesmaids, a best man and groomsmen, a weeping mother, a relieved father, organ music, songs, candles, fertility rice, and a staggering amount of champagne; a rite that is always made official by a

[8] A. W. Howitt, *The Native Tribes of South-East Australia* (New York: Macmillan, 1904), p. 650. See also J. B. Noss, *Man's Religion*, 3rd ed. (New York: Macmillan, 1963), p. 38.

signed, sealed, and courthouse-recorded certificate. It can also be most holy sacrament, for this public declaration, which authenticates a relationship basic and essential to society, can declare itself to be "performed in the sight of God." The state insists that marriage is a legal arrangement of necessity to the stability, tranquility, and continuation of society. But the church, with a backward look to its mythos, declares that what occurs is not simply a society-fostered arrangement, more or less endorsed by two families, or even a vow of love between two persons, but an "honorable estate instituted by God" even in the beginning of time, and "is, therefore not to be entered into unadvisedly, but reverently, discreetly and in the fear of God."

Religious Ritual   Although all rituals have valuable social and political implications, some are so overwhelmingly concerned with religious things that they must be regarded as sacred or cultic[9] rather than sociopolitical. We shall look at two of the truly cultic types of ritual and see them as they reflect the mythos and/or theology of two widely different religious cultures: Roman Catholic Christianity, and Zen Buddhism.

RITUAL IN CATHOLIC CHRISTIANITY[10]   The annual rituals of the Christian Church constitute a reliving of the atonement (the at-one-ment) of man with God through the birth, life, death, and resurrection of Christ. This cycle of reliving begins about four weeks before the Winter Solstice with the season of Advent, and climaxes on the first Sunday after the first full moon following the Vernal Equinox, which is Easter. From this cycle of rituals (which tells the complete story of Christ's life from before his birth to after his death and resurrection), we shall look at only three rites—those of Palm Sunday, Holy Thursday, and Good Friday. The rites of Holy Thursday and Good Friday represent, in a sense, the quintessence of the Christian myth as viewed by Catholic Christians. Sacrifice and Eucharist, that is what the whole thing is about: God giving himself *for* and *to* man.

[9] Cultic pertains to a system of religious behavior, especially the rites and ceremonies of worship.

[10] For a beautifully handled description and statement on Christian Rituals, see Alan Watts' *Myth and Ritual in Christianity*, 3rd ed. (Boston: Beacon Press, 1970). Here we refer only to three rituals of Holy Week.

The ritual year moves swiftly from the Birth of Christ to his Passion, Death, and Resurrection. There are three pre-Lenten Sundays—Septuagestima, Sexagesima, and Quinquagesima—and then forty days of Lent, which are the days of preparation for the true Mystery: the Mystery of the Redemptive Cross. The Passion ritual begins with the coming of Christ to Jerusalem on the Day of the Palms. Before the Mass of Palm Sunday there is a rite in which not bread and wine are consecrated, but branches of the palm and olive trees. This rite begins with the priest and his assistants entering the church intoning a collect, lesson, and Gospel, as in a regular Mass. They chant the Preface and Sanctus of the music of the Mass for the Dead. The priest then blesses the branches with incense and holy water, recalling in his prayer not only the palms with which Christ was greeted as he came to Jerusalem for the last time but also the olive branch brought to Noah by the dove as a sign of the end of the Flood and the beginning of a new covenant with man. The palms are distributed to the people and a procession is formed which leaves the church. The church door is then closed. Inside the church the cantors who have remained behind sing a hymn, "All glory, laud and honor, To thee, Redeemer King." The church door (representing the great Gate of Jerusalem) is again opened and the procession reenters the church singing "Hosanna in the highest . . ."

During the Palm Sunday Mass, at the time for chanting the Gospel, the clergy and the choir sing the story of the Passion according to Matthew in a dramatic form, wherein members of the clergy take the parts of Christ, Pilate, and Judas and the choir sings the words of the Hebrew mob. This Mass is repeated on Tuesday, Wednesday, and Friday with Passion stories according to Mark, Luke, and John.

Thursday is different because it is the ritual of the Lord's Supper as reportedly it was first given on the first Holy Thursday. This rite celebrates the institution of the Mass itself. The actual ritual of any Mass has two parts—part one for the catechumen (those under instruction in basic doctrines of Catholic Christianity in preparation for admission among the faithful of the Church), and part two for the faithful. The first part is adapted from the Jewish synagogue service and consists of prayers and readings. The real Mass begins with part two. It is composed of Offertory, Consecration, and Communion. The Offertory is the presentation of the bread and the wine, which at this state represents the offering by the faithful of themselves to God. In the Consecration the priest assumes the role of Christ and repeats the actions which occurred at the Last Supper, including Christ's words which declared the bread to be his true body and the wine to be his true blood. In the final division of the Mass, the Communion, the priest and the faithful gather at the altar and consume the sacred body and blood, as reportedly the Apostles did in the Upper Room. (In a Catholic Mass, the bread, in the form of a wafer is placed by the priest on the communicant's outhrust tongue. Only the priest drinks the wine.)

That this central ritual is not simply a commemoration of a divine action in the distant past, but the re-creation of that action in the present, is declared in the belief that when the priest speaks Christ's words, "This is my body . . . This is my blood," the ordinary bread and wine of the Offertory are believed to be literally transformed (transubstantiated) into the actual body of Christ and blood of Christ, with only the appearance of bread and wine remaining.

During the Mass of Holy Thursday, the priest consecrates a special host which, when the Mass is over, is placed in a chalice on one of the side-altars where throughout the night of Holy Thursday the faithful take turns keeping vigil, as did the sleepy Apostles with Christ in Gethsemane.

For Holy Thursday the purple altar cloths signifying the Passion of Christ are replaced with snowy white cloths which speak of the beauty and gladness of Christ's giving of himself in the eucharistic gift of Holy Communion. After vespers Thursday night these snowy cloths of gladness are stripped from the altar, recalling how Christ was stripped before his crucifixion. The priest, having laid bare the altar of God, then turns to his people and taking a vessel of water and a towel washes their feet, recalling how Christ, the night before he died, washed the feet of his disciples.

Then the fateful day arrives—a bad day called Good—the day of crucifixion. On this Friday the priest, dressed in somber black, on a bleak, bare altar, performs the Mass of the Presanctified. The time is hushed and agonized. The Passion in this ritual drama is the one according to John, from the agony in the Garden to the burial in the tomb. When the account is finished, the priest takes a large wooden crucifix veiled in black and holds it up before the people. The crucifix is slowly unveiled and a chant sung.

> Behold the wood of the cross,
> on which hung the Savior of the world.

Unveiled, the cross is placed before the altar. The priest removes his shoes, kneels and kisses the cross. Then the people form a procession which proceeds up the center aisle of the church. Before arriving at the cross they go down on their knees three times, as, according to the biblical story, Christ fell three times as he carried his cross to Golgotha.

During this portion of the Good Friday rite an extraordinary hymn is sung:

> Faithful Cross, the one Tree noble above all:
>   no forest affords the like of the leaf, or flower
>   or seed.
> The Creator, pitying the sin of our first parent,
>   wherefrom he fell into death by the bite of the
>   poisoned apple, did himself forthwith signify
>   wood for his healing of the hurts of wood.

Alan Watts points out that the wood or tree of the cross is of highest mythological significance.

> So many of the hero-gods and *avatars* are associated with the Tree that the central symbol of Christianity is of a truly universal nature. [The slain body of Osiris was] found within a giant tamarisk or pine-tree which had been cut down and used for the *central pillar* of the Palace of Byblos. Attis, son of the Virgin Nana, died by self-sacrifice under a pine-tree. Gautama, the Buddha, son of Maya, attained his supreme Awakening as he sat in meditation under the Bo Tree. Odin learned the wisdom of the runes by immolating himself upon the World-Tree, Yggdrasil, with a spear cut from the same tree . . . Adonis (*Adonai*, the Lord) was born of Myrrha the myrtle, and the Babylonian god Tammuz was associated in his death with the cedar, the tamarisk, and the willow.[11]

In almost all mythological traditions the tree is regarded as the center of the world. The tree of David's father, Jesse, in medieval drawings, is shown as growing from Jesse's navel. The Tree of the Knowledge of Good and Evil stood in the middle of Eden. In Christianity, the Tree (the Cross) is at the center of salvation, at the center of life, at the center of the world. "To this Tree, image of the finite world, the Son of God is nailed by his hands and feet." Upon this Tree of the world the atoning sacrifice is finally made.

---

[11] Alan Watts, *Myth and Ritual in Christianity* (Boston: Beacon Press, 1968; 3rd ed., 1970), pp. 158–159.

When Christ dies on Friday afternoon, the ritual drama of Passion ends. The candles are snuffed out, the sacred host removed from the sanctuary, the church (the world) is empty—waiting.

We have looked at the Catholic tradition for our illustrations of religious rituals because the Catholic tradition can afford us such an elaborate display of rites which are, at the same time, somewhat familiar to us in our Western World. Examples from Judaism's elaborate rituals could afford us a similarly familiar array. The Protestant tradition, especially that part which developed out of the peasant movement (the Left-Wing) of the Reformation, is much less extensive and formalized. But these, so-called, Evangelicals also have their ritual ceremonies with accompanying narrations (myths). Even the extremely spontaneous Pentecostals, gathering for a spiritual service, are ritual-myth guided. The service may seem to be a formless succession (even confusion) of singing, preaching, exhorting, praying; yet it is a deadly serious reenactment and reliving of the "birth of the church" in the first coming of the Holy Spirit fifty days after the Resurrection of Christ. It is Pentecost relived, even to the ecstasy of divine seizure and "speaking in tongues."[12] The action of a Pentecostal service may be more spontaneous than the action of a Catholic Mass, but it is no less ritual-myth.

We should also note that it is neither the amount of action nor the formality or spontaneity of the action which makes the ceremony a religious ritual. There are some powerful rituals constituted of "sitting quietly, doing nothing," as in a Quaker Meeting or in Zazen.

THE ZA-ZEN RITUAL IN ZEN BUDDHISM   Once, a long time ago, the great Gautama, after years of anguished searching for the true religion, gave up the search, the struggle, the action, the effort, and sat down under a tree. He sat quietly, doing nothing, as in "Sitting quietly, doing nothing, Spring comes, and the grass grows by itself."[13] And suddenly the search that Gautama was no longer making was concluded in the Great Enlightenment. Gautama's

---

[12] Pentecost was not really a glossolalia experience, although many people confuse it as such. On Pentecost, according to Acts, the Apostles spoke and were understood by everyone. Their speaking was not esoteric, but universal.

[13] From a Japanese Zen-Buddhist poem.

Buddhahood was accomplished, and a new, magnificent religion for mankind was born. That is the myth. It has been, since then, accoutered with the most elaborate rituals imaginable, but also with a profound ritual of practically no elaboration at all—the *Za-zen*.

Za-zen (literally, seated meditation) is the central ritual of the meditation religion called Zen Buddhism as it is practiced in the monasteries in Japan. This service takes place in the Meditation Hall (*Zendo*), which is the central building of a Japanese Zen monastery. It is a long, rectangular building, with a wide platform down the length of either side. Its only adornment is the shrine of the Buddha (*Butsudan*) standing in the center of the hall with, perhaps, a spray of flowers set before it. At the time for meditation the monks enter the hall in a procession and take their seats on the platforms in two rows facing each other across the narrow room. They sit in the traditional lotus posture, legs crossed, feet upon the thighs, hands resting in the lap, palms upward, eyes fixed upon the floor. The head monk goes forward and prostrates himself before the shrine. He then lights a stick of incense to mark the time. The head monk then takes his seat on the platform and the *Za-zen* begins. No one speaks. There is no sound in the room except that which drifts in from outside. Breathing is regulated so as to be slow, without strain, with the outbreathing emphasized slightly by a push from the belly rather than the chest. Two attendants walk slowly back and forth between the two lines of seated men. Each attendant has a stick. Any time one of them sees anyone sitting improperly or dozing off, he stops before the offender, bows ceremoniously, and proceeds to belabor him with the warning stick, until the offender has been "massaged" again into full wakefulness. When the incense has burned out, the head monk sounds a bell. It is time for relaxation and exercise. The monks get up from their lotus-posture sitting, form a column and begin to march swiftly and quietly around the room. After this exercise, they return to their meditation during the burning of another incense stick. These periods of *Za-zen* continue for three hours.

The obvious purpose of the *Za-zen* ritual is to revitalize and relive the enlightenment of the Buddha, which in Zen Buddhism is called *Satori. Satori* is a state of mind in which the usual object-subject dichotomy of ordinary living is dissolved abruptly, and the "enlightened one" intuits directly that all things are Buddha-reality. All things are harmoniously one. This "way of being" is not learned in the usual sense of learning, that is, thought out. Indeed, thought-out learning (thinking) is the antithesis of *Satori*; in fact, it is its nemesis. One achieves enlightenment (bodhi) as Gautama himself achieved it: sitting quietly, doing nothing, in a most unordinary and mind-shattering fashion.

Our concern here is not to explore the nature of Zen (for such an exploration the student is advised to read Alan Watts' *The Way of Zen,* or his *The Spirit of Zen,* and especially D. T. Suzuki's *Studies in Zen*); our concern is simply to illustrate a form of ritual-myth, which, following the primordial experience of the founder of Buddhism, is quiet, unostentatious, and non-Western.

ELEMENTS OF RITUAL

Ritual, as we have seen, is dramatic in form. It possesses action and narration. It is also a participation drama, and one that conveys religious meanings (is a symbol). We shall now look at the participation and symbolic elements of ritual.

Participation Drama   The participation character of religious drama can be seen quickly in the performance of the Christmas Story dramas enacted in Christian churches and Sunday schools each year at Christmas time. While a narrator reads the Nativity accounts from Matthew and Luke (the myth), the scenes of the Nativity (what God did for man) are performed with ritualistic, if sometimes awkward, actions and postures by selected members of the congregation. This is an almost classic example of religious folk-ritual. The myth (the dramatic narration of the divine-human encounter) and the ritual acts (the stylized actions of that encounter) are combined to effect an experience of wonder and joy in all who "behold and believe."

Two important observations should be made at this point. First, the enactment of the Christmas Story is not simply a drama, but a folk-drama. It is a drama of participation. The actors, the narrator, and the auditors are all caught up in the movement and life and spirit of the event. Which is to say, that although the ritual is often spectacular, it is not intended to be a spectacle. It is a vehicle of involvement in which the whole folk (the community of worshippers) are all communicants. They are all partakers because they all participate.

In a different setting this participation aspect of ritual is exemplified in the Jewish celebration of Passover. On that ceremonial evening the Jewish family gathers at the festive table. One of the children asks the traditional question: "Why is this night different from all other nights?" Then the head of the family answers: "We were slaves unto Pharaoh in Egypt and the eternal our God led us from there with a mighty hand." So begins the participation drama of Passover in which ritual acts and myth/narration combine to recreate the sense of God's presence and God's support in Jewish life.

Religious Symbols   First, then, ritual is participation drama. Second, it is preservation and communication of religious stories and meanings. It is a religious symbol. Paul Tillich, in his *Systematic Theology*, makes some interesting observations about the nature of symbols. He asserts that "symbol and sign are different; . . . while the sign bears no necessary relation to that to which it points, the symbol participates in the reality for which it stands."[14] Elsewhere in the same volume he states:

> The denotative power of language is its ability to grasp and communicate general meaning. The expressive power of language is its ability to disclose and communicate personal states. . . . Most speaking moves between these two poles: the more scientific and technical, the nearer the denotative pole, the more poetic and communal, the nearer the expressive pole.[15]

This is to say that denotation is the central function of signs, whereas expressive communication is the central function of symbols. A sign is arbitrarily assigned to convey information. A flashing red light at a street corner means stop. A green light could be used equally well. But symbols are not so, for the function of symbols is not to convey precise meanings, but to transport aesthe-noetic experiences, and once they arrive at full symbolic status, they cannot be arbitrarily changed. They cannot be substituted simply through

---

[14] Paul Tillich, *Systematic Theology*, 3 vols. (Chicago: University of Chicago Press, 1951), vol. 1, p. 239.
[15] Ibid., p. 124.

common agreement. For example, although the American flag does have a kind of denotative function in that it points at this country instead of that one, it is not simply a sign of this country, for it represents, depicts, excites, participates in the whole spectrum of the history and life of this nation. The symbol speaks to the American beholder of the total reality (fact and spirit) of America, of which the symbol itself is a part. It is both a piece of gaudy cloth and a nation, and it is more the latter than the former. Ritual is symbolic not signary. The concern of ritual is not to put on a show, or even simply to convey a message, but to participate in a total event which, although it is historically distant, recurs in the present enabling the worshipper to experience that mighty occurrence as if he were there. One is with the shepherds and the wisemen, seeing the fantastic birth in its simplicity and importance; one is at the Cross and at the Tomb witnessing; one is with Moses crossing the sea, standing at the mountain.

Theology and philosophy of religion may deal in signs—analyzing, criticizing, systematizing—but ritual is an art form. It speaks to the heart to elicit those reasons that "reason does not know." In saying this, we do not mean that ritual is irrational, or even unrational, or that theology and philosophy are inimical to ritual. But it speaks differently from theology and philosophy. It uses its own logic, which is the logic of evocation and nuance, as does any art form.

Attitude of Worship   Also ritual has an affective dimension different from that of theology and philosophy. In theology and philosophy, one searches for the "truth of the matter." In ritual, one desires not the truth so much as worshipful involvement. Equally important with the story being told is the attitude of the person participating in the story being told. One must give himself in worship or the ritual becomes simply a spectacle. Sören Kierkegaard tells us that it is better to worship a false God truly than a true God falsely.

> If one lives in the midst of Christendom, goes up to the house of God, the house of the true God . . . and prays, but prays in a false spirit; and one who lives in an idolatrous community prays with the entire passion of the infinite, although his eyes rest upon the image of an idol: where is there most truth? The one prays in truth to God

though he worships an idol; the other prays falsely to the true God, and hence worships in fact an idol.[16]

TARGETS OF RITUAL

Rituals are performed for a variety of reasons—to celebrate the changing of the seasons, to effect a miraculous change in the world, to accomplish a spiritual change in a person, to establish a relationship of communion between the worshipper and the divine, to make the land fertile, to make the rains come, and so on. The various types of ritual can be, for convenience, classified functionally as (1) metatechnological, (2) sacramental, (3) experiential.

Metatechnological Function   In both ancient and modern times, ritual had been used to introduce supernatural or extranatural power into natural processes. In other words, it has functioned to produce magic and miracles. We have observed this sort of thing in the religious practices of the Trobriand Islanders. Another example is the Sun Dance of the Indians of the North American plains. This dance was performed to assure the return of the buffalo for the fall hunt, and to protect the tribe from its enemies. The ritual involved fastings, self-torture, sun gazing, dancing, singing, and praying, with the entire tribe taking part in the service. Its purpose was to bring supernatural force to the assistance of the Indians in situations that were critical to their life-style and to some degree precarious. We have observed, also, that with the advance of modern scientific technology in agriculture and medicine, this type of ritual has become less and less performed in modern cultures. It is still performed in primitive cultures and in other places where modern technology is in short supply. Also, there are vestiges of it in technologically advanced cultures. There are faith healers in America, and numerous people who act on the belief that "prayer changes things." To the degree that people engage in rituals intended to infuse divine power into natural processes, ritual with a metatechnological function operates.

---

[16] Sören Kierkegaard, "Concluding Unscientific Postscript," *A Kierkegaard Anthology*, ed. Robert Bretall (Princeton, N.J.: Princeton University Press, 1947), p. 212.

Sacramental Function   As the metatechnological function of ritual aims to bring divine power into the natural environment, the sacramental function aims to bring divine power into the soul of man. In this sort of ritual the believer receives divine "grace" which is purity, perhaps, or integrity or merit, and usually—and most important of all—life after death. The worshipper gets what God has: life after death. We have noted an early form of this kind of ritual in the Egyptian cult of Osiris. The Egyptian worshipper ate the sacred body and drank the sacred blood and performed other reverent acts that he might become Osiris, and so enter the life of the Blessed Immortals. This kind of ritual was very common in the Greek Mystery Religions, for example, in the Eleusinian, Dionysian, and Orphic cults. In such cults the initiate underwent a preparatory purification, was introduced to the mystic secret, beheld sacred objects, and observed an enactment of the divine story performed as a ritual drama. Then he was received into full cultic membership and privileged to become like the God: immortal. This great power came to him (in many cults) by drinking a sacred wine (the blood of the God) and/or eating the flesh of a divine animal (the body of the God). In these ritual acts there occurred an infusion of divine power. The participant became like the God. Christianity, when it arose in the Gentile world, was greatly impressed by this notion of sacramental worship. In his letter to the Church in Rome, Paul presented a dramatic account of how the inner life of the Christian was transformed by the ritual of baptism.

> Through baptism we have been buried with [Christ] in death, so that just as he was raised from the dead through the Father's glory, we too may live a new life . . . you must think of yourself as dead to sin but alive to God, through union with Christ Jesus (Romans 6:4, 11)[17]

This type of ritual became a major form of Christian religious activity, and remains so in the Catholic Church. The Catholic Church is basically a treasury of seven sacraments through which divine power is brought into the inner life of man, and through which man obtains a power like that of Christ—to live again after death.

---

[17] *The Complete Bible, an American translation*, Old Testament trans. J. M. Powis Smith, New Testament trans. Edgar J. Goodspeed (Chicago: University of Chicago Press, © 1939).

Experiential Function   Often the aim of ritual is to vivify the awareness of the presence of God. The worshipper seeks to experience God as if they were face to face. In an extreme form this sort of ritual effects an overwhelming sense of oneness with God. In this dimension it is usually called mysticism. More often experiential ritual seems to establish, not a sense of identity between God and the worshipper, but a sense of community between them. This form of ritual has always been a central dynamic of Judaism. Quite as characteristic as their ethical-monotheism has been the Jews' awareness of God in their lives—speaking to them out of a burning bush, from the smoke of Mt. Sinai, in the voices of the Prophets, and the ceremonies of the Temple, and the prayers of the Synagogue, and the lighting of the Sabbath Candles. To know that God is with them, and that God has a burden and a mission for them, is to summarize three thousand years of Jewish life and worship.

The target aimed at in experiential ritual is an experience of the intimate presence of God in the life of the "true believer," and a sense of personal conversion, of forgiveness, and of renewal because of this experience.

Theology and ritual (rationalizing and dramatizing a mythos) are two phenomenal features of religion. Indeed, these aspects of religion are sufficient for a full-blown religion. To know the God (or Gods) and to demonstrate that knowledge with thoughtful attention and with acts of reverence, propitiation, and even adoration is sufficient for religion. The supernatural must be known, and the supernatural must be properly respected with worshipful attitudes and ceremonial dramas. Theology and ritual, especially in primitive religions, are the essential means of coming into right relation with the divine.

nine

Morality

The term religious technique, as we are using it, means a way of doing religion. Theology, as we observed, is one of the things done when people do religion. It is a technique. Also, ritual is one of the things done by people when they do religion. It is another technique. A third technique employed in religion is morality. Keeping the moral rules laid down in any given religion is another way of performing in order to achieve religion, and benefit from the values available in religion. One of the things demanded by moral religions is that the persons involved live according to certain moral rules and principles. In such religions morality is one of the ways used to please the God, or live in harmony with the God, and thereby come to enjoy the benefits promised by the religion. A moral religion is one in which, either directly or indirectly, the God is concerned with moral relations among men: a religion in which the Divine Being "cares" about how Smith treats Jones, and with how Jones and Smith behave in the community, and with how the community relates to each and both of them.

Although morality can be a tremendously important technique in religion, it is not a necessary technique. There are religions which do not employ morality as a technique. Such religions are not immoral religions; they are amoral religions.[1] An amoral religion is

---

[1] The people whose religions are amoral are not themselves amoral, or immoral, but are people who get their morality from a different source—usually from the social structure in which they live.

any religion in which morality is not a specific technique in doing the religion. Any religion that does not have a specified set or system of moral demands as a technique for effecting religious values can be called an amoral religion. In such religions the Gods care only that they be acknowledged and properly respected. Amoral religions are not devoid of moral influence. They do effect moral influence on the community, but they do so indirectly. They do not make formal moral demands upon it. They are without moral teachings. In many primitive religions the shaman exorcises demons and venerates spirits and souls and Gods, but he does not teach and/or supervise an ethical system that has been established and made demanding by the spirits or souls or Gods. However, the shaman's religion, as we shall now see, is not devoid of moral influence.

THE MORAL INFLUENCE OF AMORAL RELIGIONS

In many primitive (primordial type) religions the shaman is not only a man of primary importance in metatechnological affairs but he has a major role in maintaining social order in his community. Often, even as he operates in his capacity of shaman, he operates as the tribes' principal lawyer and judge. In dealing with amoral religious problems, he sometimes turns his authority as shaman to the solution of social and moral problems. I. M. Lewis, in his *Ecstatic Religion*, gives several illustrations of this. One is from the Akawaio Caribs of British Guiana.

The Akawaio Caribs believe that bad things happen to the tribe when someone violates a taboo and displeases the supernatural spirits. When the spirits begin to cause trouble (for example, when an epidemic occurs or the food supply is threatened), the shaman must first diagnose the cause. To do this he holds a public seance. Transporting himself into a trance state, he lets the spirits take over his personality and become the investigators searching for the culprit who by breaking a taboo has brought trouble into the community. Through the shaman, searching questions are asked and, in the face of the supernatural circumstances of the occasion, honest answers are demanded. The questions asked and the answers given are obviously on the public record. Everyone is there listening. Indeed, everyone present can participate and ask questions of his own. In this way, smoldering quarrels and enmities are venti-lated, social festers are lanced and drained, gossip and scandal are confirmed or denied, actions explained and justified, accusations openly considered. Also, it is not infrequent that the spirits, using the shaman's voice, deliver sermons "on the importance of correct conduct, denouncing moral failings, condemning transgressions, and generally reducing their victims to acquiescent contrition by a skillful combination of suggestive probes, satire, and sarcasm."[2]

The religious seance thus becomes a procedure for bringing into the open all sorts of hidden social and moral problems. Once the problems are exposed, the spirits proceed to pronounce judg-ment, through the mouth of the shaman. If the seance is a good one, their judgments are the consensus judgments of the community. Thus a religion that embraces spirits who have no real interest in human morality—a religion that is amoral—is effecting a strong influence on the tribe's harmony, solidarity, and ethics.

PRIMITIVE MORAL RELIGIONS

Not all primitive religions are amoral. Some are moral religions, and these may have acquired that characteristic either through contact with outside sources or independently.

External Source   Sometimes a primitive religion becomes a moral religion through encounter with one of the moral religions of a more advanced civilization. The outsiders come, and the primi-tive's life-style is assaulted by either propaganda or temptation. He lets down his guard, and the moral religionists move in on him. As we know, Christian missionaries have been unrelentingly insistent on clothing the naked South Sea "savages" they came to Christian-ize, and the Muslims have been very effective in "sharing" their Islamic moral codes with African natives.

The Giriama tribe of Kenya illustrates the process of moving from amoral religion to moral religion under the impact of social change and external religious influence. In the 1920s the Giriama began to change their former marginal farming culture into a seri-

---

[2] I. M. Lewis, *Ecstatic Religion* (Harmondsworth, Middlesex, Eng.: Pen-guin, 1971), p. 161.

ous cash-crop culture. With this change they began to trade extensively with the Muslim Swahili and Arabs of the coast. As this
occurred, a new affinity for Islamic ways began to develop among
the Giriama. The bulk of the Giriama, however, did not immediately convert to Islam; rather, they came into it in a circuitous
fashion. Oddly many of the Giriama began to be plagued by Muslim demons. Numerous spirit possessions occurred which could be
exorcised only by adopting the Islamic faith. The plaguing spirits
"appeared in the guise of malign peripheral demons with no
moral relevance,"[3] but to get rid of them the Giriama had to become followers of Islam with its many moral demands. These
Muslim converts are called, interestingly enough, "therapeutic Muslims." They are, for therapeutic reasons, both primitive and Muslim
at the same time. Being Muslims, therapeutic or otherwise, lays
heavy moral demands upon them, and infuses their religion with
morality.

Indigenous Moral Religions   Many primitives have acquired
their moral religions from someone else, but some have not. Moral
religion, as all religion, reaches back to origins in primitivism. Moral
religions arose naturally in those primitive societies that contained
not only spirit worship but also ancestor worship.

A shaman may be master not only of spirits (supernatural beings of nonhuman origin) but also of souls (supernatural beings of
human origins: ancestors). Often there are actually two religious
cults in the same primitive society: the cult of spirits with its
shamanistic medicine, and the cult of ancestors with its shaman
medium. Also, often, the same shaman functions in both cults. The
spirit cult is primarily concerned with problems arising from non-
moral causes: a broken taboo, black magic performed by an enemy
witch doctor, a foreign spirit invasion. The ancestor cult is concerned with moral delinquencies: incestuous relationships, adultery,
homicide.

The Kaffa people of southwest Ethiopia, although they are
mostly nominal Christians in the Church of Ethiopia, hold fast to an
old, indigenous ancestor cult that operates to preserve and enforce
the moral demands of their old-time religion. Each patrilineal clan
of the Kaffas is led by a shaman (called Alamo) who acts as a

[3] Ibid., p. 130.

medium for the souls of his patrilineal ancestors. "In this he functions as a diviner, diagnosing the cause of sickness and misfortune
within his group in terms of ancestral wrath incurred by its members when they sin."[4] The ancestors are concerned with maintaining
the solidarity and cohesion of the clans and tribe. Each Friday the
Kaffas consult with the shaman, asking him questions on matters of
importance to them. The next day they return to the shaman who,
having consulted with the ancestors, answers some or all of the
questions asked. Also, when needed, the ancestors are consulted to
diagnose and prescribe cures for illnesses and other kinds of misfortune. If the ancestors inform the shaman that the cause of distress is
to be attributed to moral misconduct or neglect on the part of one
or more of the clansmen, the shaman, in the name of the ancestors,
demands that the guilty make appropriate propitiating sacrifices to
the offended ancestors.

Kaffa ancestors demand moral rectitude. They were doing so
long before the Kaffas became, as well, members of the Ethiopian
Christian Church. Their moral religion was an indigenous religion.
They did not acquire it from someone else.

In some religions the angry ancestors themselves assail the
offending humans and punish them with sickness and misfortune
and tragedy. In other religions, however, it is not the ancestors who
punish but, rather, foreign demons and devils. In this situation,
when the people sin, break the moral rules, the ancestors, who
normally protect the family and tribe, withdraw their protection
and the wayward ones are left at the mercy of foreign malevolents.
This is the way it is with the Korekore Shona people and the Zezura
Shona people of southern Rhodesia. It was also the way it was with
the "primitive Hebrews" when they got out of line and served other
Gods.

> And the children of Israel did that which was evil in the sight of
> Yahweh, and served Baalim; and they forsook Yahweh, the God of
> their fathers, who brought them out of the land of Egypt, and
> followed other gods, of the gods of the peoples that were round
> about them, and bowed down unto them: and they provoked
> Yahweh to anger. And they forsook Yahweh and served Baal and the
> Ashtaroth. And the anger of Yahweh was kindled against Israel, and

[4] Ibid., p. 144.

> he delivered them into the hands of spoilers and despoiled them; and he sold them into the hands of their enemies (Judges 2:11–14, American Standard Version).

As we can see, with the "primitive Hebrews" a different instrument of punishment was used: not demons and devils, but human despoilers and enemies—Philistines and Ammorites and others. Also, and more important, we can see that it was a different punisher: not an ancestor, but a spirit—*the* spirit: God Yahweh.

At this point, we begin to deal with a different type of moral religion; namely a religion whose God makes the moral demands, and a religion that uses morality as a major technique in religion. In such religions, one must employ not only theology and ritual to fulfill the requirements of religion but must live by a moral code, which has been revealed or discerned as a demand made either directly or inferentially, not by ancestors, but by the dominant spiritual reality behind all life and society: by the High God. Here morality is seen as a necessary technique (if not *the* necessary technique) to "please the God" and accomplish the values of religion, that is, to be saved.

THE TECHNIQUE OF MORALITY

Along with the right theology and correct ritual, morality became, in the advanced religions, a third technique for pleasing the Gods and achieving the values of religion.

Probably the ancient Egyptians were the first people to identify moral law with divine demand. This identity of morality as a technique in religion was well advanced in the religion of Osiris, at least 2500 B.C. For a person to enter the world of the immortals (Khenti-Amenti) he had to be (besides ritualistically initiated) clean of hand and pure of heart. According to the Egyptian *Book of the Dead* a human soul had to face both God Osiris and the Gods of the forty-two Egyptian nomes. Each of these Gods was an avenger of a particular sin or crime. The soul had to make a negative confession, declaring what it had not done, in order to avoid their condemnation. The following, according to the *Book of the Dead,* is part of the confession that had to be made.

> Hail to thee, great God, lord of Truth. . . . Behold, I come to thee, I bring to thee righteousness. I knew no wrong. I did no evil thing. . . .

I did not do that which the God abominates. . . . I allowed no one
to hunger. I caused no one to weep. I did not murder. I did not
diminish food in the temples. . . . I did not take away the food-
offerings of the dead. . . . I did not commit adultery. . . . I did not
diminish the grain measure. . . . I did not lead the weight of the
balances. I did not deflect the index of the scales. I did not take
milk from the mouth of the child. I did not drive away the cattle from
their pasturage. . . . I did not dam the running water [and thus
divert from others the waters of the irrigation canals at the time of
the inundation]. . . . I did not interfere with the God in his pay-
ments. I am purified four times. I am pure.[5]

Clearly the Egyptians came to recognize that the techniques of
religion were not limited to knowing the Gods and reverently ac-
knowledging them; the techniques also included keeping the moral
laws of the Gods.

Apparently the same understanding of religion and morality
was accomplished in ancient Babylon, for we find that in the seventeenth century B.C., the great God Shamash presented King
Hammurabi with a code of laws, as God Yahweh later did to Moses.
Apparently in both Egypt and Mesopotamia morality became a
major dimension in religious life. But it was on that little section of
rocky, barren ground between the great nations north and south
that the connection between morality and religion was most signifi-
cantly made for the subsequent religions of the Western world. We
should remember, however, that both Abraham and Moses had
intimate connections in Mesopotamia and Egypt respectively.

The Hebrews came to see God as a moral being who was
pleased when men worshipped him by emulating his morality. They
conceived of the moral law as being an essential form of religious
behavior. God was pleased or displeased by the way men related to
each other. Already by the year 1000 B.C. the moral dimension was
important enough in Hebrew life to be a mandate even for kings.
For example, in II Samuel, chapters 11 and 12, there is an account
of Yahweh's displeasure at King David's disregard for the rights of
one of his subjects. We read that King David seduced the wife of
one of his soldiers, Uriah the Hittite, while Uriah was away fighting
in one of David's wars. When the wife, Bathsheba, was found to be
pregnant, David called Uriah home from the battlefront hoping the

---

[5] J. H. Breasted, *Development of Religion and Thought in Ancient Egypt*
(New York: Scribner, 1912), pp. 299–300.

unsuspecting husband would take pleasure with his wife and later think the child was his. But Uriah refused to enjoy the pleasantries of home life while his comrades bore the discomforts of war. He refused to enter his own house. David, being thus frustrated in his initial chicanery, sent Uriah back to the front carrying sealed orders to General Joab. The orders instructed Joab to expose Uriah in battle that he might be killed. The deed was done, and David took Bathsheba into his palace as his wife and she bore him a son. But "the Lord sent Nathan to David" to condemn him and to predict the death of the child as a punishment for David's immoral behavior. And, indeed, the child did die shortly thereafter because, as the author of II Samuel put it, "the thing which David had done displeased the Lord." One might question whether David's adultery was more reprehensible than God's infanticide, but this is not the point. The point is that already by the year 1000 B.C. Yahweh was being conceived as a God who was concerned with man's moral behavior. God *did* care how "Jones" treated "Smith" (David treated Uriah). The degrees of refinement in that caring were now just a matter of historical development. The Hebrews had come to believe that God had laid upon them a moral law as well as a ceremonial law. They wrote the laws of God into their Bible and that Bible became the Old Testament scripture of the Christian world.

The Hebrews continued their idea of the religious importance of right knowledge and correct ceremony, but they increasingly laid special emphasis upon ethical living until, in the words of the Prophet Micah, we hear pronounced (as an ideal at least) the complete domination of morality as the technique for pleasing God.

> With what shall I come before the Lord and
>   bow myself before God on high?
> Shall I come before him with burnt offerings,
>   with calves a year old?
> Will the Lord be pleased with thousands of rams
>   with ten thousands of rivers of oil?
> Shall I give my first-born for my transgressions,
>   the fruit of my body for the sin of my soul?
> He has shown you, O man, what is good;
>   and what does the Lord require of you
>   *but to do justice, and to love kindness,*
>   *and to walk humbly with your God* [author's italics]
>   (Micah 6:6–8, Revised Standard Version).

Along with their Hebrew precursors, Christians asserted that God could be offended not only by wrong belief and incorrect worship but also by violating man in any way abhorrent to the divine morality. Along with knowledge and ceremony, morality became a means of achieving the high morale possessed by one who lived securely in his God.

THE MORAL DIMENSION

It is the general contention of religious systems of the consummate type[6] that there is not only a moral order in man's social world but a moral order in the structure of the universe itself. It is generally contended that human behavior is so geared to life in its largest dimensions that any violation of human beings has not only social implications but metaphysical implications as well. As Winfred Garrison put it, there is a basic structure of morality in the life of man "which is beyond the power of society to make or modify," and this structure is

> first, that there shall be codes of conduct, backed by conscience and a sense of 'oughtness,' so that human community shall not exist in a state of moral chaos or nihilism; second, that these codes, whether derived from custom, enactment, or revelation, shall implement the fundamental truth that man himself has unique value and shall demand behavior consistent with man's essential worth and dignity. These requirements are fulfilled by the second term of Jesus' summary of the commandments: "thou shalt love thy neighbor as thyself."[7]

A RULE OF THUMB

Most of the consummate religions not only assert the claim of universal moral order but they all have, somewhere in their teachings, a rule of thumb for keeping the universal moral order. This rule-of-thumb formula in Christianity is called The Golden Rule: "All

---

[6] See chapters eleven and twelve for consummate religious systems.

[7] Winfred Garrison, *Protestant Manifesto* (New York: Abingdon, 1952), p. 67.

things whatsoever ye would that men should do to you, do ye even so to them." Other world religions have substantially the same rule:

In Hinduism: "Do not to others, which if done to thee would cause thee pain."

In Buddhism: "In five ways should a clansman minister to his friends and familiars—by generosity, courtesy, and benevolence, by treating them as he treats himself, and by being as good as his word."

In Judaism: "What is hurtful to yourself, do not to your fellow man."

In Taoism: "Regard your neighbor's gain as your own gain and regard your neighbor's loss as your own loss."

In Confucianism: "Do not unto others what you would not have them do to you."

In Sikhism: "As you deemest thyself so deem others."

In Jainism: "In happiness and suffering, in joy and grief, we should regard all creatures as we regard our own self."

In Zoroastrianism: "That nature only is good when it shall not do unto another whatever is not good for its own self."

IMMANUEL KANT'S POSITION

Immanuel Kant (1724–1802) went so far as to say that religion is nothing other than "recognizing our duties as divine commands." This epistemologically tough philosopher found his evidence for religion, God, human freedom, and life after death from the fact that man as man has a moral nature. Roughly Kant argued so: man possesses a moral nature; this moral nature thrusts upon him a sense of obligation. He is obliged by his own conscience to seek holiness, that is, perfect obedience to the highest good, to the highest virtue. In responding to this inborn "categorical imperative," man is necessarily driven to certain reasonable inferences about the nature of the world he lives in. Man's conscience demands that he pursue the highest virtue. He is to pursue holiness. But no human can hope to achieve perfect holiness, because (1) he himself is imperfect. Human beings, despite the moral center of their lives, are sensual and rebellious. (2) Man lives in a world that is obviously not under the control of moral principles. In short, man is a sinner and nature or history is unjust, or at least amoral. Man, a creature possessing a sense of justice, lives in a world that is not always just. If man's moral life under these circumstances is not to be taken as a farce, he must postulate the existence of (a) his own free moral will, (b) a life after death where the injustices of this life can be balanced, (c) a supreme being of perfect Good Will to whose will man responds when he strives to fulfill his duty to the moral law. Freedom, life after death, and God cannot be "known" by logical structures, but each has a claim upon man as the object of a reasonable moral faith. Kant makes man's "practical reason" (his moral consciousness) superior to his "pure reason" (his scientific and philosophical intelligence) in matters of religion. God, the Supreme Being of Good Will, is a necessary postulate of man's innate moral nature, and religion is man's "recognition of duties as divine commands."

JAMES' PRAGMATIC ARGUMENT

The American philosopher William James, in his essay "The Moral Philosopher and the Moral Life,"[8] makes an interesting practical plea for the existence of a transcendent moral order; that is, for a self-conscious God who is morally demanding. James points out that wherever there is a conscious being there is also a moral order. "The moment one sentient being . . . is made a part of the universe, there is a change for goods and evils really to exist. Moral relations now have their *status* in that being's consciousness. So far as he feels anything to be good, he *makes* it good. It *is* good for him."[9] In a world where there are a vast number of sentient beings, representing an even vaster number of desires, the ethical philosopher must try to discover what hierarchy of desires and obligations ought to take precedence and have supreme weight in the ordering of individual and social relations. To define the supreme good, the ethical philosopher must trace the "ought" to its source in some existing consciousness, for there can be no morality that does not ground itself in some self-conscious mind. To be sure, one may conclude that morality takes its foothold in the universe if only through men's minds, for "whether a God exists, or whether no God exists . . . we form at any rate an ethical republic here below."[10] But if we do not

[8] William James, "The Moral Philosopher and the Moral Life," *Essays in Pragmatism* (New York: Haffner, 1951).

[9] Ibid., p. 70.

[10] Ibid., p. 75.

reject the ordinary man's belief that there is a moral order independent of man, we must place this independent moral order also in a *thinking mind*. If there is a transcendent, extrahuman moral order, then there is a sentient God in whose mind that moral order is grounded, for the seat of "oughtness" simply cannot exist in a vacuum.

The question is: Is there such an order? A moral order independent of men? And James proposes that there had better be, or, at least, we had better believe there is. To avoid social chaos and personal disorientation, man imposes upon himself rules for living— mores, legal and ethical codes, general moral attitudes. Now, there are people who fall in line with the rules for living simply to avoid the discomfort of social disapproval. But there are other people differently oriented who embrace ethical discipline, not so much for their own benefit as for the benefit of a "hoped for world" not yet born. They dream wild dreams like the notion that men are born with certain unalienable rights, that men will one day actually beat their swords into plowshares, that pain and hunger and crime and cruelty and violence will some day be conquered; and for such dreams they are willing to sweat and bleed and even die. James divided these two kinds of people into what he called the "easy-going-mood" and the "strenuous mood." He further held that the capacity for the strenuous mood may lie in all men, but it is not always easy to arouse. It "needs the wilder passions to arouse it, the big fears, loves and indignations; or else the deeply penetrating appeal to some one of the higher fidelities, like justice, truth, or freedom."[11] Especially it needs belief in God. To be sure, in a merely human world without God life will be lived in an ethical "symphony," but, James states, "it is played out in a couple of poor octaves."[12] The strenuous mood of high ethical living is not readily called out simply for posterity—for people who will be alive a hundred years from now, or two hundred years. All this is too finite. It lacks the rousing excitement of infinite demand and mysterious obligation.

James believes that the capacity and need for strenuous moral living are so deeply a part of human possibilities "that even if there were no metaphysical or traditional grounds for believing in God,

[11] Ibid., p. 85.
[12] Ibid., p. 85.

men would postulate one simply as a pretext for living hard, and getting out of the game of existence its keenest possibilities of zest."[13] He further argues that "every sort of energy and endurance, of courage and capacity for handling life's evils, is set free in those who have religious faith. For this reason the strenuous type of character will on the battlefield of human history always outwear the easygoing type, and religion will drive irreligion to the wall."[14]

James concludes his essay with some advice to moral philosophers: "In the interest of our ideal of systematically unified moral truth, therefore, we would-be philosophers, must postulate a divine thinker, and pray for the victory of the religious cause."[15]

In this kind of thinking, William James (against the Kantian position) supports the contention that morale and not morals is the central function of religion. Using morality, motivated by a strenuous belief in God's moral will, religion affirms and demonstrates that in a religious man there is a center of gravity that balances the inward life against the outward winds of adversity enabling him to take the frustrations of life with poise, the comedies of life with good grace, and the challenges of life with an energy that bespeaks not of finitude but of infinity.

The importance of moral discipline (religious ethics) cannot be gainsayed in religion. But morality is not a substitute for religion, or the summation of religion. It is a technique in religion. Kant may tell us that religion is the recognition of our moral duties as divine commands; Matthew Arnold once said that it is "morality tinged with emotion"; A. E. Haydon said that it is the "shared quest of the good life." But they are all wrong. The function of religion is not to make man morally good, but to give him transcendence; to deal with his sense of finiteness; to give him hope, courage, confidence as he faces the human condition. Religion is *morale* centered. Ethical living may be the fruit of religion (as Paul and Calvin saw it), or a way to religion (as in Judaism and Catholicism), but it is not why people do religion. We expect "high religion" to express itself in high ethical standards. High religion produces high ethical values, just as some farms produce excellent hybrid corn. But it only con-

[13] Ibid., p. 86.
[14] Ibid., p. 86.
[15] Ibid., p. 86.

fuses the facts to define religion as ethics and morality, as it would confuse the facts to define a farm as a place where hybrid corn is grown. Again, we may refer to the account of Jesus in Gethsemane. Surely he was just as moral when he went into the Garden as when he came out of it, but the same cannot be said for his morale. He went in terrified; a man desperately in need of the hope, confidence, courage that comes from religion. He prayed not for moral perfection but for religious courage and, apparently, if we can trust the accounts, he got it.

ten

Getting It in Shape

In 1965 Harvey Cox published a book that announced the demise of religion. It had died, so Cox proclaimed, in the turning of the world into a *Secular City*. "The age of the secular city, the epoch whose ethos is quickly spreading into every corner of the globe, *is* an age of 'no religion at all.'"[1]

A year later Thomas Altizer and William Hamilton published a book that announced the demise of God. Altizer and Hamilton had looked inward and discovered that the world was suffering from an absence of the experience of God, or at least they were. They proclaimed, somewhat inconsistently, that although "God had died in our time in our history, in our experience," he really died when he willingly poured himself into the person of Jesus of Nazareth, and died with Jesus on the cross. Other "Death of God" men, of Jewish tradition, apparently concluded that God had died at Auschwitz. In his book *After Auschwitz*, Richard Rubenstein raised the question: How can a Jew believe in God? He concluded that after Auschwitz he, for one Jew, could not; that he was living at the time of the death of God.

> If I believed in God as the omnipotent author of the historical drama [the death camps] and Israel as His Chosen people, I had to accept [the] conclusion that it was God's will that Hitler committed six

[1] Harvey Cox, *The Secular City* (New York: Macmillan, 1965), p. 3.

million Jews to slaughter. I could not possibly believe in such a God nor could I believe in Israel as the chosen people after Auschwitz.[2]

Cox's death of religion was politely received by the American intelligensia, and widely read by it, but not widely read by everyone else. But the proclamation of God's death struck the fancy of certain news journals and for a while it got wide publicity, and for a while much popular attention. Now, however, some years later, neither the *Secular City* nor the books of the Death of God men command much attention. And we are, perhaps, in a position to make some sober observations about that flurry of religious excitement.

First, it is somewhat surprising that a Death of God announcement in 1966 got viewed as "news," when the same kind of announcement had been made much more logically and philosophically on a number of occasions much earlier. One can go back as far as the second century B.C. when Carneades, the Head of the Second Platonic Academy, examined the evidence and concluded, not that God had died, but that God could not possibly ever have existed. In the eighteenth century, David Hume, a brilliant Scottish philosopher, made the same argument even more systematically than had Carneades. And after Hume there were Schopenhauer, and Feuerbach, and Nietzsche and Freud—all presenting brilliant dissertations proving that God and religion had surely passed out of the picture for anyone bright enough to read their books on the subject. The notice and/or notoriety "enjoyed" by the recent announcements seems to have been more an accident of modern instant communications than a "news scoop."

The second observation to make is that apparently when the announcements were made in 1965 and 1966, as in earlier times, nobody listened. Robert Ellwood in his little book on the Jesus People asserts that what happened was that everybody played a game called "Fool the Prophets."

"Fool the Prophets" has been played on a sweeping scale in American popular and political culture in the sixties and seventies. Never have predictions and projections been more plentiful and precise. Never have the people who make popular culture taken more

[2] Richard L. Rubenstein, *After Auschwitz* (Indianapolis: Bobbs-Merrill, 1966), p. 46.

apparent delight in confounding the prognostications by finding something else to do.[3]

Lots of people heard what the "prophets" were saying clearly enough: Religion is gone, replaced by technology, megalopolis, and secularism. God is gone, dead gone; and man must learn to live not in the experience of the absence of God but in the absence of the experience of God. *But nobody listened.* Religion did not end, and God seems to have come back quite alive from Argentina or wherever else he was in 1965 to 1966. Evidence to this effect can be seen in recently taken polls which indicate that although church and synagogue attendance has declined over the past few years, a large portion (about 40 percent) of the American population still goes to church or synagogue once each week. Also, apparently God is alive and well in American hearts and minds. According to the polls, from 94 percent to 99 percent of the adult population affirms a belief in God, whereas only between 1 percent and 3 percent have no such belief, and the remainder are undecided. In Europe the belief is a little less widespread and the disbelief more widespread. But even in Europe God gets large endorsement—even from Frenchmen, who are the most skeptical of all but still array themselves 66 percent for God, 14 percent undecided, and 20 percent atheists.

The Contemporalizing of Religious Expressions   Another observation to make about the current shape of things is that Harvey Cox, Thomas Altizer, William Hamilton, and other "radical theology" people, did not mean exactly what they said, or mean it exactly as they said it. When Cox said, in effect, Religion is dead, he really must have meant: Religion is dead. Long live religion! And the others must have meant, similarly: God is dead. Long live God! What they were doing was proposing that certain kinds of religious expressions and feelings were gone, and that it was time to redo religion for the world of today. And in such proposing they were not doing anything especially new or even radical. Redefining religion is probably as old as the second generation of the first religion of mankind. Once started, the next generation surely had to redefine it to make it fit some modified contemporary situation.

Anytime there is sufficient reason, the case of religion is re-

[3] Robert S. Ellwood, *One Way* (Englewood Cliffs, N.J.: Prentice-Hall, 1973), p. 1.

stated. Sometimes a person coming at the right time is sufficient reason, for example, Moses, Gautama, Jesus, and Muhammad. Sometimes a major cultural change is sufficient reason. When Paul and the other Apostles left Palestine and moved their religion into a different cultural setting, the faith got restated. It was made to talk sense not to Jews only but also to Ephesians and Colosians and Athenians and Romans. And when it became sophisticated enough to appeal to educated people, it was reinterpreted by St. Augustine in Platonic modes of thought. When in the thirteenth century Aristotelian philosophy became the science of the day, it was restated by St. Thomas in the rational forms of Aristotle's logic. When modern states began to rise in Europe, the Christian Church decentralized and nationalized and talked a theology congenial with the newly emerging mercantile and industrial economies. When modern science introduced heliocentric and evolutionary theories, Christian theology at first fought it and then joined it. If anyone believes that anywhere today the religion of Jesus is followed, or the religion of Paul or Augustine or even Martin Luther, he is sadly uninformed. Religion does not die, but its forms change. Sometimes, almost imperceptibly, sometimes dramatically, sometimes drastically, religion takes on new shapes as it presents its old message in a new way.

The Disillusionment   It is impossible to tell how the forms of religion (or techniques as we have called them) will change in the next ten, fifty, hundred years, but they will change. What does not change is the fact of religion in the lives of people. Human finitude does not change. The joy of religious experience does not change. But the answers and expressions given and experienced constantly change, and are currently changing rapidly. The surface reason for these religious changes is that the world (through communications systems, air travel, atomic bombs, international economic intricacies) is changing rapidly, but a deeper reason for religious changes lies in growing disillusionment which reaches back fifty years in Western history. People have been increasingly disillusioned by science, by modern theology, and by society. Modern science offered a cure to all physical ills, modern theology offered a palliative for spiritual joy, and modern society offered freedom, prosperity, and security. But the payoffs did not pay off adequately.

First, science and modern technology. Science and the by-product of science, technology, came on strong with heady expectations: to know the truth, to find the answers, to control the outcome. And science has functioned magnificently. It has solved tremendous problems. But it has also created tremendous problems all the way from identity crises to ecological murder; and it has nowhere offered a solution to the human condition.

Modern theology also failed. For the modern world there arose, first, a theology that intended to translate the ancient religious message into modern language, a theology that intended to accommodate Christianity to a modern world. It did so with considerable enthusiasm and optimism. With science to solve man's physical problems, the church could develop a decent "social gospel," and work to establish the kingdom of brotherhood, the Kingdom of God on earth. And with evolution on everybody's side it would surely come about, if not tomorrow, then a little later. But that was not the way things worked out. The world went sour. It did not get better. It seemingly got worse. The Great Depression was solved not by a social gospel but by World War II, which was also not solved by either the Cold War in Europe or by hot wars in Korea and Vietnam.

Theologians began to question their liberal interpretations, and some of them turned back to a more orthodox posture. Man was a fallen creature. In no way could he ever create the Kingdom of God on earth. Christ and culture stood against each other. God was not working with man. God was far off, completely far off, completely other. From overoptimism about the powers of man to effect world change, modern theology became increasingly pessimistic. And God got farther and farther away from man's experiences in this world; and the world got farther and farther away from the "experience of God," until one day it was discovered by some searchers that no matter where they turned, God was not to be found. It was not as if they just could not, for the moment, make contact with God, but as if they had no experience of God at all. And some of them finally concluded: He is dead. We are living in the time of the death of God.

A third disillusionment came in the social structure—in thousands of ways in the social structure. Perhaps one illustration is paradigm. In the 1940s the most sophisticated people on earth, the most educated, the most scientific, the most philosophical, the most "cultured," turned upon the world with something called a Blitzkrieg and something called The Holocaust. Unbelievable! How could such a thing happen? There are thousands of explanations and excuses for how it could happen, but they do not help the disillusionment. And even after the Nazi violence, the social disillusionment did not end. It continued to grow: in little wars that kill people just as dead as big wars; in bad laws everywhere that "good parliaments" would not change; in hungry people whose petty, tyrannical governments, with the connivance of tyrannical big governments, bought fighter planes and bombers and machine guns instead of bread; in churches and synagogues that dismissed or otherwise chastised their clergymen for sympathizing with the civil disobedience of black men, in the rebellions of long-haired kids, and so on and on and on.

Some Recent Reshaping   In the midst of all of this modern disillusionment, several new forms of religious expression began to take shape in America. One new shape was called the Southern Christian Leadership Conference. A new Exodus was conceived in the hearts and minds and songs of a "bondaged people." Led by Martin Luther King, Jr., a man inspired by his Christian faith and schooled in the techniques of Mohandas Gandhi, an Indian pacifist and holy man, some black people in the South moved to the front of the bus. The impact of this "walk forward" soon extended into all of the social and political spheres of the lives of black Americans and spread nationwide. The shape of things had changed permanently, and the change was grounded in strong religious motivations.

Most of the leadership behind the black civil rights movement developed in religious organizations, and most of its power arose from religious organizations. Not all of these organizations were Christian. Of great importance in the development of the black man's rejection of the status quo were the attitude and strength of the Black Muslims who adapted the Islamic faith to their needs and ambitions. Other black people looked to Africa for their motivations to new identity and spiritual power.

A similar restiveness also activated many young white Americans. They too began to reject "the establishment." They began to cast about for an awareness of special identity and a heightening of the consciousness of selfhood. In many ways many of the young whites felt a spiritual kindred with the black cause, and with what it directly and subtly meant to the spirits of men. Some whites aided the civil rights movement by working on voter registration drives.

Most of the young whites did not join the civil disobedience of the black cause, but most of them felt a separation and an alienation in their own private homes, schools, churches, and social structures, even as the blacks felt it in the wider national structure. Rejecting the mores of established society, they began to search for alternatives. This led to an amorphous congregation of activity collectively called the hippie movement.

At least two other factors helped shape this movement. One was the common identity created by the use of psychedelic music, wild decorations, special language, and hallucinogenic drugs. The other factor molding the shape of the movement was the war in Vietnam. As they saw it, the senseless and "immoral" involvement of America in a Southeast Asian war was ample grounds for rejecting the establishment and even for despising their elders.

Many youthful Americans began to build a world of their own in places like San Francisco's Haight-Ashbury, New York's Greenwich Village, Los Angeles' Sunset Strip, and Atlanta's Peach Street, where they created a life-style including "happenings" and "trips," rock music, posters, poetry, and drugs. Many other young people who did not "split" to the special centers of the "street people" or later to communes, still joined their rebelling comrades in spirit, and in hair, dress, and drug use.

The movement was anti-establishment, and the organized religions of the American scene were establishments marked for special avoidance. The hippie people generally absented themselves from the religious denominations of their parents. At the same time, the mysteriousness of religion and its capacity for aesthetic exploitation and its potential for aiding in self-identification offered special attractions to many of them. Rejecting their parents' religions, many young people experimented with non-Western forms of religion. They explored oriental religious systems, such as Zen Buddhism, Krishna Consciousness, Transcendental Meditation, and others.[4] Whatever religious significance these experiences may have had, whatever changes they may have effected in the shape of things, they were not sweeping away Western expressions in favor of East-

[4] For a more extensive examination of these Asian imports see Carl Rashke, "The Asian Invasion of American Religions," *Philosophy and Theology* (Tallahassee, Florida: American Academy of Religion, 1973); and Jacob Needleman, *The New Religions* (New York: Pocket Book, 1972).

ern expressions as much as they were signs of the disillusionment which had infected the contemporary culture.

After a few years of Eastern religion, another religious grouping and movement of young people took shape. The pendulum swung back from East to West and American youth began to "get high" not on gurus, but on Jesus. The Jesus Movement started. One should not have been overly surprised that in a culture that sought fulfillment in numerous ways some young people would eventually be as excited about Jesus as others had been about Asian gurus. The "Jesus Kids," or "Jesus Freaks" as they called themselves, broke into American experience with the energy of a new Children's Crusade, replete with joyous smiles, Bible verses, and cheerleader enthusiasm. The aim of the visible faction of the movement, often seen preaching in public, was to bring the "Word of God" to the people. They professed with warm sincerity that their inner life was devoted to prayer, spiritual happiness, and the values taught to them but not practiced by their parents. They held that the older generation had the words of the Good News, but lacked the spirit of Jesus to make those words live in joy and glory. But they had it and meant to share it.

A close observer of American religion, Will Herberg, made an informed guess that part of the Jesus Movement usually called the Kids or Freaks, which seemed to arise as a loosely organized, almost spontaneous expression of fundamentalistic, Sunday school Christianity, would eventually dissolve into establishment, denominational religions. Getting a little older, Herberg predicted, the movement's followers would get married, get jobs, join churches, and remember (even witness to) the good old days when people had "real religion." That part of the movement called the Children of God, which was well organized into a system of Christian communes, Herberg speculated, would simply become another conservative Protestant denomination.

The fact is that no one knows what will be the impact of these various religious enthusiasms, either Asian or new fundamentalist Christian. Only time will tell. The participants themselves certainly accepted their religious views as forming a complete and lasting life-style. They intended to change the world, and to some uncertain degree they have changed it. Their efforts to change themselves and the world by techniques of Eastern meditation and/or a reinfusion of new spiritual love into the Judeo-Christian life and practice cannot be without some lasting effects. The fact is that they happened, and changed the shape of things, and once changed the shape can never be quite the same again.

Principles of Shaping   Everywhere new styles of religion are being tried, both independent of established denomination and inside established denominations. The future of any style cannot be predicted. But a historical perspective may give us some insight into the dual forces that seem to govern all religions as they move through history. Religion expresses itself in two ways: as rational, culture-related thought and activity; and as emotional, inner-directed experience. The rational pole emphasizes the ideas, vocabulary, and the established scientific and philosophical world view in which it operates. It is, properly, historically worldly. The other pole of the same religion sees the religious experience, and all of the mythological lore of that religion, as basically unique, and not to be corrupted by any foreign "modern language." At any given time both of these antagonistic poles are alive and straining against each other. Religion has its extremely rational moments. It also has its extremely emotional moments. Its long-run success comes when some degree of balance is maintained between the two. An imbalance usually occurs when the culture shifts. Our culture has shifted. There is an imbalance between the poles: between rationalism, often called liberalism, and emotionalism, often called evangelicalism. And they are struggling. Today liberalism, on the one hand, and evangelicalism, on the other, are standing opposed to each other as an internal split in both Catholicism and Protestantism.[5] How the tension will be resolved no one can possibly predict.

A deeper penetration of the religious situation, however, as we are pursuing it in this book, informs us that it is the style, the shape that changes, not the need for, nor the fact of religion in the lives of men. Religion *as such* remains constant today and tomorrow, as it was yesterday.

[5] Similar tensions and splits are to be seen in Judaism (both in America and in Israel), in Buddhism (e.g., in Vietnam), in Hinduism, in the religions of Japan, and surely in China. Indeed, today religion everywhere seems to be caught between the old ways and the new ways.

part IV

GOD AND RELIGION

*We were slaves unto Pharaoh in Egypt
and the eternal our God led us from there
with a mighty hand.*

Passover ritual

eleven

God

Some Jewish scholars believe that God's name Yahweh derived from the Hebrew verb *hayah* (היה : to be), and means basically "He who causes beings." If this is so, the word Yahweh has the distinction of being not only God's proper Hebrew name but also the proper denotation for the entire class of God. For the God-word is commonly used to designate what it is, or what is believed to be, that which *causes*. God is that which causes things to be, and to be as they are. The God-word is man's common answer to Heidegger's question, "Why are there beings rather than nothing?" The God-word functions essentially as an explanatory principle in God talk, in theology; and as an operational principle in religious behavior, in rituals and religious morality. This means that the God-word is used to explain why things are as they are, especially things that are horrendous and nonmanipulable; and how one is to operate (perform ritualistically and/or morally) to deal with the horrendous and nonmanipulable aspects of his existence.

As man rationalizes himself and his world, as he does theology, the concept of determinative power emerges in his thinking. In terms of this (discovered and/or invented) determinative power, or powers, one's life must be explained and arranged if he is going to deal adequately with his religious needs. God is the answer given by religion to the problems of the human condition, to the threat of nonbeing, to the awareness of human finitude. Religion offers the option of believing (against the horrendousness of an unrationalized phenomenon of birth-life-death) *that there is at the center of human existence a being or process, a divine reality, in which and through which a person, or community of persons, can transcend, or even overcome all the life-negating facts of human existence.*

GOD CLASS

The notion and fact of determinative power constitutes the class of God. This is what men mean, at the bottom of it, when they use the God-word, or some functional equivalent of the God-word, such as demons, Mana, Brahman, Father, or even Mother Nature and evolution. The God Class is constituted of all the concepts and terms that identify and/or explain what is the *cause* of beings, and the cause of the destiny of beings. God is that which causes and directs the destinies of worlds and men. We arrive at this classification, not completely arbitrarily, but by articulating what seems to be the common practice of religious people everywhere. When people do religion, especially when they do mythology and theology, they normally employ the God-word (or a functional equivalent) to designate what they believe to be the cause of themselves and their world; what they believe is dominating and directing, at least in general ways, the world in which they immediately find themselves. When a primitive speaks of spirits, demons, black magic, mana power, or The-Old-Man-in-the-Sky-Far-Away, he is referring to the power that causes, so he believes, things to be, and to be the way they are at the moment, and might be different at a later time. When Christians speak of God, they mean pretty much the same thing. For all the fine remarks that Christians make *about* God (calling "Him" omnipotent, omniscient, omnipresent, "that than which nothing greater can be conceived"), they are basically referring to the Father, Son, and Spirit who causes, and causes to be this way and not that. Similarly, Brahman is the causative source of all reality, and Allah created the world and directs all individual fates. To identify God so closely with the cause and destiny of things is not to say that all God concepts are fatalism concepts, that is, beliefs that all things and lives are rigidly predetermined and predestined. It is, rather, to say that all God ideas are intimately involved in "fates." God is importantly involved in the determination of destinies, and it is the amount of God's involvement in human fates, or possible involvement, that gives the God-word its dimension of destiny determination.

It is important at this point to make an observation about one of the consummate religions which seems not to possess a concept of God, much less a concept of God as determinative power. That religion is the conservative form of Buddhism, called Theravada or Hinayana. This great religion of Southeast Asia tries to take a literalist position with regard to the teachings of the Buddha. The Buddha, it is claimed, did not speculate upon ultimate reality, therefore the Theravadist monks avoid such speculation also. In the sacred writings called *Majjhima Nikaya*, Gautama (in Pali, Gotama) is reported to have instructed his followers to remember what he had talked about, and what he had not talked about. He had not said that there is an eternal world. He had not said that there is no eternal world. He had not said that the world is finite. He had not said that it was infinite. He had not said that the holy man, who has accomplished enlightenment, will exist after death. He had not said the opposite. In short, he had refused to discuss metaphysical things. He had talked only about the psychology of salvation. He reportedly said:

> What have I elucidated? Misery have I elucidated: the origins of misery have I elucidated; the cessation of misery have I elucidated. And why have I elucidated this? Because this does profit, has to do with the fundamentals of religion, and tends to absence of passion, to knowledge, supreme wisdom and Nirvana.[1]

Commenting upon this, Professor Daniel Bassuk stated that the Theravadists declare the experience of enlightenment to be of divine nature, but beyond this they make no declarations or even speculations. Whatever God is, or even if God is, is of no major concern. The purpose of religion is to free man from the dislocations of human living which are attendant upon human desire and craving. Whatever the causative and determinative power is, it is not the means to religious liberation. The power to save is a human power.

The Theravadists hold that Buddha did not go beyond this

---

[1] *The Majjhima Nikaya*, as found in Henry Clarke Warren's *Buddhism in Translation* (Cambridge: Harvard University Press, 1922), p. 122.

point in religious doctrine; therefore, they do not go beyond it. Nevertheless, underlying the concept that man is situated in dislocation (is in life, out of joint) is the inference that there is power that causes that dislocation—causes things to be, and to be as they are, which is what the God-word fundamentally denotes.[2]

DIMENSIONS OF THE GOD CLASS

The Universal Dimension   In defining God as "that which causes," it becomes apparent that the God-word has two related dimensions. First, there is what can be called the universal dimension. The God-word stands for the power (or powers) responsible for the existence of all things, events, and beings. This is the All-Cause. This is the primitive's High God, who once long ago created the world, and the tribe, and established the customs and the rules; this is the Judaeo-Christian "Creator of Heaven and Earth"; this is the Hindu's issuer of the Kalpa; this is the Theravada Buddhist's unspeculated framework of reality. In this dimension the God-word refers to the power that is causative of all things. In this quintessential dimension the word stands for the power that causes mountains and rivers and rainbows and universes—everything—and thus the cause of many things which may or may not have much religious significance to a given worshipper or a particular theology. The heavens may declare the glory of God, and the earth showeth his handiwork, but one may hardly notice the fact, and may find such things as the moons of Saturn, or the planet Mercury, or the galaxy of Andromeda of no practical religious significance at all. Even the Hebrews who often sang God's praises as the God of nature did not really base their faith on any kind of nature worship. They acknowledged God as the God of creation (the author of nature), but it was as the God of history that they engaged him religiously. Which brings us to the point of saying that besides the universal dimension of the God Class, there is also a religious dimension.

The Religious Dimension   Besides a word to identify universal creation, the God-word is also used to designate the dynamic cause

[2] For further consideration of Gautama, Buddhism, and God, see Charles Hartshorne and William Reese, *Philosophers Speak of God* (Chicago: University of Chicago Press, 1963, © 1953), pp. 411–415.

of what concerns man ultimately, that is, man's ultimate values. By ultimate values in this context we mean anything held to be of critical value to the welfare of an individual person, or to the welfare of a community of persons, or even to all mankind, especially when the thing so valued is in jeopardy. It is in the context of circumstances that are horrendous and nonmanipulable that the God of religion (and not simply creation) comes into his own. When finitude crushes down upon a person, it is not the God of starry heavens or wondrous earth that men call upon, but the God of threatening power, terrifying portent, shattering anxiety. The God of religion is the God which stands astride the human issues of life and death, devastation and joy, estrangement and reconciliation. This is the God to whom, in man's moments of finite nudity, he turns to find meaning in his rock and succor in his helplessness, the God in whom or through whom rescue from finitude is believed possible. "God," writes Bernhardt, "is the religious name for the dominant phase or controlling power in reality as a whole, the power to which we must submit ourselves in our search for [and preservation of] religious values."[3] It is to this God that the Psalmist prayed:

> Judge me, O God, and plead my cause against an
>   ungodly nation:
>   O deliver me from the deceitful and unjust man.
> For thou art the God of my strength, why has thou
>   cast me off?
>   Why go I mourning because of the oppression of
>   mine enemy?
> O send out thy light and thy truth;
>   Let them lead me:
> Let them bring me unto thy holy hill,
>   And to thy tabernacles.[4]

THE NAMED GOD

In dealing with God as a central aspect in religion, men are inclined to do more than simply respond in awe and wonder, or fear and trembling. They are also inclined—one might say almost impelled—

[3] William Bernhardt, *Iliff Review* (Denver: Criterion Press, Winter 1946).
[4] Psalm 43: 1–3, King James Version.

to specify God: discern or assign the attributes of God and discern or assign God's name. God is particularized: given "sectarian" images.

Apropos of this was the answer given by a professor when one of his students asked: "Did God create man, or man create God?" The professor said, "Yes." Being urged to elucidate, the professor pointed out that it is an obvious fact, corroborated by science, that once there were no men on earth, but now there are men. This must mean that there was a being or a process that created or caused man to become. Whether this was accomplished by divine fiat, or as an emanation from a divine source, or out of a process of evolution does not alter the fact that man was a created creature. Therefore, there was a God-who-created-man reality some place in the world; ergo, God created man. But beyond this, once created, or sometime thereafter, man, being a creature of reason and imagination with a passion for words, turned back upon the God which created him to describe, if he could, the nature of his creator. In doing so, this man created (and yet creates) concepts of what God was like. Man assigned attributes to God; he defined God; he named God; he gave God various kinds of qualities, such as life, love, intelligence, personality, and so on. And this God talk then became an important dimension in the life of the "human creator," because this talk was then taken to be true. God was really like that. In this sense, at least, man creates God. The professor's answer remains, Yes.

In this illustration the professor dealt first with the simple affirmation that something caused man to be. But men do not settle for saying simply that there was a "something" which caused them to be. They name it. They describe it. They discover or invent its characteristics. They particularize God. There are a few men in the world (for example, the holy men of India—the sannyasis) who simply meditate upon God undescribed (Nirguna Brahman), but most people, for religious reasons, must "see" God somehow and somewhere. They particularize God in order to get God into some kind of meaningful and manageable form. They name God so that God can be thought about religiously and ritualized meaningfully. To deal with God religiously, to secure religious values, men use words to describe God and God's relationship to the world and men.

THE CATEGORIES OF PARTICULARIZATION

God is described in innumerable ways, but generally in the East and in the West the innumerable descriptions fall into two categories of description: (1) a living being, (2) a creative principle, or ground of being. We shall look at these two categories, and also at the category of those who eventually despair of describing God: the category of ineffability.

God as a Living Being   In primitive religions, as we have observed, men believe that the world is populated with spirits and souls (animism). The spirits and souls are not simply free-flowing powers; they are living powers. Spirits and souls have "personalities." They have minds, feelings, wills. They respond in personlike fashion: lovingly, angrily, moodily, happily. Many of the spirits of both primitive and ancient men have nonhuman forms, but not all of them. Many appear in the forms of men and women. There was the Old One, far away and long ago, who made everything. He was "a man." There was the primordial Yahweh who walked in the Garden of Eden in the cool of the day, looking for his man Adam and his woman Eve. Such Gods were more than merely alive; they were manlike (anthropomorphic).

The Greek philosopher Xenophanes once observed that if an ox had a God, that God would be as a great Ox. So with men; their God was often a man "twelve feet tall." For example, the Greeks (especially with Homer and Hesiod) particularized their Gods anthropomorphically. Mercury, the God of speed, was a young man-God with winged feet. Aphrodite was a beautiful woman-goddess of delightfully erotic propensities. Zeus, King of the Gods, was a handsome, bearded patriarch. The Jews, also, particularized their God in this fashion. God was for them a grand, solitary, personal being, awful and frightening, yet, paradoxically, the God of a people whom he loved with infinite tenderness. Yahweh was lord of their lives, their immediate protector, their daily companion. In contemporary times (in response to some who have said that God has died, which implies, of course, that God was once alive), little jokes have been made which are exceedingly anthropomorphic in their implications. Some student wrote on a lavatory wall at Harvard: "God is not dead. He just doesn't want to get involved," and here and there one saw bumper stickers which read, "God is not dead.

He is alive and well in Argentina." It all added up to the same particularization: God is the great manlike one. The inverse of God creating man in his image, in Genesis chapter 1, is that God is also in man's image.

God as Principle of Creativity or Ground of Being   As we have seen, God in "his" most primitive form was probably neither animistic nor anthropomorphic. The first particularization of God was probably simply power: Mana, as Bishop Codrington's Melanesians named it. Mana is invisible power which causes things to be special. It is not itself pictured, but is identified according to what it does. It is not unlike the way we think of electricity, except that Mana is involved in all sorts of things and situations: in a stone that sparkles more than others or is harder, in a stronger wind, or a swifter river, or a more terrible thunderclap. It is seen in trees that grow taller than others, in birds that fly faster or higher, in animals that are more powerful or ferocious. It is in the warrior who wins battles, the artist who paints beautiful pictures, in the shaman who not only has Mana but who knows how to manipulate and even make Mana. Mana is simply multifarious, localized extranatural or supernatural power. It is not good or bad, moral or immoral. It is just powerful, and it is not animal-like or manlike.

Something distantly similar to Mana is to be seen in the Hindu's God Brahman and the Chinese God Tao. They are not manlike either. The consensus of the Hindu Upanishads is that God, whether material or spiritual, is THAT (not he or she) which is the cause of all worlds. God is simply all-inclusive, unitary, spiritual energy. It is the ultimate "substance," infinite in essence and self-sufficient. It is not a person, or personlike. It is, rather, sheer creative power. The Tao, also, is the Way of Heaven and Earth, not a personal creator and ruler of heaven and earth.

In the religions of the West (Judaism, Christianity, and Islam) God is the "person" who created the world, and is to be regarded as different from it. The world is natural, God is supernatural. God stands above all things as their creator and as the willful power that determines their destinies. This kind of God talk tends to take God out of nature, and even out of the world, and make God the wonder of all wonders. God has created the world; the world vaguely reflects his "image," but he is not truly in the world. This, however, is not the direction in which the maturing Eastern religions went.

They developed in the opposite direction, and God became not something out of this world but something in it. God became the soul of the world (Brahman), and the creative process and direction of the world (Yang/Yin and Tao). Here God is imminent. Of this position William Bernhardt writes:

> God, no matter how conceived, is believed to be within the cosmic totality . . . the term God . . . symbolizes some phase, character, structure or behavior pattern of the Environing Medium . . . [as G. T. W. Patrick, in his *The World and Its Meaning* put it] God is "the soul of the world, an indwelling spiritual presence, a creative, organizing and perfecting power, the source of our moral, religious and aesthetic ideals."[5]

God as Ineffable (a God Unknown)   In both East and West, sensitive religionists became leery of all of the things they were saying about God. They began to suspect their God talk as imperfectly describing what God was really like. For example, as the Jews moved more and more toward their consummate religion, some of them became uncomfortable with so much particularization of God Yahweh. They felt, at times quite keenly, that God was not like anything they were saying about him; that he was, in fact, beyond any true description. In Hebrew thought and practice God's name became too sacred to be used regularly. They began to address God with circumlocutions such as My Lord (Adonai), or as The Name of the Lord (Ha-shem), or as Creator (Boray), or as Our Father Who Is In Heaven (Avenu She-ba Shamayim).[6] They began to avoid using God's name Yahweh. God's name was not spoken, except once each year by the high priest in the innermost part of the Temple, the Holy of Holies.

In the Middle Ages, theologians in Judaism, Christianity, and Islam proposed speaking of God's attributes only negatively. Thus, to say "the living God" would mean not that God had life as a man had life but only that God was not dead. To attribute knowledge to God would not mean that God knows as man knows but only that

---

[5] Bernhardt, *Iliff Review*, Winter 1946.

[6] Other epithets for God were Ha-Makom—The Place, the Omnipresent; Ha-Gibor—The Power; She'chinah—The Divine Presence; Rachamah—The Compassionate; Ha-Kadosh Baruch Hu—The Holy One Blessed Be He; El or Elohim—God.

God was not ignorant. The oneness of God did not mean that God was as the concept one but only that God was not plural.

This uneasiness of talking about God (particularizing God) in the Near East religions, was the modus vivendi of certain theologies in India and China. To discerning Hindus, Brahman was experienceable but unutterable. Those who had experienced Brahman literally had nothing to say. The Chinese Taoist Lao-tzu put the ineffability of God Tao in these words:

> The Tao that can be expressed
>   is not the eternal Tao;
> The name that can be defined
>   is not the unchanging name . . .[7]

From this point of view, to speak of God (whether God be called mana power, spirit, ox, tall man, principle, oblong blur, or even to call God he, or to say that God is one or good or exists) is to commit an error. One might call it "the fallacy of false naming," or the "fallacy of the pseudonym." If God is ineffable, then to particularize God is to commit an error, if not a sacrilege. Such particularization, however, has a very practical function. It gets the God-word, the God experience, into some kind of manageable dimension so that one can conceive of *him*, or worship *him*, or understand *him*, all for religious purposes; namely to deal metatechnologically and/or metapsychologically, or mythologically, or theologically, or ritualistically, or morally, with him.

The question might be put to such theologies: If one cannot define God in any adequate way, why not give up the attempt? Why not disband theology? The answer to such a challenge could be given on both psychological grounds and pragmatic grounds. Man cannot stop talking about ultimate things as long as man is man. He must deal with his religious needs. He must interpret his existence to himself in terms of his ultimate values, and in terms of that which he believes creates, sustains, and finally destroys those values. He will talk about God simply because man is a talker. He is the linguistic animal. He has a veritable lust for words. He must speak, for not to speak is not to be human. To be human is to search for meaningful life and the key to meaningful life (unlike the instinct-guided other animals) is, for man, to search for the mean-

[7] These are the opening lines of the *Tao Te Ching* ascribed traditionally to the sage Lao-tzu.

ing of life as it arises in the divine encounter. So man always searches with words to express God's nature, and will continue to do so as long as he is man. And although his nets of words (according to the notion that God is ineffable) have never captured God, and never will, they have become increasingly better meshed and finer and richer, and man, if not God, has been greatly edified. The admonition, then, would appear to be not to stop engaging in the fallacy of false naming but only to recognize that the pseudonym is a pseudonym.

God and the Demonic   We have mentioned, in several places, belief in demons and devils. A little, dangling question might be: Where in God talk, where in theology, does the Devil, by whatever name he is called, belong? The answer is that demons and devils belong to the Class of God quite as much as Yahweh and Tao belong there. The God Class, as the ultimate power structure, confronts man both positively and negatively. It creates and supports him and his values. It also assaults and destroys him and his values. In both instances man is confronted with the power that causes things to be and to be as they are. He may call the one good and the other bad, but in fact they both belong to the same class, and his calling them this or that is simply a particularization, primarily for religious reasons.

For analytic purposes we could dispense with the demonic in this brief fashion, but because the Devil and his ilk have become so popular in recent times, it behooves us to return to the Devil in a later chapter and, as they say, "give him his due." We should, also, do this because early in this book we proposed that religion can be conceived of as predominantly mankind's long suffering effort to identify with divinity on the one hand and exorcise the demonic on the other. In chapter sixteen we shall concentrate on the effort for identity. Before that, in chapter fourteen, we shall look briefly at the Devil and exorcism.

God and Atheism   We are also now in a position to deal with another little, dangling question; namely, What exactly is atheism? Who is an atheist? We have observed that when doing theology, man refers to God on two levels of meaning: the universal level, which refers to God as the Creator or source of all beings and events, and the religious (particularizing) level, which describes what God is like. To be a genuine atheist one would have to deny the reality of God on both levels. Besides all sectarian Gods, one would have to deny that there is any being or process that causes and directs things and events. Such a person would deny that there is any meaning or value any place in the universe, except the little, nauseous amount of meaning and value that man himself creates. There are few atheists of this genuine stature. Jean-Paul Sartre and Albert Camus would qualify, but Karl Marx would not qualify. Marx believed in the inevitable, meaningful, redemptive, perfecting process of history. He called it dialectical materialism, which is to say that at the heart of human history there is a dynamic that propels mankind toward a final destiny, toward a utopian order. In other words, there is a power resident in the social order itself which compels and determines the lives of men.

But, one might question, how can one say that Marx was not an atheist, except by splitting hairs, or reading the term into an abstraction that nobody ever uses? After all is not an atheist simply a person who calls himself an atheist, who denies the reality of God, and then, perhaps, calls religion an opiate of the people, to boot? And the answer could be: If that is what one means by the word atheist, then call Marx an atheist, and anybody else an atheist who denies some particularization of God. But then, of course, everybody becomes an atheist from somebody's point of view, for we all reject somebody's God as unreal. The fact is that few people deny that there is a dynamic determinant affecting their ultimate values: a metaphysical reality in terms of which they must relate to achieve adequate courage to live with zest not simply because of, but in spite of, the lives they experience. Most often where people "commit atheism," where they deny God, is at the point of particularization, at the point of a God made up in some sectarian theology. They reject somebody's idea about what God is like. This surely amounts to what could more properly be called pseudo-atheism. The true atheist, the genuine atheist, must be that rare soul who has struggled through to the end of theological and philosophical speculation and has been forced to conclude, in anguish, that there really is nothing there in which and through which he can transcend all the life-negating facts of his human condition. Such a person deserves to wear the epithet atheist. He has earned it in agony and despair; he is not some sophomore who is simply rebelling against his father's Baptist God.

twelve

God Coming of Age in the West

The idea of God in primitive religions seems to be far different from the idea of God in "civilized" religions. At first glance there would seem to be little affinity between a God Class composed of Mana, Spirits, Souls, and Demons, and a God Class dominated by a Yahweh or a Brahman or a Tao. Yet the lesser Gods of primitives fulfill the same function in primitive religions as the greater Gods of civilized religions. In each case, the Gods represent the power or the powers to which religious people try to relate in their efforts to transcend, or even overcome, the life-negating facts of their human existences. The function is the same. It is the degree of sophistication that is different. Primitive people see God through primitive eyes; civilized people see God through civilized eyes. Indeed, civilized people are seeing the primitive Gods "come of age." The various Gods of the dozen or so major religions in the world today are all Gods which emerged in the metamorphoses of very ancient and primitive forms of religion. All the great world religions go back either directly or indirectly to primitive beginnings, and to primitive-type Gods.

In this chapter and the next, we shall look at the metamorphoses and maturing of God concepts in several of the world religions. It should be recognized that this will be done only in broad outline. Neither time nor space is available for anything approaching a complete examination of this subject. The metamorphosis and maturation of any God concept in any major religion is extremely complicated, with almost endless intercultural connections and nuances. Nevertheless, it is important to try to get a "sense" of the unfolding of the idea of God. The concern here, then, is to give only the broad outlines of the coming of age of God in Iran, Palestine, India, and China. But before going directly to those ancient times and places, it is important to establish several terms to assist the analysis: primordial religion, consummate religion, and kairotic episode.

Primordial Religion   By primordial religions we shall mean those religions whose God Class is composed of many supernatural powers and beings; those religions that do not conceptualize a universal power but conceive of supernatural power as being multifarious and localized. The Gods are many and the God powers are limited to various locations in the world and/or to specific situations in the world. For example, the Trobrianders of the South Pacific live in a world they believe is populated by a multitude of spirits and souls,[1] each and all of which are limited in what they do and where they do it. Again, the Yahweh of ancient Hebraism was the protector and war leader of the Hebrews (that was his job), and he was where they were. At the same time, there were other Gods in Palestine; the baals, which were agricultural Gods, each having a specific fertility power for a particular plot of ground. And outside of Palestine, and away from the Hebrew tribes, there were all sorts of Gods, of other people, doing other jobs, in other places.

The God Class of primitive and ancient people, generally speaking, was (1) multifarious: composed of many spirits and souls, and (2) localized: the spirits and souls had specific powers and places. Consummate religions resulted when these two factors were inverted.

Consummate Religion   A consummate religion is one in which the concept of universe has been accomplished, and God is no longer attached to a specific place, or limited power. Man lives in a universe, and God has become a universal power; indeed, God has

---

[1] We should draw a distinction between spirits and souls. Spirits are supernatural powers and beings of nonhuman origin such as Gods, Goddesses, angels, devils, demons, and similar divinities. Souls are supernatural powers and beings of human origin—the ghosts and souls of ancestors.

become *the* universal power. For example, unlike the primordial
Yahweh of the wilderness experience who was a God in Palestine
and a private Hebrew God, the Yahweh of the post-Babylonian
exile, was a God of all men everywhere—a God of absolute and
universal power.

As, over the millennia, certain primitive people advanced out
of the Stone Age and a nomadic existence into the use of metals,
stable agriculture, and urbanization, a new step was taken in God
talk. Men began to say that the multitude of destiny-determining
powers in the world were essentially a unity of some kind; that
behind the spirits and souls there was an ordering power. The notion of universal order emerged. The ultimate source of determinative power (God) became focalized; seen as one, or two, or perhaps
a few, but no longer innumerably multiple. Instead of the primordial notion of localized power there developed the notion of universal power. God power was seen as operating universally. There
might be spirits (lesser Gods, Goddesses, divinities, demons), but
they were themselves agents of one ultimate power (or of a few
ultimate powers). They were all dominated by a great God and
were empowered by that God, and, at the same time, the notion
developed that the souls of men had their genesis in and from the
same ultimate power that controlled the spirits. The world became
a universe for man.

The Kairotic Episode   The third central term for our analysis is
kairotic episode. A kairos is a special time, and in our use of it we
shall mean those special times and episodes in which and through
which the Gods of the great world religions of today grew into
maturity. This coming of age took place almost imperceptibly between c. 800 B.C. and 500 B.C. in Iran, Palestine, India, and China.
The consummate religion of Iran (Zoroastrianism) particularized
the universal power as dualistic and personalistic—there were two
ultimate Gods who were anthropomorphic in character. In Palestine
the consummate God was conceived as monotheistic and personalistic—there was only one God and he was at least somewhat
manlike in character. In India (in Hinduism) the ultimate power
was a monistic, all-pervading, nonpersonal power. More needs to be
said at this point, for Hinduism was a transcendent monistic, nonpersonal pantheism. What it transcended was the phenomenal world,
the world that man normally knows and lives in. Religion functioned

to guide man out of this phenomenal world. In Taoism, which was also monistic, nonpersonal, and pantheistic, the negations of Hinduism were reversed. In Taoism religion functioned to guide man into the way of the world, the true way: the Tao.

We shall now take time to look in broad outline at the God-word as it came of age in the classical theologies in Iran, in Palestine, in India, and in China.

FROM PRIMORDIAL TO CONSUMMATE RELIGION IN IRAN

The ancient Iranians came to the semiarid plateau of Iran from Central Asia. Although information about their religion at the time of their migration is scanty, it appears to have been what we are calling primordial; that is, a religion in which the God Class was composed of multifarious and localized spirits and souls. The spirits (*mainyu*) were divided into good spirits (*ahura*) and evil spirits (*daevas*), with some of the spirits important enough to be called Gods. In addition to supernatural beings of nonhuman origin, the Iranians also believed in the existence of the souls of deceased persons—the Fravishis, or Fathers (ancestors).

The kairotic episode for Iranian religion came, probably, sometime in the seventh century B.C. when the prophet Zarathustra (in English Zoroaster) instituted the reforms which eventually unified all of the spirits and souls under one supreme God, and then later under two supreme Gods, from whom alone all causative power was derived. Zoroaster proclaimed that there was one supreme Holy Spirit (Spenta Mainyu) whose name was Wise Lord (Ahura Mazda, or Ormazd). This chief God effected his power and will in the world through lesser spirits (mainyu), which might more properly be called divinities than Gods. With Zoroaster the transformation of the old primordial religion was certainly under way. Its arrival at a consummate unified hierarchy of spiritual power was accomplished later by the priests (the Magi) who followed the Prophet in the centuries after his death. Eventually the Zoroastrians affirmed that all causative power flowed from a unified system: from a common, although dualistic, source.[2] As early as Zoroaster,

---

[2] This idea of dualistic source had important influence on the latter-day theology of Hebraism (Judaism) and the theology of Christianity.

there was the idea that Wise Lord was not unopposed in the spirit world. There were spirits that were in rebellion against him. Those rebellious spirits were led by the prince of rebels, a negating God called Evil Spirit (Angra Mainyu, or Ahirman). Angra Mainyu later came to be called Shaitan or Satan, the same Satan we find in Christianity. All of the good spirits were organized under, derived their power from, and worked for Wise Lord. All of the bad spirits were organized under, derived their power from, and worked for Evil Spirit.

The division of ultimate power into two sources became increasingly pronounced in later Zoroastrian theology. Apparently Zoroaster himself taught a monotheism in which Evil Spirit was simply a rebelling spirit, leading other spirits in rebellion, but in later theological developments Evil Spirit became the archfiend almost equal to God. And in some of the later writings of the Avesta (the Zoroastrian scripture), Wise Lord and Evil Spirit were regarded as having been of equal status in creating the world. Wise Lord created all things of excellence, beauty, goodness, but Evil Spirit matched each of these good things with a bad thing. About this, John Noss writes:

> Portions of the later Avesta almost made Angra Mainyu coequal as well as the contradiction of Ahura Mazda. For example, the world was regarded as their joint creation. In the first chapter of the Vendidad, Ahura Mazda is portrayed as telling Zoroaster the story of his struggle with Angra Mainyu at the creation of the world. He pictures himself as creating the various Iranian districts and endowing them with every excellence; unfortunately, as he admits, Angra Mainyu was on hand, too, busily creating an evil for every good—killing frost of winter, excessive heat in summer; snakes, locusts, ants; the wicked rich, evil sorcerers, non-Aryan lords of the land; human vices, lust, witchcraft, doubt, disbelief, and so on. . . . Angra Mainyu's capacity for mischief was in fact boundless. The Twenty-second chapter places the number of diseases created by him at 99,999, a stupendous number to the people at that time. But there was a final touch. He was the author of Death.
>
>   The evil power that Angra Mainyu possessed was many times multiplied by the demons he created to assist him.[3]

Not only were the spirits, good and bad, unified under Wise Lord and Evil Spirit but the generic distinction between spirits and

---

[3] J. B. Noss, *Man's Religions* (New York: Macmillan, 1956), pp. 482–483.

souls disappeared, and the souls of men were also unified in this one universal spirituality. Zoroaster identified the souls of living men as battlegrounds where Wise Lord and Evil Spirit waged war. The spiritual destiny of each person was determined by which side he chose to be on in this battle. If he chose for Wise Lord, he would in life after death join Wise Lord in Heaven. If he chose for Evil Spirit, at death his soul would join Evil Spirit in the torments of Hell.

Personal Gods   The two consummate Gods of the mature Iranian religion were personalistic Gods. To say that a God is personalistic is to say that the God possesses the characteristics of a human being (male or female). The God is anthropomorphic. The God possesses at least what man possesses in the way of self-consciousness, intelligence, and will. The God may be a great deal more than a human, but he is not less than human. Both of the Zoroastrian Gods were particularized so. Wise Lord was a personlike being who was the source and power of all the good things man enjoyed. Evil Spirit was a personlike being who was the source and power of all the bad things that hurt man.

(God Yahweh of the Hebrew religion was also personalistic, but God Brahman in India and God Tao in China were not personlike. They were both nonpersonal Gods, as we shall see.)

FROM PRIMORDIAL TO CONSUMMATE RELIGION IN PALESTINE

The ancient Hebrews were a tribal people, speaking a Semitic language, and living in the arid areas of the Near East. Before the Hebrews, as a people, were heard from in history, similar people had filtered out of the Arabian desert into Mesopotamia and Egypt. The Hebrews, thus, once they arrived on the scene, were just one of many Semitic people in that part of the world, struggling to establish and maintain themselves. According to tradition, the Hebrews originated as a separate people through the leadership of the clansman Abraham and his kinsmen, who migrated from Mesopotamia into the Palestinian area (also called Canaan). Hebrew identity was furthered by the leadership of Moses when he effected the escape from Egypt of at least some of the Hebrew people who had migrated that far south, had settled and lived there, and had finally become enslaved and oppressed there. The Hebrew identity as a nation of people was finally established (a thousand years before the common era, B.C.E., that is, before the Christian era) when the various Hebrew tribes, better to effect their invasion of Canaan/Palestine, united their tribes under the kingship and military leadership of Saul.

When the Hebrews began their push to establish themselves in Palestine, c. 1200 B.C.E., they found themselves opposed by other Semitic people who had arrived ahead of them: Phoenicians, Arameans, Moabites, Edomites, and others, as well as a non-Semitic people, originally from Crete, known as Philistines. They also found an array of Semitic Gods and divinities. Of special importance and influence in subsequent Hebrew religious thought and practice were the baals or baalim, who were believed to be the localized Gods, the lords of the land. They were the Gods credited with producing crops in Canaan. On many of the hilltops of Palestine, and in many of the groves, the local baals were duly recognized by those who depended on the crops of those particular pieces of land. Each plot of land had its own baal, or rather, each plot of land was "owned" by a particular baal. These baals already in Palestine were taken over by the Hebrews as they became established on the land because the Hebrew God, Yahweh, acquired somewhere in the Sinai Peninsula, was not a farmer God but a nomadic God, a war God, and particularly a God of history, not of nature.

The multifarious and localized character of the ancient Hebrew religion was further seen in the Hebrews' veneration for stones and pillars. Apparently these stones and pillars were originally believed to be alive, to be supernatural in and of themselves. Later they were regarded as the dwelling places of demons or minor Gods. Also, as would be expected among a desert people, wells and springs and streams had a special sacred character. Trees, especially evergreens, were believed to be full of spirit-energy. Groves became holy places. Professor Noss informs us that

serpents were universally feared (and as universally revered) for being demonically sly and cunning, if not indeed possessed by fiery spirits (known to the later Hebrews as seraphim, "burning ones"). Goats were regarded as incarnations of "hairy ones" (Hebrew se-irim). As for untamable wild things of the desert—panthers, leopards, hyenas, wolves, and foxes—they were the savage flock of demon gods of the wasteland.[4]

The Hebrews believed in spirits of human shape also (like the *jinn* of later Arabia), and even in seductive female night-demons, like Lilith who, in Hebrew tradition, led Adam astray. All of these various spirits and divinities, both good and bad, were given a name current among Semitic people: *el,* or in the plural *elim* or *elohim,* a word with the general meaning of superhuman or divinity. As we have it, the name of Abraham's God was El Shaddai—God of the Mountain. As in other primordial religions, the ancient Hebrews identified the various superhuman divinities as either spirits of non-human origin (*ruach*), or as the souls of man (*nephesh*).

For all the multifariousness and localization of their divinities, the Hebrews after Moses had one God in particular. This was the God who, according to tradition, spoke to Moses from the Burning Bush, effected the escape of the tribe from Egypt, established a Covenant at Mt. Sinai, and guided and protected the Hebrews for forty years in the wilderness. This was, also, the God which later tradition would like us to believe, was to the ancient Hebrews the one and only God of the universe. But the facts were otherwise. Whatever may have been Moses' posture, the Hebrew people who left Mt. Sinai were not monotheists. At best they were henotheists, holding to one God in particular, their own God, in a world populated by numerous Gods. Moses may have been a monotheist, even an Egyptian monotheist of the Ikhnaton (Aton) variety, as Freud suggested, but his people, or the Hebrew people he led out of Egypt, never bought it. Not for another eight hundred years did they buy it, even though in the eighth and seventh centuries the great Prophets of Israel and Judah tried to persuade them, and one King, Josiah, literally drove the "false gods" and their "false priests" out of Jerusalem. Apparently not even the great King David (1000 B.C.E.), one of Yahweh's true champions, saw his God as more than the God of a people, a history, and a place. In I Samuel 26:18–20 while David is fleeing from the wrath of King Saul, who surely intended to destroy the man he feared would usurp his throne, David made this plea:

> Why must your majesty pursue me? What have I done? What mischief am I plotting? Listen, my lord, to what I have to say. If it is

4 Ibid., p. 486.

the Lord who has set you against me, may an offering be acceptable to him; but if it is men, a curse on them in the Lord's name; for they have ousted me today from my share in the Lord's inheritance and have banished me *to serve other gods!* [author's italics][5]

The real religious position of the Hebrew people before the Babylonian Exile has been most succinctly summarized in the final, fifth-century, edition of their history: in the second chapter of the Book of Judges we read:

> The Israelites did what was wrong in the eyes of the Lord, and worshipped the Baalim. They forsook the Lord, their Father's God who had brought them out of Egypt, and went after other gods, gods of the races among whom they lived; they bowed down before them and provoked the Lord to anger; they forsook the Lord and worshipped Baal and the Ashtaroth[6] (Judges 2:11–15, *The New English Bible*).

The numerous baals (and their consorts, baalaths) each had a place of worship on some hilltop or elevated ground, or in a grove. Canaanite priests conducted services at these shrines. Sacrifices were made there and nature worship was performed. Also there were special festivals, in spring, early summer, and fall, in which a fertility Goddess was given special prominence. Astarte (the Hebrew Ashtoreth) was by far the most important of such divinities. She was usually represented as naked, and not always gentle or kind. She was, when aroused, a very primitive and powerful force: primordial sexuality. It was chiefly in connection with her worship that the Canaanites practiced temple prostitution. In the divine marriage between Astarte and the Baal of Heaven,[7] which the Canaanites celebrated in the autumn, Astarte was the earth become woman, and the Baal of Heaven was the husband who fertilized her.

The Hebrews, turned farmer in Palestine, found it convenient to adopt most of the Canaanite agricultural worship. Yahweh was a nomad's God, the God of a people, a God of history, not a farm

---

[5] *The New English Bible* (New York: Cambridge University Press, 1971).

[6] Ashtaroth is the plural of Ashtoreth, (the Phoenician and Canaanite Goddess Astarte; and the Babylonian Ishtar), Goddess of fertility, reproduction, and sexual love.

[7] Besides the multitude of local baals there was the Baal of Heaven, a storm God and chief among the lesser baals.

God. He was still *their* God, but the more agricultural they became, the more need they found for the metatechnological assistance of the baals and the baalaths, the Baal of Heaven and Astarte, and others. Without deserting their faith in Yahweh as the God who presided over the nation and guided them in war, the Hebrew farmers became worshippers also at the shrines of the resident agricultural Gods.

As time passed at least some Hebrews must have become convinced that Yahweh was not just the God of Hebrew history and religious life but was the power behind the agricultural divinities; he was, in fact, the God of nature. Evidence of this was in the fact that in the days of the Judges the Yahweh shrine at Shiloh held only the Ark of the Covenant, but in later times the shrines at Bethel and Dan contained bull-images, that is, nature symbols. Apparently the God who had led the Israelites through the wilderness was becoming identified as the God who also provided fertility to field and flock. The exalted, austere God of Moses was in danger of devolving into a local nature power.

In the ninth century B.C.E., serious protests against all forms of Baalism began to be raised, and with these protests the first theological steps were taken by the Hebrews away from their primordial Gods toward their consummate one God. With Elijah the prophetic protest began in earnest. Appearing in Israel when King Ahab, under pressure from his foreign wife Jezebel, was moving to make the Tyrian form of Baalism dominant in Palestine, Elijah made his dramatic stand in defense of Yahwism. He tried to demonstrate that Yahweh was the most powerful God, and the only God for Hebrews. Elijah's successor, Elisha, carried on this battle to a sweeping political and religious revolution, but, even though Baalism received a hard blow, it continued and recovered. One thing, however, was accomplished for Yahweh. His supremacy over any and all baals was established. Baalism would be practiced henceforth only as a secondary and peripheral cult.

In the eighth century B.C.E., the greatest of the protestors for Yahweh began to appear in Israel and Judah: Amos, Hosea, Isaiah, Micah, Jeremiah, Ezekiel, Deutero-Isaiah. And they said: (1) there is only one God, creator and father of the whole universe and all mankind; (2) he is a God who wants from man not "lambs of a year old," or "first fruits," or "rivers of oil," but justice and mercy; (3) and, from his bride Israel, he wants fidelity and love. "On that day she shall call me 'my husband' and shall call me no more 'my Baal'; and I will wipe from her lips the very names of the Baalim; never again shall their names be heard" (Hosea 2:16, 17, *The New English Bible*). These magnificent champions for Yahweh stumped the land both north and south, and they got a hearing, but often only a hearing. The people were reluctant to give up the fertility worship of the baals. They must have feared to do so because of possible ill effects that might result if they gave up a form of worship and metatechnology that had served them so long. Besides, the sternly ethical religion of the Prophets must have appeared to them as bare and cold when compared to the sensuality of a fertility religion.

Nevertheless, the Prophets' reform did get a serious and dramatic hearing from King Josiah[8] of the seventh century B.C.E. The problem in Jerusalem in Josiah's day was not Baalism but imported Assyrian Gods. This invasion of foreign Gods had occurred as part of Judah's attempt to curry favor with the great, threatening national power of Assyria. Josiah's father, Manasseh, had gone so far as to build shrines, even within the courts of the Jerusalem Temple, to the Gods of both Babylon and Nineveh. He also set up asherah to Ishtar, and he even sacrificed one of his own sons to the child-devouring God Molech. It was against such abominations that Josiah, in the eighteenth year of his reign, inspired to do so by the "discovery" of the Book in the Temple—and, one may surmise, by the urging of Hilkiah the High Priest—launched his Yahweh reform. It all began in 622 B.C.E., and it swept clean all the idolatrous religious practices condemned in the Book.[9] Joshua did not stop with Jerusalem, but ranged throughout Judah as far as Bethel, destroying the worship places of all false Gods, both foreign and domestic.

But the reform, begun with such energy, was not completely successful. Josiah was killed at the Battle of Megiddo, and some of the drive went out of the reforms. The people lacked Josiah's enthusiasm. The fact was that besides being too severe (e.g., all worship was to take place only in the Temple in Jerusalem), the people were still not convinced. They had not really acquired the mentality

[8] For an account of this see II Kings, chapter 22 f.

[9] The Book, so called in II Kings, chapter 22, is now identified as having been actually the book now called Deuteronomy.

of a consummate religion. They were still semiprimitive/primordial. Yahweh remained for them one of many, and Baalism, even though outlawed by the new law, continued. Something more was needed to transform the old Hebrew (primordial) religion as practiced by the people into a new (consummate) religion.

That something, that kairotic episode, came in the form of a national catastrophe: the destruction of Judah by Babylon, and the subsequent seventy years of captivity and exile in a foreign land. In Babylonia, on the banks of the River Chebar, baal worship was no longer an issue. The baals were back in Palestine, no longer a concern to the Jews.[10] The critical question now was what would happen to Yahweh. Was it over with Yahwism too? Would these Hebrews from Judah become lost and Yahweh forgotten, as had been the case with the Hebrews from Israel when that nation fell to Assyria 135 years before? The happy fact was that neither the Hebrew "nation" nor its special God were lost. Indeed, the God, as conceived and preached by the great Prophets, finally came into his own; became finally transformed from a primordial (one-among-many localized) status to a consummate (one only and universal) status. Since the days of Josiah, the Hebrews had believed that Yahweh could be worshipped only in his Temple in Jerusalem, but now the Temple was no more and the Jews were far from Jerusalem. So now what the great Prophets had said made pragmatic sense (just as worshipping the baals formerly in Palestine had made pragmatic sense): Yahweh, the Prophets had proclaimed, was everywhere. Amos had said it plainly enough

> Are not you Israelites like Cushites to Me?
>   says the Lord.
> Did I not bring Israel up from Egypt,
>   the Philistines from Caphtor, the Aramaeans
>   from Kir? (Amos, 9:7, 8, *The New English Bible*)

Yahweh was God of all nations. The God of everywhere. With further help from two Exile Prophets (Ezekiel and Deutero-Isaiah) Yahweh became, once and for all, for the Sons of the Covenant, the only God anywhere, whose sphere of activity was the whole world. "Before me was no God formed, and after me there shall be none" (Isaiah 43:10).

---

[10] During the Exile the name Jew came into use, and from that, Judaism.

The time had come when the "shema" would become the ir-revocable center of all Jewish religious thought and action: *Shema Yisroel, Adonai Elohanu, Adonai Echod:* Here, O Israel, the Lord our God, the Lord is one.

God had come into his majority in Israel, and the ancient He-brew religion had finally fully arrived as a mature, consummate religion. There might still be divinities besides Yahweh, but all of them (even the latter-day Satan) would receive their creaturehood and power from the one and only God, creator and moral ruler of the entire universe: He who causes beings.

thirteen

God Coming of Age
in the East

FROM PRIMORDIAL TO CONSUMMATE RELIGION
IN INDIA

Before 2000 B.C., India was inhabited by a dark-skinned people called Dravidians. Then at some time in the middle of the second millennium there came pouring over the passes of the Hindu Kush Mountains in the northwest, a tall, light-skinned Indo-European stock, who called themselves Aryans. They drove the Dravidians southward. Later these Aryans would push their way into southern India and the Dravidians would be reduced to serfdom. Once settled in northwest India, the Aryans began to establish a new religious tradition for themselves. Their first sacred writings, called Vedas, were developed. One of the Vedas, the *Rig-Veda*, was an anthology of religious poetry in ten books, containing over a thousand hymns. The hymns were prayers addressed to various divine beings. Three of these divine beings probably came with the Aryans into India. They were Gods shared with other Indo-European peoples. There was Sky Father (Dyas Pitar), and there was Earth Mother (Prithivi Mater), and there was Mitra, God of loyalty and morality. These three Gods were rather vaguely depicted in the Vedic poems. Much more prominent in the *Rig-Veda* were those deities that were representative of the environment of northwest India. Prominent among these were blustering Indra, a storm God, a war God, and the patron God of Aryans; Rudra, a fierce and dreaded God who caused the destructive storms that swept down from the high, snow-covered Himalayas;[1] Vishnu, a God not prominent in the *Rig-Veda,* but destined to become one of the major deities of later Hinduism. The *Rig-Veda* expounded many other nature divinities also: Vayu, the wind; Ushas, the dawn; Yama, the first man to die who then became a God and ruled the afterworld; Varuna, God of moral law; Rita, God of orderliness. The ancient Hindus[2] also had, interestingly, some ritualistic Gods: Agni, God of fire, especially the sacred alter fire; Soma, God of the ecstatic intoxication of the soma plant (possibly a hallucinogenic mushroom); and Brahmanaspati, the deified power of sacred prayer. Brahmanaspati was especially important in later Hinduism because this impersonal power inherent in prayer was the embryo concept that was destined to advance into the great God Brahman of consummate Hinduism. The Aryans of India in the second millennium B.C. possessed a primordial religion, which was composed of numerous supernatural beings, each of which had a local and special function.

Then, around 800 B.C., in the later Vedic writings, some theological speculations began pointing in the direction of a consummate religion. The Hindu religion was beginning its kairotic move. There were beginning speculations which suggested that the powers of the universe were somehow unified in a system. In the late hymns of the *Rig-Veda* three grand figures, which were more than localized nature Gods, suddenly appear. One was Vishvakarman, whose name means "He whose work is the Universe"; another was called Prajapati, which means "Lord of Creatures"; a third was Purusha, the "Soul of the World." Also, Hymn 129 of the Tenth Book of the *Rig-Veda* was addressed to "That One Thing," which apparently was a causative principle that existed even before there was a universe, and must have been the ground from which the universe came forth.

The ritualistic God Brahmanaspati also began to change. Earlier in the *Rig-Veda,* Brahmanaspati was the power inherent in the sacred prayers. Now this prayer-power began to take on larger and larger dimensions of power. It was about this time, in the seventh

[1] Rudra was an early form of the later important Hindu God Shiva, the destroyer.

[2] The Persian word for India was *Hind;* thus the inhabitants of India became known as Hindus.

century B.C., that the Aryans began moving down from northwest India into the Ganges Valley, where they overran the territory and made serfs of the Dravidians they found there. In taking the southern part of India, the Aryan nobility (the Kshatriyas) were kept busy fighting and governing, so it fell more and more to the priests (the Brahmins) to develop and administer religious affairs. In doing so they naturally began to emphasize the importance of the priestly function. The concept of holy power inherent in sacred prayers was greatly expanded. It was finally claimed that the sacred prayer formula, once uttered, was so powerful that not only nature and men but even the Gods had to obey it. In other words, the old Aryan Gods were beginning to fall under a unifying power: the power of ritual. Ritual became increasingly important, and a new literature began to appear. This literature was called the *Brahmanas*. Primarily it was for priests, intended to instruct them on how to perform their sacred prayers and rituals, but mingled with these instructions were statements that indicated a growing notion that there was something unifying the powers of this world: a principle and/or power of creativity and unity. Apparently, it was occurring to some Brahmin priests that the holy power of prayer (Brahman-aspati), which could alter cosmic events and force obedience from both men and Gods, must be some kind of ultimate power. Was it, perhaps, the central power of the universe?

Between 700 and 300 B.C., the Hindus engaged in one of the greatest speculative periods in the history of religions. Another new literature was produced. It was called the *Upanishads*. This literature was profoundly concerned with the nature of ultimate reality, and although no final, single doctrine of ultimate reality was established in the *Upanishads*, they generally concluded that the true reality—the ground of being, the high and final God, whether material or spiritual—was "an all-inclusive unitary reality, beyond sense-apprehension, ultimate in substance, infinite in essence, and self-sufficient; it [was] the only really existing entity. This reality [was] most commonly called *Brahman*."[3] By this time the word Brahman no longer meant the power of prayer. It now meant the power of being. Brahman had become the impersonal matrix from which the whole world had issued forth and to which it would eventually return. "Verily, this whole world is Brahma[n]. Tranquil

---

[3] J. B. Noss, *Man's Religions* (New York: Macmillan, 1956), pp. 139–140.

let one worship IT as that from which he came forth, as that in which he will be dissolved."[4]

The religion had arrived at its consummate form. All power was unified in the universal Brahman. All the phenomenal world had arisen from Brahman. Whatever was real was God Brahman. And this was especially true of human souls. Not only were all Gods and nature a manifestation of Brahman, but man too was a manifestation. The soul of man (atman) and Brahman were identical. To think of men as separate, individual selves was to be in spiritual ignorance and outside Hindu salvation. The soul of man and the world-soul (paramatman) were the same. Also, although Hinduism still had its personal Gods, they were all simply particularizations of Brahman.

In a long and profoundly intellectual kairotic period in India, the God-word had passed from a primordial (multifarious, localized) status to a consummate status in which a single, nonpersonal power unified all things and made them one. Hinduism had arrived at a nonpersonal, monistic pantheism: a truly consummate religion.

The consummate religion of India was not only nonpersonalistic, monistic, and pantheistic; it was also "negating." What it negated was the world as it appears to be. The religion of the early Aryans had been robust, optimistic, and direct. It took the world straight, as it appeared to be, and did religion accordingly. But in the later Hindu thought all of this changed. It changed from a religion in which the world was simply affirmed to be as it appeared to be, into a religion that profoundly denied that the world was as it appeared to be. The function of religion was not to deal directly with the immediate appearance of things but with the subtle and hidden reality of things. It was not to save man in "this world" but to guide him beyond these appearances into the "real world."

At least three conditions conspired to transform Hinduism from world-affirming to world-denying. These conditions were the Caste System, the Law of Karma, and the Doctrine of Reincarnation or Transmigration of Souls.

First, the Caste System   A rigid social stratification of society developed in Hinduism when, about the seventh century B.C., the

---

[4] *Chandogya Upanishad*, Chand. 3.14.1, trans. R. E. Hume, *The Thirteen Principle Upanishads* (London: Oxford University Press, 1934), p. 209.

Aryans moved from northwest India down into the Ganges Valley. They conquered the Dravidian natives and immediately made them into a serf class (the Shudra). The three other large classes of Hindu society were the nobles (Kshatriyas), the priests (Brahmins), and the commoners (Vaisyas). These castes became increasingly rigid to the point where not only were intermarriages forbidden but even friendly social intercourse was forbidden. Besides these castes there was a growing number of people who were "outcastes," those who for one reason or another had been expelled from caste. They were the miserable dregs of society, impoverished, untouchable, hopeless. By 500 B.C. the castes had divided into hundreds of sub-castes with added social restrictions. The whole thing was becoming oppressive. People were being shut off in every direction. And this restrictiveness was given a moral and religious justification by identifying caste as effected by Karma and Reincarnation.

Second, the Law of Karma and the Doctrine of Reincarnation Quite early, possibly from the Dravidian natives, the Hindus came to believe that life was repeated: people were reborn, and the status of their rebirth was determined by their thoughts, words, and deeds in a previous life. Karma was the law of just deserts. One got, or became in the next life, what he deserved. As the *Chandogya Upanishad* puts it, "Those who are of pleasant conduct here . . . will enter a pleasant womb, either the womb of a Brahman, or the womb of a Kshatriya, or the womb of a Vaisya. But those who are of stinking conduct here . . . will enter the womb of a dog, or the womb of a swine, or the womb of an outcaste."[5]

In Hindu thought one was doomed to return to this world with all the suffering and pain, with all its anguish of finitude, again and again, unless and until through a life of religious devotion and/or altruistic works and/or spiritual insight, his soul attained sufficient moral and spiritual purity to make possible its escape from the Wheel of Rebirth, and its return and reunion with God Brahman. Hinduism, in its most exalted form, was mysticism. Rejecting this world of falseness, it directed men finally to seek escape by entering Nirvana, by becoming completely identified, not with one's self and one's world, but with the God behind the world, with the reality beneath all phenomenon, with Brahman.

[5] Ibid., Chand. 5.10.7, p. 233.

The final maturity of God in India led to world rejection. In one sense, the idea that "all is God-Brahman" declared that all was right because everything was basically divine. But in another more practical sense this notion became world-negating and pessimistic, for it denied any true individuality to persons, depriving the independent person of all significance. It crushed one with a sense of unreality and made his worldly life a helpless, hopeless existence in which a pessimistic world-withdrawal was the only way out of the human condition and the anguish of finitude. In India the multifarious supernatural powers became unified in one basic power. The localized supernatural powers became united in a universal power. An early primordial world optimism became pessimistic and world-renouncing. As God Brahman became all, the world and individual men became nothing, or worse than nothing; they became delusions.

FROM PRIMORDIAL TO CONSUMMATE RELIGION IN CHINA

The religious practice of the early Chinese was typical of primordial cultures. It was a mixture of nature worship and reverence for ancestors. The worship of nature included a belief in a Sky-God, first called Upper Ruler (Shang Ti) during the Shang (eastern) Dynasty, 1766–1122 B.C., and later, during the Chou (western) Dynasty, 1122–249 B.C., was called Heaven (T'ien).[6] Besides the

---

[6] In Chinese mythology, there were, besides the Sky-God, many other spirits of sufficient importance to be regarded as Gods. There were Yü Ch'ao, who taught men to build houses; Sui Jen, who taught men to make fire; Fu Hsi, who taught men to domesticate animals, use iron, fish with nets, write, forecast with eight trigrams, make music; Shen Nung, who taught the arts of agriculture and medicine; Huang Ti, who invented bricks, vessels of clay, the calendar, and money. But even before these great personages there had been the first man, P'an Ku, who had become a God after he had, with hammer and chisel, during a period of 18,000 years, separated heaven from earth, hewed out the places of the celestial bodies, dug out the valleys, and piled up the mountains on earth. When he died various parts of his body became the five sacred mountains of China: T'ai Mountain in the east, Sung Mountain in the center, the Heng Mountains of the north and south, and Hua Mountain in the west. His breath became the wind, his voice the thunder, his flesh the fields, his sweat the rain and, finally, the insects on his body became people.

Sky-God, the ancient Chinese believed that all of nature was alive with spirits. Many of them were good spirits, beneficial, friendly spirits, but many more were demonic. From earliest times the Chinese had something close to paranoia concerning devils and demons. They believed that devils and demons thronged around every human dwelling, haunted lonely places, infested roadways, especially at night, lurked in forests and mountains. There were demons in the water, in the air, in the ground. There were animal demons, bird demons, fish demons, and snake demons; and man-eating demons, vampires, ghouls, by the hundreds and thousands. Probably never was there a people more afraid of devils and demons than the Chinese, or a people who ever did more to protect themselves from bad spirits, on the one hand, and get assistance from good spirits, on the other hand.

Of all people, the Chinese were, also, the most solicitous of the dead. The cult of ancestor worship was exceedingly old and important in Chinese history. The purpose of the cult was to ensure prosperity and to avoid adverse influence from the powerful souls of departed family members. Indeed, the dead were regarded as full-fledged living members of the family capable of advancing the welfare of the family, or, if offended, afflicting it with punishment. The ancestors were to be honored, respected, eulogized, remembered with prayers and sacrifices, and consulted in all matters of family planning and fortune.

The kairotic movement away from multifarious and localized spirits and souls toward a single, universal God-power began sometime after 1000 B.C., when Chinese philosophical speculation moved to invent or discover two concepts of central importance. One was called Yang/Yin. The other was called Tao. Chinese philosophers and theologians became increasingly observant of the flowing polarity in all things, both in the heavens and on the earth. They observed light and darkness (day and night) flowing into and out of each other; hot and cold, each a condition of the other; male and female each separate, yet not alien, not really completely different; each was a little of the other. Yang/Yin might be symbolized by the banks of a river. There was the sunny bank and there was the shady bank, yet both were banks of the same stream. Unlike the Zoroastrian divine aliens (Wise Lord and Evil Spirit), the Chinese Yang/Yin blended into each other—both parts of the same whole. The Yang principle, although containing elements of Yin, was the dominant mode: male, bright, dry, active, warm. The Yin, on the other hand, was female, dark, moist, cold, passive. All things in the world got their nature or character from the dominance of one or the other of these two energy principles. Indeed, the universe itself was an activity of Yang and Yin. Heaven was full of Yang. Earth was mostly Yin.

With Yang/Yin the Chinese arrived at a universal energy system, but they were not content simply to have a theory for the becoming, being, and passing away of things and events. They looked deeper and discovered or invented the harmony and order of nature as a whole. They concluded that there was a character and a direction to all the Yang/Yin activity in the universe. The world was ordered, directed, controlled by the Way, by the Tao. They drew a distinction between the mechanism of the universe (the Yang/Yin process) and the powerful *Way* in which, as by an inner necessity, the mechanism ran. This Way was conceived to have been before all else, before the Earth, before the Heavens, and even before the principles Yang and Yin. First, there was the plan, the "way to go" (which is what Tao means), and then there was the going. The Way was preestablished—a way of harmony, integration, cooperation. Thus, it was the basic way of nature to move toward peace, prosperity, fulfillment. Indeed, if it were not for the perversity of men and the wickedness of devils and demons all would be well in this world, for to be well is the way of the high God; the single, universal, nonpersonal ultimate power—Tao.

Tao is as much the ground of beings in Chinese thought as Brahman is in Hindu thought, but the Tao is immanent in a way that Brahman is not, for Tao affirms the world in its natural course. Tao is the glory of *this* world, seen in the flight of a bird, the blooming of a flower, the birth of a child, the flowing of a river, the changing of the seasons. Unlike Brahman, Tao does not direct one out of the world but into it. The Western benediction "Go with God," is an even more proper wish for those who follow the way of the Way than for those who follow the way of the Nazarene, for to go with God Tao unresistingly, unaggressively, flowingly is to live *wu-wei*, which means to live and act in such a way that there occurs no interference with the natural way, with the way things should go.

Although the two native religions of China (Confucianism and Taoism) differ greatly in their interpretation of the true way of the

Tao, they both affirm the Tao as the definitive power behind all spirits and souls, and all things and events. The Confucians say that the Tao (often called by them Heaven) gives the proper rules for the way a father and son should relate to each other; an elder and a younger brother should relate to each other; a husband and wife to each other; elders and juniors to each other; rulers and subjects to each other. There is a Way. If it is followed, good life, happiness, tranquility, prosperity flow forth naturally. So say the Confucians. But the Taoists, unhappy with codes and restrictions, say "No, not by Heaven's rule, but by Nature's way." Flow with nature. Reject the mind's rebelliousness. Suppress the aggressive attitude. Feel the wind and go with it. See the sunset and become enchanted by it, merge into it. Taste the honey and be delighted. Do not try to create order; surrender to it as it moves Yang/Yin in all natural things and events.

The fact is that Confucianism is a consummate religion arising from the practice of ancestor worship so ancient in Chinese life, whereas Taoism, also a consummate religion, flows from the strain of nature worship which was equally ancient in Chinese life. Both affirm the Tao, the single, universal nonpersonal, ultimate power of the universe, but each does so from only one part of the ancient Chinese religion tradition. It is probably because of the different emphasis made by Confucianism, on the one hand, and Taoism, on the other, that these two great religions have been able to exist side by side with little conflict over the centuries, and how it is that so many Chinese are both Confucian and Taoist at the same time.

fourteen

The Devil's Due

Not since the witch burnings in Salem has the Devil seemed to have gotten as much attention as he has been getting recently. As if by popular demand, he seems to be doing a repeat performance, replete with demons, witches, satanism, and witchcraft. And the word "exorcism," which only a short time ago most people had never heard of, is about as common as "plastics" or "astronaut." Not that the Devil has not been around the whole time in this religion or that one. He just has not been around so obviously. Ernest Jones, in his *On the Nightmare*, tells us that

> the idea of evil supernatural powers, although perhaps not absolutely universal, is exceedingly widely spread among ruder peoples, and was so with civilized peoples of antiquity. On investigating specific instances more closely, however, it is striking to note how very rarely these powers were purely evil in nature. With almost the sole exception of the Persian Ahriman . . . one may say that before the advent of Christianity there was no definite conception of a supernatural being professionally devoted to evil.[1]

Jones makes two points which we should pursue somewhat further: (1) the notion that most devils are not totally evil, and (2) that the Persian Ahriman and the Christian Satan are exceptions. They are totally evil.

[1] Ernest Jones, *On the Nightmare* (New York: Liveright, 1951), pp. 156–157.

Semidemonic Gods   In Hinduism the great God Shiva is a demonic God who is, in fact, only half-fiendish. In ancient Hinduism, as indicated in chapter thirteen, there was a God named Rudra. Rudra was Shiva's predecessor, and he was the fierce author of the devastating storms that swept down from the Himalayas. He destroyed people. He was held in fear and awe, but he was, also, appealed to in prayer as if he might listen and be kind. Furthermore, was not Rudra the one who ruled the mountain passes where the medical plants grew? Surely he was not entirely malevolent, for sometimes the winds from the mountains were gentle winds, and the medicine was good.

Later Rudra was called Shiva, which means "auspicious," and his title was *Mahadeva*, which means "the Great God." The Great God destroyed, but not simply for the love of destruction; he killed, but not simply for the love of killing. He did so to make room for new creation. Shiva was in the fall of the leaf, but if the leaf did not fall, the spring could not come. Shiva was demonic, but not totally so. The same cannot be said for the Zoroastrian-Christian devil God: Satan.

The Professionally Demonic Gods   Jones simply referred to Ahriman (also called Angra Mainyu) as another totally evil supernatural power in addition to the Christian "supernatural being professionally devoted to evil." But Ahriman was more than just another devil. Ahriman was a direct predecessor of the Christian Satan.

The Satan of Christian doctrine is not as ancient as is usually surmised. There are, in the Jewish Bible, the Old Testament, other supernatural powers besides God Yahweh, but they are not given much stature. They never stand against God as archenemies, but are, rather, powers tolerated by him, and even used by him for his own purposes. The Serpent of Eden, for example, is not Satan in disguise, but one of God Yahweh's creatures who is cursed only after he tempts the woman. Again, the Satan who appears in Job is not at all like the later figure called the Devil. Rather, Job's Satan appears to be a part of God Yahweh's court playing the role of dialectical adversary in God Yahweh's department of justice. Indications of a power systematically opposing God in Hebrew thought do not appear until the Book of Chronicles, written in the third century B.C. Earlier, around the eighth century B.C., in the Book of II Samuel, chapter 24, one reads that the "Lord tempted"

David to carry out a census of the people, and then when David did this, punished him for doing so by sending a plague to reduce the numbers of Hebrews, after which the Lord "repented him of the evil." This same story is told again in First Chronicles (21:1), five centuries later, only this time it is not God Yahweh but Satan who tempts David. Between the eighth century and the first century something had happened. The Hebrews had become acquainted with the religion of the Persians (Zoroastrianism or Mazdaism) which did conceive of a supernatural force of evil standing in constant opposition to a supernatural force of God: God Ahriman (Angra Mainyu) against God Ormazd (Ahura Mazda).

After the Babylonian Captivity, and especially in a period of two centuries before and the two centuries after the birth of Christ, an extensive biblical and extrabiblical literature emerged in which there was a fully developed demonology headed by a first-class Devil. This Devil was not simply an angel dialectically opposing God or tempting God's children, but a Devil who was God's archenemy, a Satan of apocalyptic dimensions, the Fiend of Hell, who would eventually be identified as Lucifer,[2] an angel who had instigated a revolt, had been defeated, and had been, with his diabolical host, driven from Heaven. To support the supposition that after being driven from Heaven the fallen angels had invaded the earth, it became customary to cite that obscure passage in

[2] The identification of Lucifer with Satan was a contribution of the Church Fathers. It was the result of a wrongly interpreted biblical passage: Isaiah 14:12. The Prophet Isaiah had compared the king of Babylon, surrounded as he was with worldly splendor, prior to his death, with Lucifer, which is the Latin equivalent of the Hebrew word hillel, the light-bearer, the morning star; that is, the planet Venus when it appears above the Eastern horizon prior to daybreak. Just as the brilliance of Lucifer/Venus surpassed that of all other stars, so the splendor of the king of Babylon surpassed that of all other monarchs. And just as Venus quickly disappeared from the sky, so did the king of Babylon quickly disappear. Eusebius of Caesarea, Tertullian of North Africa, Jerome and Gregory the Great, all fathers of the Christian church, misunderstood Isaiah's passage: "How art thou fallen from heaven, O Lucifer, son of the morning, how art thou cut down to the ground which didst weaken the nations" (Isaiah 14:12, King James Version), as referring to the fall of a rebel angel. The result of this mistake was that the name Lucifer was subsequently used as a synonym for Satan. The two names, however, were not generally so identified until the time of St. Anselm, Archbishop of Canterbury (1034–1093), who, in his *Dialogue de causa Diaboli*, considerably elaborated the story of the fall of Lucifer/Satan from Heaven.

Genesis 6, which tells how the Sons of God took the daughters of men as wives and produced a progeny of mighty men. Originally this passage was probably a popular legend about giants, but in later Jewish and Christian thought it became a means of explaining how evil spirits and demons got into the world. In the book called First Enoch we are informed that the giants bred offspring who were invisible and incorporeal and who were dedicated to doing evil. Furthermore, these spirits and demons were under the command of the chief of fallen angels who was sometimes called Mastema, sometimes Belial, sometimes Beliar, and sometimes Satan.

Since it emerged into the literature of the Jews and Christians just before and after the beginning of the common era, the figure of Satan has been pictured in several dimensions. There was the figure of the diabolical fiend of the book of Revelation, who greatly resembled the demonic God Ahriman of the Zoroastrian religion. Later in secular literature there was the figure of Satan most dramatically portrayed in Milton's *Paradise Lost:* a figure of tragic majesty—a rebel whose cause was permanently shattered; a rebel puzzled and remorseful, trying to understand his own behavior; a rebel who was realist enough to know that he was forever lost and could blame no one but himself; a rebel eternally committed to promoting sin and death, but who also had a conscience.

After the stature attained in Revelation and *Paradise Lost,* the figure of Satan was sadly degraded into the mockery one sees in the Satan of witches and witchcraft—the Satan with horns and hooves and a tail, copulating with drug crazed witches on Walpurgis Night, which is a far cry from the giant figures of the Persian Ahriman, or the Fiend of Revelation, or the Lucifer of *Paradise Lost.*

By the time of Jesus and the rise of the Christian church an elaborate demonology had developed in Jewish thought, much of which was taken over by the new religion. In the New Testament it was taken for granted that there was an archfiend and a host of demonic spirits; and that Satan, who was lord of this world, was by the coming of Christ doomed, and at the Second Coming of Christ would be finally defeated and destroyed. As time passed in Christian history, Satan became identified with the serpent of Genesis and with other demonic beings named in the ancient tradition: Beelzebub, Abaddon, Apollyon, Levithan, Behemoth, Belial, Lucifer. Also, pagan additions were made to the figure until eventually the giant of the Apocalypse became a parody, a travesty, a joke. Jakob Grimm, in 1835, in his *Deutsche Mythologie*, observed that the devil idea was a composite of various figures. "He is at once of Jewish, Christian, heathen, elfish, gigantic and spectral stock." But mostly he was Persian.

In the Middle Ages this Persian, Jewish, Christian, heathen, elfish, gigantic, spectral Satan became the God of an inverted religion known as witchcraft, or, at least, so we have been told.

WITCHCRAFT

In common usage, witchcraft is a vague term often used to stand for sorcery, magic, necromancy, voodoo, or almost any other trafficking with spirits and/or demons. One hears of black witches and white witches and gray witches, and little witches out for tricks or treats on Halloween. But real witchcraft is something else. There have been witches and sorcerers and magicians back beyond when the mind of man runneth not to the contrary, but, following most modern scholars on the subject, we shall contend that "witchcraft does not antedate 1350 and many authorities would declare this as a century too soon."[3] Witchcraft was a cult movement which purportedly developed in the Christian Middle Ages when God was replaced by Satan as the object of worship and as the source to which men turned to deal with horrendous and nonmanipulable aspects of their miserable existences.

Theories on the Origins of Witchcraft   There are a number of speculations on the origin of witchcraft. We shall look at four of them: (1) It was a cult created by the Devil from ancient times—the "orthodox view." (2) It was a surviving primitive cult in the midst of Christendom. (3) It was a perverted response of people to their conditions of misery and hopelessness. (4) It was a fantasy created inadvertently by a kind of heresy-mania that infected the Catholic Church during the Middle Ages.

First, the "orthodox theory" goes something like this: In the

[3] Julian Franklyn, *Death by Enchantment* (London: Hamish Hamilton, 1971), p. 9.

beginning there was only God, magnificent and alone, omnipotent, omniscient, omnipresent, the absolutely perfect, "than which nothing greater can be conceived." But there was one thing wrong. There was no one except God to appreciate his absolute perfection. Indeed, one might almost suspect that God was lonely. He had no companions, no community, no communication. This problem was solved by an act of creation. God created the heavenly host—angels and archangels—to see and adore him. Now, God could have created automatons to sing his praises: good beings who could only be good—beings who loved and adored him because they were completely programmed to do so. But even greater would be the adoration not of robots but of free beings—beings who could choose to adore God or not to adore him. That kind of adoration was superior, and that kind of being God created. But there was a danger, and the danger became manifest in one of the most powerful and beautiful of all of the angels: the one named Lucifer. Lucifer fell under the sin of covetousness. He wanted to be God. Desire stirred in him. Avarice swelled in him. Deceit spoke to him. He became a subversive, seducing other angels to help him fulfill his ambition. His power grew. The time came. He rose in revolt. War erupted, with Lucifer and his cohorts on one side and God and his loyal angels on the other. Under the logistical competence of God's General, Michael, Lucifer was defeated and cast from Heaven into the outer-darkness, along with his corrupted angels, now hideous and demonic.

By this revolt, the choirs of heaven were somewhat depleted. To rectify this, God set up a kind of experiment. He would create a new world and put on it free beings (mankind) and let them prove themselves before admitting them to take the vacant seats in Heaven. So the physical world was created, and a man and woman placed on it. They were innocent and free, unrestricted except by one commandment: they were not to eat of the Tree of the Knowledge of Good and Evil. And so, for a time, Adam and Eve dwelt in Paradise. But out there, in the outer-darkness, there was Lucifer/Satan, angry and vicious, still desiring to thwart God in any way he could. So he came in the guise of a serpent and he told the woman that if she and her husband ate of the forbidden fruit, they would not die, but would know what God knew, and would in that way become Gods. She ate of the fruit and gave some to her husband. The experiment failed, so God drove the man and his woman from the Garden and turned his back on them. Satan moved in and took over, and Adam and Eve began begetting the generations of "fallen men." Some time later God tried again, using Noah as his starting point. But this too failed. Time went by and God tried a third time, this time with a Chosen People.

Through the history of these Chosen People, God wrought, by hard learning, a firm realization in man that man could not be God, or even create a perfect world. When enough of the Hebrew people came truly to believe this, and to wait for the coming of the promised Savior, God made his final and magnificent move. He sent his Son, his very being, into the world to suffer and die for the redemption and perfection of those persons who would cleave only to Christ and forever renounce the Prince of Darkness, Ruler of the Earth, the Devil.

With the coming of Christ, Satan went into a frenzy. At first he tried to tempt Christ to join him. When this failed, he loosed his wrath upon Christ's Church, and through the power of Imperial Rome tried to wipe it out. When this too failed, Satan went underground, and through stealth and dark, nighttime action, secured as many men and women to worship him as he could seduce, giving them power and pleasure in exchange for their souls. Against God's Church he arrayed not only himself and his demons but thousands and millions of human witches: depraved creatures who performed black magic, devoured babies, worshipped at an evil mass, engaged in sexual orgies, and bedeviled and corrupted as many priests, nuns, virgins, Christian matrons, and honest God-fearing men as possible.

In this view Satan has ontological and apocalyptic status. He is a structure out of God's own being, that is, out of God's original loneliness or desire for community, and is the major negative force in history, to be finally thwarted only at the end of time. And witchcraft is one of the major devices that Satan employs to thwart God's desire to have the souls of men and women with him in Heaven.

Second, a more modern theory of the origin of witchcraft is proposed by Margaret Alice Murray. She holds that when one examines the records of medieval witchcraft, one is actually dealing with the remains of a pagan religion, which predated Christianity in Europe and which stubbornly resisted the invasion of Christianity, even to the death. As Christianity became more firmly established, the "Old Religion" retreated to the less frequented parts of the countryside and was practiced by the more ignorant members of the European community. Murray is proposing that there existed a well-defined religion coexisting with Medieval Christianity. This religion was later interpreted as devil worship by the Christian authorities. The witch trials, which spanned three centuries, marked the effort of the Christian Church to extirpate its rival.

Murray's reconstruction of the Old Religion includes the existence of covens dedicated to the worship of a horned God, which was a nature deity going back to neolithic times. She further argues that witchcraft was a well-organized belief system that made appeal not only to ruder folk, but even to such superior souls as Thomas à Becket and Joan of Arc.

After Murray's thesis became popular, and after the last of the English laws condemning witchcraft were removed from English statutes, several persons came forward to claim and demonstrate that Murray's witch cult had survived even into the twentieth century. Gerald B. Gardner published *Witchcraft Today,* with an introduction by Margaret Murray. Sybil Leek surfaced and exposed her own coven in the New Forest, in Hampshire, England. Alex Sanders, self-styled king of the witches, set out on a well-publicized effort to recruit witches into the Old Religion.

This is all quite fascinating: there was an Old Religion; it got a bad name and was driven underground by the avidity of conquering Christianity; but it survived and is alive and well today in places like New Forest, Miami, San Francisco, and other modern places. But, unfortunately, Miss Murray's thesis is not everywhere highly regarded. Few competent scholars will buy it. Apparently she is a good Egyptologist, but with witchcraft she seems to have let her desires and her imagination run away with the facts. Many authorities hold that she was just plain sloppy in her work on witchcraft.[4] However, her theory is usually regarded with favor by modern practitioners of witchcraft, if not by anthropologists and historians.

---

[4] For example, Henry Ansgar Kelly points out that in her account on Witchcraft in the *Encylopaedia Britannica* she is, first, willing to use Lord Coke, an early seventeenth-century jurist, as her definer of the term witch: "a person who hath conference with the Devil to consult with him or to do some act." That sort of thing one might pass over as unimportant, but when she actually makes a scholarly attempt to define "devil" and misses, that is a different matter. She states: "The word 'devil' is a diminutive from the root from which we also get the word 'divine'. It merely means god." Kelly points out that if Miss Murray had

A third thesis on the origin of witchcraft is that it was a perverted response induced by the misery, the squalor, and the frustrations of medieval life. Witchcraft, thus identified, existed as a
rebellion against the restrictions of the Medieval Church and the
impotence of the Christian God to deal with the misery and priva-
tion in which the masses of Western man lived between the decline
of the Carolingian Empire and the coming of the Modern World.
Ernest Jones comments upon the impotence of the Christian God
by observing that the Church increasingly identified the miseries of
life with the activities of Satan. Pestilence, war, famine, and oppres-
sion were all caused by Satan, and no amount of appealing to the
Christian God seemed to improve the people's plight. Thus many of
the peasants of Europe

> in despair at the obvious failure of God and the Church to relieve
> their misery, greedily absorbed the doctrines of the wonderful
> powers of the Devil, so that not a few took refuge with him. . . .
> The extent of the belief in the Devil's influence on even the most
> trivial everyday happening was so colossal that one cannot read the
> records of the time without thinking that Europe was being visited
> by a mass of psychoneurosis of an unusually malign type.[5]

The miserable masses of Europe were not finding adequate
solace in the teachings and practices of the Church. Some of them
turned elsewhere. In turning elsewhere, to what did they turn? To
the religion that ancient Lucifer established? To Murray's Old Religion of pagan origins? Or possibly to something else: to the simple
sorcery and magic and conjuring carried on by independent witches
and magicians; to some explorations into demon worship; to the
kinds of superstitions and practices engaged in by some people in
the backwoods places of Europe and America even today? Small
groups may have been organized around a witch or wizard. Secret

---

simply read the Britannica article on "Devil," she would have been properly
informed that the true derivation of the word comes from the Greek translation
of the Hebrew word "satan." The *de* element corresponds to the prepositional
prefix *dia*, which means "through," and the *vil* element to *ballein*, which means
"to throw." Again, Murray blithely states that "it is a well-known fact that when
a new religion is established in any country, the god or gods of the old religion
become the devils of the new." This is not only not a well-known fact but it is,
in fact, seldom the fact. See H. R. Kelly, *The Devil, Demonology and Witchcraft*, revised edition (Garden City, N.Y.: Doubleday, 1974), pp. 55–56.

[5] Jones, *On the Nightmare*, p. 164.

meetings may have been held. Spells cast. Drugs taken. Orgies performed. But nothing like the vast and highly organized underground religion envisioned by the heresy-hunting Inquisitors of the Church, or Margaret Murray's Old Religion.

A fourth thesis on the origin of witchcraft is the "fantasy theory." The medieval records describing the nature and extent of witchcraft must have been extravagantly overstated by the Church's heresy-hunting inquisitors. In reading them one has ample reason for suspecting that he is dealing quite as much with fantasy as with fact.

In 1967, when Professor Evans-Pritchard retired from his Chair of Anthropology at Oxford, the Association of Social Anthropologists of the Commonwealth decided to hold a conference in his honor. Because of Professor Evans-Pritchard's interest in witchcraft (he had published in 1937 an extremely influential book on the subject), it was decided to make witchcraft the theme of the conference.

Among the persons who read papers at that conference was Norman Cohn. He titled his paper "The Myth of Satan and His Human Servants," which he opened with this statement:

> This paper is concerned with a fantasy and the part it played in European history. The fantasy is that there exists a category of human beings that is pledged to the service of Satan; a sect that worships Satan in secret conventicles and, on Satan's behalf, wages relentless war against Christendom and against individual Christians. At one time in the Middle Ages this fantasy became attached to certain heretical sects, and helped to legitimate and intensify their persecution. A couple of centuries later it gave the traditional witchcraft beliefs to Europe a twist which turned them into something new and strange—something quite different from, and vastly more lethal than, the witchcraft beliefs that anthropologists find and study in primitive societies today. And the fantasy has also frequently been attached to the Jews—and not only in far off times but in the late nineteenth and early twentieth centuries when it helped to prepare the way for the secular demonology of the Nazis. It is a long story but a perfectly coherent one, and it is excellently documented.[6]

[6] Norman Cohn, "The Myth of Satan and His Human Servants," *Witchcraft Confessions and Accusations*, ed. Mary Douglas (London: Tavistock Publications, 1970), pp. 3–16.

In his paper Professor Cohn examines the long and often grisly witchcraft story. Satan, identified as the heart of the fantasy, is traced back to Christian, Jewish, and Persian origins. It is pointed out that the Fathers of the Christian church regarded the deities of the pagan religions as demons who served Satan's purposes. Thus the Church took a dim view of any kind of trafficking in the sorcery and magic of the pagan cults. In this attitude the early Church prepared the ground for the great demonization of human beings which was to take place centuries later in Western Europe.

In spite of the Church's rejection of paganism, the observances of pagans were not always ruthlessly suppressed, and many became incorporated into the practices of the Church. But in the early years of the twelfth century things began to change radically. Up to that time there had been few heretical sects in Western Christendom, but from that time on they began to appear and proliferate, especially in the urban centers of northern Italy, France, and in the Rhine Valley. These sects were often supported by noblemen, clergymen, merchants, and artisans. They were, thus, to be taken seriously by both ecclesiastical and secular authorities, who became increasingly intolerant of any deviations regarding matters of faith. Heretics were systematically ferreted out, imprisoned, and even burned at the stake. Cohn informs us that "It was in the context of this struggle against heresy that, for the first time in Western Europe, groups of human beings were described as Satan-worshippers."

In 1022 several canons of the cathedral of Orléans were condemned as guilty of heresy and burned at the stake. Their heresy consisted primarily of rejecting the Catholic concepts of Eucharist, Baptism, and the efficacy of invoking the intercession of saints. They advocated, rather, the coming of the Holy Spirit through the laying-on of hands, and the receiving of "heavenly food." This receiving of heavenly food set imaginations running among the opposition. A contemporary chronicler, Adhémar de Chabannes, reported that these "heretics" had been bound into a Devil sect by eating the ashes of murdered children. In this abominable rite, Satan appeared to them, sometimes as a Negro and sometimes in the guise of an angel of light, and commanded them to reject Christ, even while pretending publicly to be true followers of Christ. They were also commanded to abandon themselves to every sort of perverted vice. Some eighty years later one, Paul,

Monk of Chartres, with similar imaginative freedom, reporting on the Orléans incident said:

> They came together by night, each carrying a light. The demons were invoked with particular formulae, and appeared in the guise of animals. Thereupon the lights were extinguished, and fornication and incest followed. The children born as a result of this were burned and their ashes were treasured like holy relics. These ashes had such diabolic power that anyone who tasted even the smallest bit of them was irrevocably bound to the sect.[7]

That the heretics not only associated with demons but actually worshipped Satan was "demonstrated" by the English chronicler Walter Map (or Mapes), who lived in France at the end of the twelfth century. He described meetings that took place in Aquitaine and Burgundy in which Satan appeared as a black cat and was adored by the satanists. In 1233 Pope Gregory IX issued a bull describing how, at heretical assemblies in Germany, Satan appeared as a black cat, or as a frog or toad, or as a furry man, and how the company would give him the obeisance kiss and then embark on perverted orgies. But it took yet another seventy years before such accusations became part of an actual trial for witchcraft, and then the trial was not against real heretics, but against the Knights Templars of France. The Knights Templars were an order of warrior monks who for two centuries had protected the conquests achieved by the crusaders in the Near East. The order had become enormously wealthy, even to the point of becoming an international banker with whom kings and popes did business. In 1307 Philip IV, King of France, who had already despoiled the Jews and the Lombard bankers, turned covetous eyes toward the Templars' wealth. The Templars were accused of defiling Christ by trafficking with and worshipping the Devil, in the form of a black cat, or as an idol called Baphomet. They were accused of doing all the things that witches do—black magic, sex orgies, Devil worship. The Templars were arrested and tortured so severely that some died under the torture, and others "confessed."

Quite supportive of Cohn's "fantasy theory," we might observe that most of what we know about witches was told us by witches

---

[7] "Paul, Monk of Chartres, Liber Aganonis," *Cartulaire de l'abbaye de Saint-Père de Chartres*, ed. M. Guerard, Tom. I. Paris, 1840, p. 112. Quoted by Cohn, p. 9.

under torture. So many witches "confessed" to the crime of witch-craft and then told all, that we have data to burn. The only trouble with the data is that most of it was obtained just that way—with burnings and other sorts of equally effective persuasions. The ac-cused witch faced a tough set of inquirers (even professional In-quisitors), as Julian Franklyn tells us:

> To be engaged in supporting Satan against God was an act of major treason for which the punishment was death. Since no one could be expected to admit guilt unless forced to do so, it was reasonable to use force to extract confession. . . .
> Every witch brought to trial on the Continent of Europe went through the torture-chamber. Notwithstanding that there was suffi-cient evidence against the accused to burn her, to which she added her voluntary confession, torture was applied to ensure that the confession was genuine, and complete: the agony inflicted would invariably extract desired additions.[8]

Under torture anyone accused of trafficking with Satan sooner or later "confessed" to everything her/his tormentors wanted to hear. Did you participate in a Mass of desecration? When the screws were turned sufficiently, the eyelids cut off, the hands doused with oil and set on fire, the "witch" said, Yes. Did you have carnal relations with Satan? Yes. Did you fly to the Sabbat on a broom? Yes. Did you curse the miller's wife and cause her to die? Curse the farmer's cow and cause it to go dry? What else did you do? And what the witch confessed to—orgastic cavortings, and naked dances, and murderous cursings—got widely publicized at the trials, and was duly noted and recorded in various learned *Treatise(s) on Heretics and Witches,*[9] and in *Handbook(s) on Witchcraft,*[10] and in court records as widely separated as Toulouse, France, London, England, and Salem, Massachusetts. The odds are that the vast majority of people executed for witchcraft were not witches, or even magicians or sorcerers, but that their confessions added enormously to the store of misinformation about witchcraft which today confuses both laymen and scholars.

Out of overzealousness the inquisitors created the typical

---

[8] Franklyn, *Death by Enchantment,* pp. 72–73.
[9] Paulus Grillandus, published c. 1525.
[10] Francesco Maria Guazzo, published in 1608.

208   GOD AND RELIGION

stereotype of witchcraft, with its witches and warlocks meeting in
secret covens and at sabbat assemblies that were presided over by
Satan and where the cannibalizing of infants and sexual orgies were
performed.

> In this way the inquisitors built up a fantasy of a mysterious sect,
> endowed with supernatural powers, which at Satan's bidding was
> waging incessant war on Christians and Christendom.
>   This sect was wholly imaginary. Whereas heretical sects did at
> least exist, there was no sect of witches.[11]

The early inquisitors created a witchcraft mania that was to
sweep large areas of Western Europe long after the Inquisition had
ceased to function there. The persecutions which began in the fourteenth century came into full swing in the sixteenth and seventeenth
centuries. In these latter centuries they were carried out mostly by
secular authorities, some Catholic, some Lutheran, some Calvinist.
It cannot be determined exactly how many people were executed
for witchcraft in those two centuries, but responsible estimates
place the figure at not less than 200,000 and perhaps upwards to a
million. And for what? According to Norman Cohn, for a fantasy. A
fantasy for murdering which did not end in the seventeenth century
but only went dormant, to revive again in pogroms against the Jews
in the nineteenth century, and in the Nazi holocaust in the twentieth
century.

Witchcraft and the Jews   Professor Cohn sees the Nazi destruction of European Jewry as a direct result of the "fantasy of witchcraft." By the eighteenth century the witchhunt mania in Europe
had played out. There were still a few people hunted down and
killed in backward areas, accused of practicing sorcery, but the idea
of a Satanic cult of witches had lost its appeal. This, however, was
not the case with the idea that there were still servants of Satan in
the world. In the nineteenth century the idea revived in the myth of
Jewish world conspiracy under the auspices of Satan.

During the early years of the medieval period there had been
little serious conflict between Christians and Jews. But when, in the
twelfth century, heretics came to be regarded as servants of Satan, a
similar fate befell the Jews. For the first time they were accused of
such things as ritual murder of Christian children, of defiling the

[11] Cohn, "The Myth of Satan," p. 11.

consecrated wafer of the Holy Eucharist, and of practicing black magic and worshipping Satan. From the twelfth to the eighteenth centuries, Jews suffered privations and restrictions and martyrdom such as they had never known from Christians before.

With the French Revolution came an emancipation for the Jews, which spread from one country to another during the nineteenth century. But with emancipation there came, also, a wave of panic among the non-Jewish people, stimulated partly by the fact that once freed many Jews quickly achieved influence (in banking, journalism, radical politics) quite out of proportion to their numbers. But, Professor Cohn insists, the roots of the panic lay much deeper, and he refers to the book of Gougenot des Mousseaux, *Le Juif, le judaïsme et la judaïsation des peuples chrétiens,* published in 1896, which not only stated the hidden case but became the source book for modern, political anti-Semitism. Des Mousseaux was convinced that the world was in the grip of a mysterious body of Satan worshippers, whom he called Kabbalistic Jews. He said that there was a secret demonic religion that had been established by the Devil at the very beginning of time. The grand masters of the cult were Jews. The cult centered in the worship of Satan, and its ritual consisted of orgies, interspersed with episodes when Jews murdered Christian children to use their blood for magical purposes. The book claimed to unmask a Jewish plot to dominate the whole world through the control of banks, the press, and political parties.

Out of this demonological fantasy there emerged another document created by the Russian pseudo-mystic Sergey Nilus: the *Protocols of the Elders of Zion.* This fantasy of Jewish Satanism, appearing in 1905, was later to obsess the mind of Adolph Hitler. In summary, Professor Cohn states:

> At the heart of Hitler's antisemitism is the fantasy that, for thousands of years, all Jews, everywhere, have been united in a ceaseless endeavor to undermine, ruin, and dominate the rest of humanity. And although in Hitler's mind and in Nazi ideology this fantasy is dressed up in the pseudo-scientific garb of racism, the fantasy itself stems from quite another source.[12]

That source was the fantasy of witchcraft, the fantasy that the Devil was alive and well and had thousands and thousands of secret human servants who were endowed with uncanny and infinitely

[12] Ibid., p. 15.

sinister powers. Through such believing, enormous amounts of hatred and a fantastic device for murdering without qualms of conscience could be achieved, and most horribly was achieved in the extermination of perhaps a million witches in Medieval Europe and six million European Jews in our own time.

Exorcism   The Christians knew how to deal with witches and witchcraft: exterminate brutally, everywhere and often. The church also knew how to deal with the demons and with Satan: exorcise them.

When one exorcises one uses ritual and/or incantation to drive out of, or away from, some person an evil spirit which has possessed that person's body and/or mind. We shall look at two examples of exorcisms that come from opposing religious camps in very modern times. One is intended to exorcise Christ; the other to exorcise Satan.

The first exorcism is one performed by a California-based cult called "The Church of Satan." This is done in a service called *La Messe Noir* (the Black Mass).

One of the purported features of medieval witchcraft was the desecration of the Catholic sacrament of the Eucharist in a ritual called the Black Mass. According to various accounts a parody of the Catholic Mass was enacted at each sabbat gathering. Consecrated hosts were either stolen from Catholic churches or consecrated on the spot by apostate priests. Some accounts state that a slice of blackened turnip was used as the host in the Black Mass. However it was done in past times, there is available for examination a published ritual of the Black Mass as it has been performed in current times in The Church of Satan.[13] In this ritual a priest, assisted by several other persons, including a woman who lies naked on the altar, performs a Mass to the glory of Satan, in which Christ is exorcised.

After a number of invocations and prayers and symbolic gestures have been performed, the canon of the Mass is reached, at which time the priest consecrates the host and chalice declaring over each in turn: "This is the body of Jesus Christ." "This is the cup of voluptuous carnality." With the bread and wine duly consecrated, the mass enters the phase called Repudiation and Denuncia-

[13] See Anton Szandor LaVey, *The Satanic Rituals* (New York: Avon, 1972).

tion, which is actually an exorcism. The priest, addressing Jesus and Satan, declares:

> Thou, thou whom, in my capacity of Priest, I force, whether thou wilt or no, to descend into this host, to incarnate thyself into this bread, Jesus, artisan of hoaxes, bandit of homages, robber of affection—hear!
>
> Since the day when thou didst issue from the complaisant bowels of a false virgin, thou has failed all thy engagements, belied all thy promises. Centuries have wept awaiting thee, fugitive god, mute god! Thou wast to redeem man and thou hast not; thou wast to appear in thy glory, and thou sleepest. Go, lie, say to the wretch who appeals to thee, "Hope, be patient, suffer; the hospital of souls will receive thee; angels will succor thee; Heaven opens to thee." Impostor! Thou knowest well that the Angels disgusted at thy inertness, abandon thee! Thou wast to be the interpreter of our plaints, the chamberlain of our tears; thou wast to convey them to the cosmos and thou hast not done so, for this intercession would disturb thy eternal sleep of happy satiety.
>
> . . .
>
> O lasting foulness of Bethlehem, we would have thee confess thy impudent cheats, thy inexpiable crimes! We would drive deeper the nails into thy hands, press down the crown of thorns upon thy brow, and bring blood from the dry wounds of thy sides.
>
> And this we can and *will* do by violating the quietude of thy body, profaner of the ample vices, abstractor of stupid purities, cursed Nazarene, impotent king, fugitive god! . . .
>
> O Infernal Majesty, condemn him to the Pit, evermore to suffer in perpetual anguish. Bring Thy wrath upon him, O prince of Darkness, and rend him that we may know the extent of Thy anger. Call forth Thy legions that they may witness what we do in Thy name. Send forth Thy messengers to proclaim this deed, and send the Christian minions staggering to their doom. Smite him anew, O Lord of Light, that his angels, cherubim and seraphim may cower and tremble with fear, prostrating themselves before Thee in respect to Thy power. Send crashing down the gates of Heaven, that the murders of our ancestors may be avenged!

At this point the celebrant inserts the host into the vagina of the nude woman lying on the altar; removes it and declares:

> Vanish into nothingness, thou fool of fools, thou vile and abhorred pretender to the majesty of Satan! Vanish into the void of thy empty Heaven, for thou wert never nor shalt thou ever be.

The celebrant takes the chalice, drinks from it, then holds it out to the assembled company and says:

> Look, the cup of voluptuous carnality, from which comes joyous life.

The cup is then shared by the assemblage. After which there is a benediction and the mass ends.[14]

Whether or not LaVey's Black Mass is in format anything like the Black Mass of medieval witchcraft, it does strike the same note of angry rebellion: God has failed. Christ has failed. He is an impostor; let him be desecrated by the human spawn of Satan, debauched in the carnal sheath of a naked woman and assigned to oblivion by the power and glory of His Infernal Majesty, the Prince of Darkness, "our protector and friend."

To exorcise Christ is a rarity in exorcism: one might even say a parody on a parody, for as all good exorcists know, it is Satan and his evil spirits who are the proper subjects of exorcism, as we shall now observe, in an example from Catholic ritual. In the rite of Baptism for adults,[15] used until recently in the Roman Catholic Church, Satan and two other evil spirits are exorcised no fewer than six different times. The first of the six exorcisms occurs at the church door. The catechumen (the one to be baptized) stands outside. In responsive questions and answers, the priest asks who he is and what he wants. The catechumen declares his desire for faith and eternal life. The priest then asks the catechumen to renounce Satan, which the catechumen does. The priest questions the catechumen's understanding of faith. Then "the priest blows three times upon the catechumen's face and says once: Depart from him (her), unclean spirit, and give place to the Holy Spirit, the Consoler." Thus the first demon (the demon of Adam's transgression: the demon of "original sin") is exorcised.

The ritual continues with proper blessings and prayers, still at the church door, until the rite arrives at the "Blessing of Salt." Salt symbolizes preservation, but the salt must be purified and blessed. It is purified by exorcising the demonic element it contains. The priest says:

---

[14] All the above quotations are from Anton S. LaVey, *The Satanic Rituals* (New York: Avon, 1972), pp. 49–51.

[15] See *Collectio Rituum*, 1964.

O salt, creature of God, I exorcise you in the name of God the Father Almighty and in the love of our Lord Jesus Christ and in the strength of the Holy Spirit. I exorcise you by the living God, the true God, the holy God, the God who brought you into being. . . .

The ritual then continues with a symbolic placing of the de-demonized salt in the catechumen's mouth as "a symbol of wisdom" and "life everlasting."

Then, still at the church door, in three separate, successive ritual steps, Satan is exorcised with powerful prayers and scriptural references. The three separate statements of exorcism are:

Therefore, accursed devil, acknowledge your condemnation, and pay homage to the living and true God; pay homage to Jesus Christ, his son, and to the Holy Spirit, and depart from this servant of God. . . .

Hear, accursed Satan, I adjure you by the name of the eternal God and of our Savior Jesus Christ, depart. . . .

I exorcise you, unclean spirit, in the name of the Father, and of the Son, and of the Holy Spirit. Come forth, depart from this servant of God. . . . Therefore, accursed devil acknowledge your condemnation and pay homage to the living and true God; pay homage to Jesus Christ, his son, and to the Holy Spirit, and depart from this servant of God. . . .

Whether or not there is such an absolutely evil being as Satan, or whether or not there is a host of demonic imps and black angels fouling the life of man, satanism and demonism have been violent beliefs in Christianity, and remain, if not so violent as before, fixed and tantalizing aspects of the Western Christian scene, as is abundantly evidenced by the voluminous amounts of popular writings on witchcraft and satanism devoured by Western readers, as well as the fantastic popularity of William Peter Blatty's spine-chilling, demon-chasing novel called *The Exorcist*. If 6,300,000 copies were sold before the movie itself started setting attendance records, one may safely surmise that there must be a few people left who have an inordinate interest in a very old and macabre way of thinking.

part V

RELIGION AS
EXPERIENCE

There is no Bodhi tree
Nor strand of mirror bright.
Since all is void,
Where can the dust alight?

Hui-neng

ſifteen

Religion:
Exoteric Expression

With all this, religion still turns out to be not simply a methou ͻ, dealing with metatechnological and metapsychological problems but is itself an experience of great satisfaction and immense personal worth. Religion is not only something for people (functional) but is something to people (an experience, even an ecstasy).

We have said that religion arises from human frustration. It moves to overrule anxiety and meaninglessness. It structures life with sustaining morale. It cumulates into commitments and aspirations and moral demands of the highest order. It discerns and depicts God. But anyone truly sensitive to deep religious experience would not want to settle for only this much, for it does not account for the private aspects of religion (for the sentiments, passions, love, spiritual knowledge, elation, ecstasy) which are to the believer, the worshipper, the mystic, the most precious and definitive characteristics of all. Even if we could solve technologically all of the problems of human finitude, there would still be devotees of religion, for there would still be those who had discovered that religion is not only something that people do but something that happens to them. It is an experience: even an ecstasy. I. M. Lewis, in his book *Ecstatic Religion,* begins by saying that "belief, ritual, and spiritual experience: these are the cornerstones of religion, and the greatest of them is the last."[1] Having looked at the first two

[1] I. M. Lewis, *Ecstatic Religion* (Middlesex, England: Penguin, 1971), p. 11.

cornerstones—belief/theology and myth/ritual—we shall now look at the last, without which religion would be no more than a business or a game.

In trying to discern the dimension of experience in religion, we shall observe, first, several expressions of religious experience that are predominantly exoteric in character, that is, open to external observation and description: religion as sensuous, religion as sexual, religion as love, and religion as Charity/Agapé. Second, in the next chapter, we shall observe several religious experiences that are esoteric in character, that is, privately personal: religion as a noetic experience (the inner knowledge of conversion), and religion as an ecstasy (divine seizure, worship, and mysticism).

SENSUOUSNESS

That religion is accoutered with sensuousness is abundantly obvious. Man's greatest (and sometimes not so great, but always sincere) artistic efforts have been directed to making religion a sensuously attractive experience. Magnificent buildings, exquisite colors, elaborate pageantry, superb dramatics, the best of music and dancing and poetry; indeed, the superior artistic accomplishments of man grace and enhance the sensuous enjoyment of religion. Even the more drab traditions of Christian pietism and Protestant evangelicalism have heightened sensuous enjoyment with lively hymn tunes and vividly sensuous (even sensational) preaching.

I have a sharp memory of my own shocked discovery of the importance of the olfactory sense in my own religious life. Reared a Roman Catholic, I eventually left that Church and became an evangelical Protestant, but for some reason I never "felt religious" in a Protestant service of worship. Yet I could simply enter a Catholic church and sense immediately something mysteriously religious. I became aware of this odd circumstance, and even wondered occasionally if the "Catholic God" were not depriving me because of my desertion of "Holy Mother the Church." And then one day as I happened to enter a beautiful Catholic cathedral, and got that usual experience of religiousness, I had presence of mind to ask myself why. And immediately I knew why. It was the smell: the lingering odor of incense and burning candles. It smelled right! The thing wrong with a Methodist Church was that it did not smell religious. For sure, sensuousness is part of the religious experience.

As we have already noted at length in chapter eight, ritual and myth are artistic forms. Frederick Streng, in his *Understanding Religious Man*, calls this liturgical art, visual theology. This is the art that self-consciously attempts to express the content of a given religious tradition. It "includes especially the images of gods, saviors, and saints, and the architecture of holy places."[2] In this kind of art, the artist, like the prophet, tries to become a medium through which God, or infinite reality, is manifested to man. Through dramatic action, the action of God is exposed. For example, in religious dance, God's movements are shown.

> Dancing in a circle or in a long, serpentine line dramatized the divine actions of creation or the battle between the powers of life and the dark forces of nature. The movements and verbal expression in the archaic drama and dance were based on formal elements revealed not only in these art forms but also in the myth and other rituals. Here one could dance a prayer.[3]

Various religious traditions have different styles of artistic expression. In Christianity, for example, much of the art focuses on Jesus Christ, on his image, on his cross, on various stylized images that represent Christ—a lamb, a babe, a fish. In Hinduism, the foci of religious art are widely scattered. There are many images, and forms "to depict the infinity of the divine."

> The "otherness" of God is expressed also through various suggestions of the "nonnatural": multiple arms or many eyes, or skin that is gold or dark blue. Perhaps the unique Hindu quality is best expressed in the image of the union of opposites in the combination of gods and goddesses (for example, Shiva and Shakti).[4]

Islamic religious art exemplifies another style of religious art. Here, following the biblical restrictions on divine images, the Muslim artist has developed the fantastic art of Arabic design. Beginning with a simple mosaic design, the design is repeated, until it begins to generate variations of the original design *ad infinitum*. God, who in Islamic thought is intricately involved in the lives and fates of men, emerges visually not as an anthropomorphic God but as a magnificent pattern, an infinite design.

[2] Frederick J. Streng, *Understanding Religious Man* (Belmont, Calif.: Dickenson, 1969), p. 85.

[3] Ibid., p. 86.

[4] Ibid., p. 86.

Streng also takes note of the fact that among some religious thinkers (Paul Tillich, Jacques Maritain, Ananda K. Coomaraswamy, and D. T. Suzuki) and in some religious traditions, art expresses religion not in directly religious subjects but in ordinary, everyday subjects.

> *Any* aesthetic performance, regardless of explicit content, arises from the pressure of life's experiences which are grounded in ultimate reality. It is this ultimate ground or spiritual essence in which the artist and observer participate when each is sensitive to beauty.[5]

A young professor of philosophy was once questioned by an irritated sophomore student to justify why he, the student, should be expected to read and struggle with something like Plato's *Timaeus* or Kierkegaard's *Unscientific Postscript*. The professor replied to this question with a question: Why have a bowl of flowers? One would expect that a philosophy professor would tell the student that both Plato and Kierkegaard had something worthwhile "to say" to him, but the professor chose to hint at a deeper answer. Perhaps, even in concrete experiences, it is possible to experience ultimate and profoundly religious things.

Plato and Kierkegaard may not be very ordinary and concrete experiences for many people, but the drinking of tea surely is for anyone. Yet the drinking of tea, under the proper form, is both an artistic and religious experience. The following is a description of the Tea Ceremony described for us by D. T. Suzuki. He writes:

> . . . Let me describe a tea-room in one of the temples attached to Daitokuji, the Zen temple which is the headquarters of the tea-ceremony. Where a series of flagstones irregularly arranged come to a stop, there stands a most insignificant-looking straw-thatched hut, low and unpretentious to the last degree. The entrance is not by a door but a sort of aperture; to enter through it a visitor has to be shorn of all his encumbrances, that is to say, to take off both his swords, long and short, which in the feudal days a samurai used to carry all the time. The inside is a small semi-lighted room about ten feet square; the ceiling is low and of uneven height and structure. The posts are not smoothly planed, they are mostly natural wood. After a little while, however, the room grows gradually lighter as our eyes begin to adjust themselves to the new situation. We notice an ancient-looking kakemono in the alcove with some handwriting or a picture of Sumiye type. An incense-burner emits a fragrance

which has the effect of soothing one's nerves. The flower-vase contains no more than a single stem of flowers, neither gorgeous nor ostentatious; but like a little white lily blooming under a rock surrounded by in no way sombre pines, the humble flower is enhanced in beauty and attracts the attention of the gathering of four or five visitors especially invited to sip a cup of tea in order to forget the wordly cares that may be oppressing them.

Now we listen to the sound of boiling water in the kettle as it rests on a tripod frame over in the square hole cut in the floor. The sound is not that of actually boiling water but comes from the heavy iron kettle, and it is most appropriately likened by the connoisseur to a breeze that passes through the pine grove. It greatly adds to the serenity of the room, for a man here feels as if he were sitting alone in a mountain-hut where a white cloud and the pine music are the only consoling companions.

To take a cup of tea with friends in this environment, talking probably about the Sumiye sketch in the alcove or some art topic suggested by the tea-utensils in the room, wonderfully lifts the mind above the perplexities of life. The warrior is saved from his daily occupation of fighting, and the business-man from his ever-present idea of money-making. Is it not something, indeed, to find in this world of struggles and vanities a corner, however humble, where one can rise above the limits of relativity and even have a glimpse of eternity?[6]

Here is an art form that is simply doing something well and sensitively, which reveals and heals and saves, and which is, thereby, an expression of and an experience of religion, sensuously operating in the ordinary life of man. Similarly a farmer plowed his fields in straight furrows not merely because that made planting and harvesting more efficient and easier but because, as the farmer expressed it, "A straight plowed field is a pretty thing to see. It's like going to church."

SEXUALITY

That religion expresses itself sensuously is abundantly obvious. That it has sexual expressions is, perhaps, not so obvious, but is also a fact.

[6] D. T. Suzuki, *Zen Buddhism* (Garden City, N.Y.: Doubleday, Anchor, 1956), pp. 293–294.

The excitement and mysteriousness of sexuality must have bee
both fascinating and awesome to primitive and ancient man. The al
pervasive nature of the sex instinct, its imperious demands, it
mystery, its pleasures must have brought it early into the ambit o
religious belief and ritual. The startling nature of sex must hav
appeared quite magical to the primitive mind, as indeed it ofte
does to the civilized mind. Everywhere throughout nature the mira
cle of fertility operated extravagantly, displaying abundance of nev
life in animals, plants, and women. Around such a phenomenon i
was natural that an aura of religiousness would develop, and i
many cases a priesthood to systematize it. Once ritualized, phalli
worship influenced many aspects of religion from the defloration o
virgins, to the ritually depicted fecundation of the Earth Mothe
by the Sky God in the annual rites of spring, and to the elaborat
programs of temple prostitution carried on in such places as Baby
lon, Corinth, and, even for a while, in Jerusalem.

Without pursuing this matter unnecessarily far, we shall ob
serve a few examples of sexuality in several of the world religions
past and present.

First, in Greece: Sexuality among the Gods   In numerous crea
tion myths the sex act accounts for the origin of the world. In Gree
and Roman mythology, for example, the primordial chaos was af
fected by Love and from this, Earth and Sky were formed. Earth
and Sky then mated and gave birth to the Elder Gods (the Titans)
Two of these Elder Gods mated and bore five children: Zeus
Poseidon, Hades, Demeter, and Hera, who along with their childre
became the Gods of Mt. Olympus. All of whom were like Greek
twelve feet tall, with all the virtues and vices of Greeks exagger
ated, including an appetite for sex. Of all the Gods, Zeus was the
most powerful. He was the supreme ruler of men and Gods, but fo
all his power he had some weaknesses. The Fates and Destiny ofte
opposed him successfully. He was not omniscient. He was some
times fooled by both Gods and men. Also, he had a devastating
weakness for shapely females, both divine and mortal. Out of this
affection/affliction, Zeus had numerous love affairs that resulted in
some famous progeny (both divine and human): the Three Graces
the Nine Muses, Diana, Apollo, Mercury, Minerva, Hercules,
Perseus, and others. Zeus was actually married to Hera and had
three offspring by her: Mars, Hebe, the Goddess of youth, and

Vulcan. As might be expected, Hera was justifiably jealous of Zeus' escapades, and some of Zeus' female companions felt Hera's wrath beyond what they actually deserved. The nymph Callisto was one.

Callisto was a nymph of rare beauty who belonged to the company of Diana the Huntress. One day Callisto lay down for a rest in a forest glade. Zeus spied her and was immediately smitten with passionate desire. He transformed himself into the form of Diana and wakened the slumbering nymph. Unsuspecting at first, Callisto permitted this "Diana" to embrace her, but quickly the lovely nymph was alarmed by an ardor too intense to be considered sisterly. She began to fight desperately, but to no avail. Zeus had his way. When Diana discovered that Callisto was no longer a virgin, she drove the poor nymph from her company. And then, when Callisto gave birth to Zeus' child, Hera who had discovered her husband's infidelity with the nymph, moved in for her revenge. She turned the hapless nymph into a shaggy bear. Callisto's son, named Arcas, grew to manhood and himself became a hunter. One day while hunting in the forest he came upon a bear and was about to kill her. But at the last moment, Zeus, finally contrite, intervened. Sending a whirlwind to catch up mother and son, he set them down among the stars in the heavens, where they can still be seen: the Great Bear and the Little Bear.

On the female side of divine sexuality there was, of course, the famous and infamous Aphrodite. She was not an Olympian by birth (or even a Greek), but probably had her origins in the fertility Goddess Ishtar of Mesopotamia. The Greek myth had it that she was born from the foam of the sea near the island of Cyprus and was taken as a visitor to Olympus by gentle Zephyr, where she so charmed the Gods with her beauty that they all wanted to marry her; but Zeus gave her to the ugliest of all the Gods, his son, the lame Vulcan. This may not have been exactly what Aphrodite wanted, for she soon fell into the habit of being unfaithful to her husband, or, perhaps, it was not spite that led her astray but her warm-blooded nature. Nevertheless, stray she did, and on one occasion quite embarrassingly so. (It was reported that the Gods and Goddesses of Olympus all liked this story very much, and kept it alive as a choice piece of gossip.) It was Apollo who first became aware of the fact that Aphrodite and Mars were meeting clandestinely, even in the bedroom of the house where she and Vulcan lived. Apollo reported this to Vulcan, who was at first angry, and then vengeful. He devised a punishment in the form of an embarrassment. Vulcan, who was the most inventive and dexterous of the Gods, proceeded to fabricate a net of bronze with links so fine that they were invisible to the naked eye. This he spread over his marriage couch, and then hid himself nearby. When Aphrodite and her lover slipped into the room and began to make love on that bed, Vulcan quickly drew the net tight and imprisoned the two lovers in shameful embrace. He then threw open the doors of the bedchamber and invited all the Gods and Goddesses to view the spectacle.

All of this may resemble an X-rated movie; our purpose, however, is not pornographic but to illustrate that in some religions, among some Gods, sexuality was a very active dimension.

Second, Religious Prostitution   We have already observed that fertility ceremonies were performed annually in the Baal religion of ancient Palestine. The same kind of fecundation rituals were common practically everywhere in the ancient and primitive world. In addition to such sexually involved religious practices as fertility rites, rites of passage (from childhood to adulthood), virgin defloration, and marriage, there developed also in many religions the practice of temple prostitution. As we observed, not even the Yahweh-worshipping, moral-minded Hebrews escaped this sort of thing. In the days of Manasseh, especially, Jerusalem was invaded by the fertility Gods, and along with those Gods, temple prostitutes, both male and female.[7] Nevertheless, overt sexuality was rarely more than a peripheral aspect of the Hebrew religion, and temple prostitution was short lived. Manasseh's son Josiah in 622 B.C. put a stop to it when he made a sweeping reform in favor of Yahweh-worship. The same was not so of Israel's great northern neighbor.

In the cult of Mylitta (the Babylonian Aphrodite), prostitution was fully endorsed as a formal part of public worship. There were temple prostitutes, and there was also sexual congress for religious reasons between men and women who were not normally religious prostitutes. The Greek historian Herodotus has given a graphic, perhaps eyewitness account of one aspect of this sex-centered worship.

The Babylonians have one most shameful custom. Every woman born in the country must once in her life go and sit in the precinct

[7] See II Kings, 22:7.

of Aphrodite, and there have intercourse with a stranger. Many of
the wealthier sort, who are too proud to mix with the others, drive
in covered carriages to the precinct, followed by a goodly train of
attendants, and there take their station. But the larger number seat
themselves within the holy enclosure with sheaves of string about
their heads, and here there is always a great crowd, some coming
and others going; lines of cord make out paths in all directions
among the women, and the strangers pass along them to make their
choice. A woman who has once taken her seat is not allowed to return home till one of the strangers throws a silver coin into her lap,
and takes her with him beyond the holy enclosure. When he throws
the coin, he says these words: "I summon you in the name of the
goddess Mylitta." The silver coin may be of any size; it cannot be
refused, for that is forbidden by law, since once it is thrown it is
sacred. The woman goes with the first man who throws her money,
and rejects no one. When she has had intercourse with him, and so
satisfied the goddess, she returns home, and from that time on no
gift however great will prevail with her. Such of the women who
are tall and beautiful are soon released, but those who are ugly have
to stay a long time before they can fulfill the law. Some have waited
three or four years in the precinct. A custom very much like this is
found in certain parts of the Island of Cyprus.[8]

We should make a special observation about the sex act as a
religious act. There is an almost infinite difference between people
engaging in a sexual debauchery and people performing a religious
rite in which sexuality is present or even predominant. Sexuality in
religion creates its own "occult atmosphere," whereas sexuality in
debauchery does not. There was a vast difference between an ancient Roman orgy and an ancient fertility ceremony. In a Roman
revel, which was a large drinking bout interspersed with other
sensual pleasures, the aim was pure pleasure, and at best might
have had some kind of cathartic value—a means of letting off
steam. In the cultic rites that employed sexuality, the aim was not
pleasure, but religious ecstasy. This latter type of performance was
a supernatural occasion and in it sex was used as a means of heightening a religious mystery. The purpose was not to enjoy sexual
excitement, but to experience religious emotions. The Maenads
(raving women) of a certain form of the Dionysian religion, who

---

[8] *History of The Passion Wars*, 2 vols., trans. Geo. Rawlinson, (Chicago:
Regnery, 1949), I, par. 199.

danced with bodies convulsing in orgasmic frenzy, were said not to be "in sex" but rather to be in "enthusiasm," which, in the Greek meaning of the word, means "God-possessed." Even in the medieval witches' sabbats, the indications are that the participants were in "enthusiasm," in a state of trance and dissociation.

Third, Sexuality and Islam   In the Muslim *Qur'ān* both sensual enjoyment and sexual pleasure are promised as the rewards of the true believers. In Paradise the righteous "shall be in a pleasing life, in a lofty garden, whose fruits are nigh to cull—'Eat and drink with good digestion, for what ye did aforetime in the days that have gone by'" (The Infallible). "Verily, the pious [shall be] in gardens and pleasure, enjoying what their Lord has given them. . . . Reclining on couches . . . wed to large-eyed maids" (The Mount).

Fourth, Repressed Sexuality   Christianity, with its austerity, has had a history of driving the sexuality of religion underground—into the subconscious. An elderly, very lovely nun of the Catholic Church, while addressing a large audience, spoke of the joy of being part of a religious order. She pictured vividly the fact that unlike most women, she would be buried in her "wedding dress"—in the habit of her order, which was, according to her, the gown she was wearing the day she became "the bride of Christ." There was nothing untoward or immodest in her remarks. She was simply reporting that wives can be virgins and remain so if they are married to God. Indeed, that God can be related symbolically in marriage is solemnly declared in the very act of the marriage ceremony.

> Dearly beloved, we are gathered here . . . to join this man and this woman in holy matrimony, which is an honorable estate, instituted by God, and signifying unto us the mythical union which exists between Christ and his Church.

In this same kind of reference the *Song of Songs* (Solomon's Song) is of interest here. It is a passionate poetic dialogue between a dark-skinned woman of great beauty and a magnificent white-bodied man, and it is a part of the Jewish Bible and the Christian Old Testament. What this poem is supposed to be has been given a number of interpretations. It has been called an allegory of the relationship between the divine and the human. (If so, it is an exceedingly sensual and sexual one.) It has been called a drama celebrating the marriage of Solomon to Pharaoh's daughter. It has been called an epithalamium composed for a royal wedding. It has been called a love poem. Some scholars believe that it was originally a fertility rite in a fertility cult popular in the Near East, and in Jewish experience even as late as the fifth century B.C. The cult was concerned with the union of the Baal of Heaven and the Mother Earth Goddess. Involved in the cult were ritual practices intended to promote the return of the vegetation and the assurance of a good harvest. A prominent feature of the cult was the death and resurrection of the God. He died in the spring as the sown seed or in summer at the parching of the vegetation by the blistering sun. When this happened his wife and lover, the Goddess, sought him in the underworld, and when she found him and he was restored, they celebrated their marriage in a joyous fashion. Whichever interpretation one subscribes to, he must admit that sex and religion are closely related in this scripture, as they are in the marriage ceremony and also, at least with some, in the chastity of nuns.

Fifth, Yahweh Remains Asexual   In spite of aberrations (e.g., permitting such things as fertility cults and temple prostitutions to occur in Israel), the Jews were first among religion builders to emasculate God—to remove sexuality from the Godhead. God Yahweh stood aloof and alone, without consort, without phallic symbolism. To be sure, as the God of creation he was the inventor of the sexual process, but he never himself engaged. He said, "Be fruitful and multiply" and he called his creation "good." Sexuality was divinely ordained. Only the misuse of sex was evil. As a part of God's law, Jews are supposed to marry and enjoy the intimacies of sexual pleasure. Indeed, some rabbis tell us that the Sabbath is not properly kept unless husband and wife make it joyous with coitus. Lovemaking is proper and good; it is ordained of God, but in no direct, personal way is it an activity of God.

One reason why Christianity was such a scandal to Judaism was the purported impregnation of Mary by God's Spirit. To propose that Mary's pregnancy was something that God did to her was blasphemy in the extreme. For 1200 years the Hebrew religion had struggled against the sexuality of pagan Gods. It is not surprising, then, that they were not about to revert to a former "evil in the sight of the Lord."

It should be noted that although the founders and protectors of Judaism avoided the phallic symbol as a symbol for God, they, on numerous occasions, used a marriage metaphor in reference to Yahweh. The Prophet Hosea, for example, who is often called the prophet of love, tells a beautiful story of a marriage that shattered in the perversity of a wayward wife who deserted husband and children and ran off with another man. Before long she and her lover fell on hard times and she turned first to prostitution and finally was seized to be sold into slavery to pay their debts. The husband, who still loved his wife in spite of her violation of their marriage, learning of her situation, rescued her by buying her back. He then restored her to her former position as wife and mother in his home. All she had to do was repent her ways and become a faithful wife. Hosea's account was a metaphor of the relation between Yahweh and Israel. God, the loving husband, would restore Israel, his whoring wife, if only Israel would repent and live in fidelity.

In numerous places in the Jewish scriptures, Yahweh is depicted not in the role of fertility God, not as a God of sexuality, but as a husband to a people—to Israel. He is seen not in the dimension of sexuality but in the dimension of love.

LOVE

The fact of sensuousness in religion and the endorsement of sexuality is not to be denied. Aphrodite (sexuality) is a part of religion, though disguised at times she may be. Also, Eros (love) is part of religion. Eros is the God of those who are "in love," not merely "in sex." Love as Eros is both different from sexuality, and more than sexuality. C. S. Lewis, observing how Eros differs from Aphrodite, says in his *Four Loves:*

> Now Eros makes a man really want, not a woman, but one particular woman. In some mysterious but quite indisputable fashion the lover desires the Beloved herself, not the pleasure she can give.[9]

Speaking of Eros/Love in the context of religion, William Evans states in his article in *The International Standard Bible Encyclopedia:*

[9] C. S. Lewis, *The Four Loves* (New York: Harcourt Brace Jovanovich, 1960), p. 135.

Love, whether used of God or man, is an earnest and anxious desire for, and an active and beneficent interest in, the well-being of the one loved.

And St. Paul, in his letter to the church in Corinth, identifies other characteristics of Eros/Love:

Love is patient and kind; love is not jealous or conceited or proud; love is not ill-mannered, or selfish, or irritable; love does not keep a record of wrongs; love is not happy with evil, but is happy with the truth. Love never gives up: its faith, hope and patience never fail (1 Cor. 13:4–7, *Good News for Modern Man*, American Bible Society, 1966).

Although sexuality is part of Eros as it exists between man and woman, it is not all of Eros, or even the essential part. And where love exists between man and man, friend and friend, neighbor and neighbor, God and man (as affection, brotherhood, respect, agapé), sexuality is scarcely a characteristic at all.

In Eros/Love it is the person himself/herself who is precious and desired and loved, not simply what that person can do for the lover. The statement sometimes heard— "He wants a woman"—is almost completely misleading. He wants pleasure, and a woman is simply the vehicle for his pleasure. This is far different from the fact of being "in love." To be in love is to desire a person, not a thing; to want to see that person happy, to give that person happiness. In such a relationship sexual pleasure, and even friendship, are simply additional boons in the relationship.

However, Eros/Love does not only flow from the lover's passion to give; it also is motivated by the lover's need for "nesting." It is when the beloved returns love that the capacity of Eros/Love is fully demonstrated, and the desired *miracle* occurs. A lover finds joy in simply loving, but finds something even more joyous when the beloved responds in kind. A mutual penetration takes place, a common ground of being is accomplished, and the two lovers are no longer alone in the world, or alone in themselves. There is a nesting in each other. The story of the creation of the first woman from the rib of the man may not be scientifically factual, but it is superbly true metaphorically. God had placed Adam alone in the Garden, and Adam was lonely. So God created all sorts of possible companions for him—singing birds, lithely beautiful animals, fascinatingly colorful fish in the pond. But Adam remained locked inside himself in a world of things out there: a lone and lonely subject, in a world of objects, until She was formed, bone of his bones, flesh of his flesh. And with her coming, loneliness ended. And this, we are informed, is why a man and a woman leave parents, and the world out there, and cleave to each other, "and they become one flesh," yes, and one spirit.

In religion it is God, or someone or something that God loves, who is the beloved. As examples of this, one might note (1) the biblical commandment: "And thou shalt love the Lord thy God with all thy heart, and with all thy soul, and with all thy might." In this it is God himself who is to be loved. But (2) in the teachings of the rabbis it is especially God's Law (Torah) which is to be loved. Indeed, it is said that if one could either believe in God or keep God's Holy Law, but not both, he should keep the Law, for God wants more that man should love the Law than that they should love him. Also (3) in Christian tradition it is Christ who is truly the beloved, Christ who is the object of the believers' greatest devotion. Interestingly, certain "Death of God" theologians contended, and perhaps accurately, that Christianity could survive without God, but not without the beloved Jesus. It is obviously a fact that Christians as Christians love what God loves; namely his Son. And (4) Christians are not the only people who love the manifestation of God on earth; the Hindu disciples of Vishnu-Krishna do the same.

How one loves the beloved God is, of course, affected by the tradition in which the loving happens, and by the individual doing the loving. Some love adoringly, as the worshippers of Krishna and Christ. Some love loyally, as the Jews keep the Law that God loves. Some love sentimentally; they walk in the garden alone, with dew on the roses, and they talk and walk and have an adolescent love experience. Some fall down weeping in the torn love of Good Friday and the devastation of Crucifixion. Some love God by loving wife, child, neighbor, stranger, enemy, and all who are in need: "When did I see you hungry? thirsty? naked? in prison?" (See Matthew 25:31*f.*)

Concerning this last kind of God love (loving God by loving men), we might note, again, that the Jewish-Christian command to love one's neighbor as one's self, and to do unto others as one would be done by, is to be found in virtually the same form in all of the major religions of the world. The reason for loving one's fellow man, at least in the Near Eastern religions, is because God loves them. And equally, the reason for loving God is because God loves us. The writer of the letter called First John puts it as follows:

> Dear friends! Let us love one another, for love comes from God. Whoever loves is a child of God and knows God. Whoever does not love does not know God, because God is love. This is how God showed his love for us: he sent his only Son into the world that we might have life through him. This is what love is: it is not that we have loved God, but that he loved us and sent his Son. . . .
>   . . . if this is how God loved us, then we should love one another (John 4:7–11, *Good News for Modern Man*).

God loved man and sent his Son, so say the Christians. Out of love for man Krishna came, and the other Avatars of Vishnu also, so say the Hindus. Once a Jew wrote God's love for Israel in a passionately vivid account preserved today in the eleventh chapter of the Book of Hosea.

> When Israel was a child, I loved him,
> And out of Egypt I called my son.
>
> . . .
>
> How can I give you up, O E'phriam!
> How can I hand you over, O Israel!
>
> . . .
>
> My heart recoils within me,
> My compassion grows warm and tender.
>
> I will not execute my fierce anger,
> I will not again destroy E'phriam
> For I am God and not man,
> The holy One in your midst,
> And I will not come to destroy.
>   (Hosea 11:1f, Revised Standard Version)

CHARITY/AGAPÉ

Important as it is, Eros/Love is not the last word in love. There is, some claim, a love that is devoid entirely of the dimension of need on the part of the lover. It is completely gift love, and God is the giver; God is the lover. With no need to be loved, God simply, openhandedly, loves. Rain falls on the just and unjust alike. Krishna comes for everyone, as does Christ. God's saving message through the Prophet Muhammad is for all mankind. The Buddha's wisdom is open to all men. Israel's ultimate kingdom is not for Jews only.

It is contended that God loves because it is God's nature to love. God *is* love, and his loving is always outbound, toward people. And in many cases it is not even in the intention of the Giver. God gives without forethought, without knowing, simply because he is what he is. According to Greek mythology, the primal chaos first stirred by Love; from thence all else emerged. According to Hindu philosophy, God Brahman is, and all else is simply himself given. In other systems of religious thought, God gives intentionally, lovingly: he gave Moses to the Hebrews in his loving desire to rescue them from bondage in Egypt; he gave himself in his Son, the Christians say, to suffering and death, because he loved mankind.

This love has a name of its own. It is called Charity or Agapé; both words in original usage mean love. Charity/Agapé is gift love, especially the divine gift of life: life now, and in many religions, life to come.

Charity/Agapé is not limited only to God action. People too can love givingly, and when they do, they are, in many religious traditions, being most like God. In the New Testament letter called First John (4:10), it is declared that "God is love and whoever lives in love lives in him." And if one lives in love at times not even knowing it, he is perhaps more like God than when he plans and works to be charitable. There is a story told about a young man and a bishop riding on a train, in the club car with several other men. None of them knew each other. But several of the men soon identified themselves as businessmen and began to talk about lucrative businesses. One wished he could get into the oil business; another wished he had gone into plastics; another sang the praises of IBM. One said that he just wished he had a million dollars and would not have to be in any business at all. Finally the young man, upset by the lack of human concern, the lack of idealism that he found among the talkers, blurted into the conversation that he only wished that he could live his life knowing that he was helping people. In the embarrassed silence that followed, the bishop interposed a slightly different point of view. He said, "To want to live your life knowing that you are helping people is a most admirable ambition.

There is only one greater." The young man asked him what could possibly be greater. And the bishop replied: "To live your life doing good without knowing it."

Be that as it may, there would be one tremendous benefit in having a God who not only loved, but loved purposefully. Such love would go even beyond the nesting love of Eros, and would provide the saving love of divine forgiveness and acceptance. Jacques Maritain makes the point in his *Existence and the Existent*. First, he points out that a person is known inwardly, as he really is, only by himself, if at all. That other men see him as an "it," as an object. To be known as an object is to be forever unknown and wounded in one's identity.

> It is to be always unjustly known—whether the *he* who sees condemns . . . or whether . . . the 'he' does honor. . . . A Tribunal is a masquerade where the accused stands accoutered in a travesty of himself. . . . The more the judges stray from the crude outward criteria with which formerly they contented themselves, and strive to take account of degrees of inner responsibility, the more they reveal that the truth of him whom they judge remains unknowable to human justice. Interrogated by such a tribunal, Jesus owed it to Himself to remain silent.[10]

We have suggested that this wound of broken identity can be at least soothed in the nest of Eros/Love. Maritain proposes that it can be healed in the embrace of God's love. Only God knows a person in his subjectivity, in his inwardness. Only to God is a person open and known. And even if God condemns for what he knows, the broken identity is repaired. The person is understood. The idea that we are known completely, that no secrets are hidden, may reduce us at first to fear and trembling, because of the evil that is inside us. But, as Maritain proposes,

> on deeper reflection, how can we keep from thinking that the God Who knows us and knows all those poor beings who jostle us and whom we know as objects, whose wretchedness we mostly perceive—how can we keep from thinking that God Who knows all these in their subjectivity, in the nakedness of their wounds and

[10] Jacques Maritain, *Existence and the Existent*, trans. L. Galantiere and B. Phelon (Garden City, N.Y.: Doubleday, Image, 1960; published earlier, 1948), pp. 83–84.

their secret evil, must know also the secret beauty of that nature which He has bestowed upon them? . . . To know that we are known to God is not merely to experience justice, but is also to experience mercy.[11]

Being known, our identity is healed; being seen in both evil and beauty, we are forgiven and accepted, not for a little while, as with our beloved, but forever with God.

[11] Ibid., p. 85.

sixteen

Religion:
Esoteric Experience

The religious experience occurs in a special kind of consciousness, often called the mystical consciousness. It is a consciousness that results when the believer and the essence of a divine reality unite in some kind of incarnation. This can occur in an incarnation of *possession,* as in Shamanism, where the human being is seized and invaded by the divine reality; or it can happen as an incarnation of *presence,* as in worship, where one simply senses the nearness, the availability, the presence of the supernatural or extranatural divine reality; or it can happen as an incarnation of *identity,* as in mysticism, where the normal human consciousness bursts asunder and a new egoless, ineffable consciousness expands the human mind into a divine mind.

We shall look directly at these three kinds of religious experience (possession, worshipful presence, mystical identity), but first we shall take time to observe that the religious experience is noetic in character: it is not simply an ecstasy, but a way of knowing. Besides the kind of rationalized knowledge that theology affords, there is, in the experience of religion, a directly intuited knowledge: esoteric knowing, intuitional knowing, which without formal logic or dialectics makes known its "truth" directly, forcefully, and usually irresistibly.

ESOTERIC KNOWING

Besides the empirical and rational methods of obtaining knowledge, which we observed in chapter five, and knowledge from revelation, which we observed in chapter seven, there is another kind of knowledge which arises out of inner and immediate experience. One knows, for example, what it is to have a toothache, or what it is to be afraid, or to be in love, or to think, or to be saved. This kind of knowledge might properly be called "enlightenment." A light in the mind gets turned on and one "sees" things one has never seen before. One knows something directly that could not possibly be known in any other way. This is esoteric knowing. It is subjective and private, and it is tremendously significant. It is the kind of knowing that informs and certifies aesthetic values, for example, that certain music is beautiful; and ethical values, for example, that human beings have rights; and religious values, for example, that God is real and that one has been spiritually renewed.

The knowledge indigenous to religious experience occurs primarily in the private awareness of a human consciousness, and this is especially so in the case of mysticism. Mysticism is esoteric knowing of the highest order. But because we shall examine mysticism later in this chapter, we shall defer at this point to another kind of religious experience in which enlightenment occurs: conversion, and observe three examples of it. One example is of an Eskimo conversion and enlightenment; one is a Hindu conversion and enlightenment; and the other is the autobiographical account written by John Wesley of his own conversion and enlightenment.

Conversion Knowing   The Danish Arctic explorer and ethnographer Kurt Rasmussen records the following account told him by an Eskimo shaman who, as a neophyte, had gone into solitude in the wilderness in search of divine inspiration. There, he told Rasmussen,

> I soon became melancholy. I would sometimes fall to weeping and feel unhappy without knowing why. Then for no reason all would suddenly be changed, and I felt a great inexplicable joy, a joy so powerful that I could not restrain it, but had to break into song, a mighty song, with room for only one word: Joy, Joy! And I had to use the full strength of my voice. And then in the midst of such a fit of mysterious and overwhelming delight I became a shaman. I could

see and hear in a totally different way. I had gained my enlightenment.[1]

The Eskimo shaman experienced enlightenment, which is an inner
knowing; a vision of ultimate truth. This report is not unlike that
told of the great Siddharta Gautama, founder of Buddhism. Gautama too went into solitude searching for divine inspiration. For six
years he was an unsuccessful searcher. He tried, perhaps too hard,
by giving himself rigorously first to the practice of meditation and
then to severe ascetic discipline—the two common paths to salvation in India. But none of it was of any avail. Then one day, after
years of enormous effort, he gave up trying and sat down under the
Bodhi-tree. There it abruptly happened: suddenly, completely, he
knew the answer. He experienced enlightenment, and with it liberation. Siddharta suddenly knew something he had never known before. He knew a principle of life which at once both shattered
human reality and re-formed it new. There is a story that Gautama,
after he had become enlightened (i.e., Buddha), was asked if he
were a God. He said, "No." Then he was asked if he were a saint.
Again he said, "No." Finally he was asked, "Then what are you?"
And he answered, "I am awake." His conversion was an awakening,
a discovery of transforming knowledge. He saw a new way, and
seeing it became a new man—a liberated man.

The account of John Wesley's esoteric experience is of the same
life-shaking character as that of the Eskimo shaman and the
founder of Buddhism, although it is, with a certain British reserve,
dramatically understated in Wesley's *Journal*. Like the Buddha and
the Eskimo, John Wesley too was a searcher after divine light. He
was a professor at Oxford University and had gone to the New
World, to the Colony of Georgia, and in a kind of low-key religious
frenzy, obviously searching for something he did not find. Except he
saw it, as it were, afar off, in the faith of the simple Moravians
(Peter Böhler, in particular) he met on shipboard. But he did not
get it himself until, on his return to London, he let himself be
persuaded to go to an anabaptist-type meeting. The following is
part of the entry of Wesley's diary for May 24, 1738:

[1] Kurt Rasmussen, *The Intellectual Culture of the Iglulik Eskimos*, Copen-
hagen, 1929, p. 119.

In the evening I went very unwilling to a society in Aldersgate Street where one was reading Luther's preface to the *Epistle to the Romans.* About a quarter before nine, while he was describing the change which God works in the heart through faith in Christ, I felt my heart strangely warmed. I felt I did trust Christ, Christ alone for salvation; and an assurance was given me that He had taken away *my* sins; even *mine*, and saved *me* from the law of sin and death.[2]

Esoteric knowing possesses religious significance because it is that knowing which brings man into encounter with the transcendent source and meaning of religion. This source and meaning are experienced as being in some sense the ultimate reality, the ultimate truth, or at least that reality to which man owes his final allegiance.

Transforming Knowledge   Another important thing to observe about this kind of knowledge is that it does not just inform the mind; it transforms the life. Or, probably more correctly, it is not the knowledge that transforms, but the coming of the knowledge. Something happens (conversion, for example) and when it happens the person, as he is "informed" is also "transformer." It is the transformation, the happening, that makes the difference. We shall now proceed to examine more closely the religious "happenings" of possession, presence, and identity.

THE POSSESSION GAME

Joseph Campbell, in his *The Masks of God: Primitive Mythology* points out that "the mask in a primitive festival is revered and experienced as a veritable apparition of the mythical being that it represents—even though everyone knows that a man made the mask and that a man is wearing it."[3] This primitive ability to be seized with belief is not simply a primitive ability. Sophisticated, civilized persons are also capable of being so seized with belief. For example, in the celebration of the Eucharist, the Catholic knows that he is eating bread, and often rather palate-sticking, tasteless bread at that, but he "plays" the part of believing until he is seized with the believing. It is not unlike children pretending that there are

[2] *The Journal of John Wesley*, Epworth Press, 1938, Volume 1, pp. 475–476.
[3] Joseph Campbell, *The Masks of God: Primitive Mythology* (New York: Viking, 1959), p. 21.

ghosts in the bedroom until there really are ghosts in the bedroom. Even when the religious practices are known to be different from what they represent, they become religious practices when the game of "as if" takes on the aura of "as is," and the man behind the mask does not simply represent the God; he *is* the God. The bread does not simply remind one of Christ; it *is* the Christ. The person involved must be seized by the game if it is to be a game that counts as real religion for him.

Some people have difficulty "psyching" themselves from the attitude of "as if" to the attitude of "as is." Their modern skepticisms must be purposefully set aside. They must ease themselves into the game, let the ritual aura take over, before they can return to the capacity of childlikeness, which has been all but lost in the machinations of a modern world that makes few accommodations (except during festival times) for the innocence of true believing. This, however, is an affliction that affects only those people who have come to live in the modern, twentieth-century world of science, business, and technology. Much of the rest of the world (and the world of the past) has no such difficulty.

KINDS OF DIVINE POSSESSION

Professional Possession   Everywhere in the phenomenon of religion, we observe persons who are caught up in a frenzy of religious excitement. They become what is called spirit-possessed or demon-possessed. Sometimes this possession has a kind of professional character. The persons possessed are possessed on purpose at their own command. In the Book of I Samuel, we read how in the days of Samuel and Saul and David there were "companies of prophets" who met at the hill shrines in Palestine and led by lute and harp and fife and drum were filled with "prophetic rapture" and danced naked and in ecstasy. There are, of course, today the Near Eastern dervishes, that is, the members of various Muslim orders of ascetics, some of which practice the achievement of collective ecstasy through whirling dances and the chanting of religious words. And there are in all primitive communities shamans and Shamanism.[4] I. M. Lewis in his book, *Ecstatic Religion*, tells us that

---

[4] The word *shaman* comes from the reindeer-herding people, the Tungus of Siberia, and literally means "one who is excited, moved, raised."

a shaman is a priest who has become possessed by and/or possesses one or more spirits. He is a master of spirits, summoning them at will to assist in his religious duties.

> A shaman is a person of either sex who has mastered spirits and who can at will introduce them into his own body. Often in fact, he permanently incarnates these spirits and can control their manifestations, going into controlled states of trance.[5]

Besides a kind of professional ecstatic seizure, there is also, throughout religion and religious history, a more general form of spirit possession which we shall refer to as compensatory seizure—compensatory in the sense that although it may seem to be demonic and undesirable, it is often, in fact, an experience full of compensations for the person possessed.

Compensatory Possession   As we have seen in our consideration of the demonic, most of the people in bygone days, and many people today, accept the idea of demons possessing human beings as obviously (even by observation) true. Sometimes demons even possess human beings sexually; for example, the sons of God (angels) in Genesis "who came in unto the daughters of men, and they bore children of them"; the incubi and succubi who seduced both men and women. Also the "victims" did not always consider themselves especially victimized. Possession is not always regarded as something terrible. Indeed, more often possession instead of being depriving is compensatory. In getting at this aspect of spirit possession, I. M. Lewis points out that many instances of what appear to be demonical illnesses as viewed by primitive men are, by primitive women, transformed into both compensatory events and therapeutic ecstasies.

Lewis is convinced that spirit possession and possession cults are strongly motivated by the unconscious need to protest the inferior status imposed upon the cultists by the general society in which they live. This, he thinks, is especially true where women are concerned. Those forms of possession regarded initially as illnesses are virtually restricted to women, and they are "thinly disguised protest movements directed against the dominant sex."[6] When

[5] I. M. Lewis, *Ecstatic Religion* (Harmondsworth, Middlesex, Eng.: Penguin, 1971), p. 51.
[6] Ibid., p. 31.

pathogenic spirits come possessing they seem to do so capriciously, with no apparent rhyme or reason. They do not come to punish the wicked. They have no concern for moral behavior. They do not defend the society's ethical code. As this is the case, one would expect to find that the spirits are quite indiscriminate in their selection of human prey, but Lewis points out that this is not exactly the case. The spirits "show a predilection for the weak and the downtrodden . . . the underprivileged and oppressed." The phenomenon of possession is especially prevalent among women in those cultures where women are arrogantly repressed by male domination.

In such cultures the women, far more than the men, are assailed with illnesses caused by spirit possession. But in this context, Lewis makes the interesting observation that in many cases the "added misery" is in fact a blessing in disguise. The woman is compensated by the attention she gets in her "illness," and, one might suspect, from the domestic inconvenience caused her husband and the expense he must bear to get her cured; that is, to get her exorcized.

From Lewis we get some indication of this sort of thing as it occurs among the Somali people of northeast Africa who live in what is now called the Somali Republic. The Somalis are Muslims. Their culture is completely male-dominated. Somali women are to be at all times weak and submissive. But being weak and submissive does not always have its rewards in a responsive male gentleness and concern, for the Somali culture is rigidly puritanical. Any open display of affection and love between men and women is unmanly and sentimental and must be suppressed. Furthermore, as polygamy is permissible, a wife may be at any time affronted by the establishment of another, younger, more attractive wife in the household. As elsewhere in Islam, Somalis believe that demons (jinn) lurk everywhere ready to attack and possess unwary persons. These creatures are thought to be greedy, desiring dainty foods, luxurious clothing, jewelry, perfume, and other finery; and perhaps not surprisingly, women are the prime targets of these spirits. The spirits are called *sar*, and the afflicted woman is said to have been seized by the sar. The sar spirits demand various forms of luxurious gifts. These requests are voiced through the lips of the afflicted woman and uttered with an authority that the woman normally would not dare to assert. The spirits, also, have their own language which is interpreted, for a fee, by a female shaman. It is only when the costly demands have been met, as well as the expense involved in mounting a cathartic dance attended by other women and directed by the shaman, that the victim can be expected to recover, and even then the recovery may be only temporary.

Because the men believe in sar spirits, they are inclined to accept the idea of sar possession of their women. However, sometimes the men become skeptical and begin to suspect the genuineness of some of the seizures. Normally the husband will endure a few bouts with the sar spirits, but if they happen too often and his wife becomes a regular member of a circle of sar devotees, the husband's patience may wear out, and he may begin to exorcise his domestic problem himself. "If a good beating will not do the trick (and it often seems effective), there is always the threat of divorce." That usually works, so Lewis reports.

We are saying, then that spirit possession, even when regarded as an illness, as an affliction, may effect a sense of power and importance in the life of the possessed which is not otherwise possible.[7]

Ecstasy Possession   The greatest rewards of spiritual possession, however, are not found in a few trinkets or in a temporary psychological lift that comes from escaping briefly from repressive social restraints. It comes in the ecstasy of a consciousness that has become dislocated and fled to some ethereal heights or has been taken over by an enlightening and joy-giving spiritual being. We referred to the "conversion" of the Eskimo shaman as he expressed it to the Danish explorer and ethnographer Kurt Rasmussen. From melancholia and weeping suddenly the Eskimo, about to become a shaman, was transported into a great, inexplicable joy. In the midst of mysterious and overwhelming delight, he became a shaman. He could experience things in a totally different way, and this had happened, he went on to say, "in such a manner that it was not only I who could see through the darkness of life, but the same bright

[7] Various explanations are given for the phenomenon of mental dislocation or possession. Sometimes it is explained naturalistically; sometimes supernaturalistically. For example, the frenetic dancing which seized whole communities in Europe in the fifteenth century was diagnosed in Holland as demonic possession and was exorcized, while in Italy it was diagnosed as resulting from the bite of a tarantula spider; thus the name Tarantism.

light also shone out of me, imperceptible to human beings but visible to all spirits of earth and sky and sea, and these now came to me to become my helping spirits."[8]

Francis Thompson speaks with bitter-sweet eloquence of the tragedy of resisting the conquest of divine possession; of those who flee the pursuing spirit "down the nights and down the days . . . down the arches of the years," pleading outlaw-wise, running from the hound of heaven;

> From those strong Feet that followed, followed after.
>> But with unhurrying chase
>> And unperturbed pace,
> Deliberate speed, majestic instancy
>> They beat—-and a Voice beat
>> More instant than the Feet—
> "All things betray thee, who betrayest Me."[9]

It is the joy which comes in submission, in being possessed by the pursuing spirit, that is the reward the shaman seeks, and Jacob wrestling in the night, and Gautama, pale and emaciated, sitting under the Bo-tree, and Wesley outward bound for the Colony of Georgia.

The experience of divine possession is so intimate that it is often symbolized as a marriage. We have already observed this in the interpretation that sees Hosea's story of the husband and the wife as being the relationship between God and Israel, and in the Christian wedding ceremony that declares that the joining of the man and the woman in matrimony signifies the mystical union which exists between Christ and his Church. But beyond this is the idea that the relationship is not simply symbolic marriage, but actual marriage. Lewis gives two accounts in which this is the situation. First, taking his information from Verrier Elwin's *The Religion of an Indian Tribe* (London, 1955), he reports that a man of the Saora Tribe of Orissa, in India, claims that he married a spirit girl who presented him, in the course of time, with three fine spirit boys, the celestial counterparts of his earthly children.[10] Lewis also

---

[8] Rasmussen, *op. cit.*, p. 119.

[9] See Francis Thompson's "The Hound of Heaven" (London: The Bodley Head) for the full text of this superb poem.

[10] I. M. Lewis, *Ecstatic Religion* (Harmondsworth, Middlesex, England: Penguin, 1971), p. 60.

duplicates a Voodoo marriage certificate which records the mystical union of a woman with her spirit mate Damballah. The certificate officially records that on the sixth of January, 1949, at three o'clock, Damballah Toquan Mirissé and Madame Andrémise Cétoute appeared before the Registrar of Port-au-Prince and were "united by the indissoluble bond of the marriage sacrament." The marriage was certified according to Article 15.1 of the Haitian Code, and witnessed by persons whose names appear thereon.

PRESENCE AND IDENTITY

Worshipful Presence   Some people would hold that Whitehead's statement, quoted at the beginning of our study, that religion is what a person does with his solitariness would more correctly be what happens to a person in his solitariness. Religion is not what we do when we are alone, but what happens to us when we are alone, or more accurately what we become when we are *truly* alone. It is not simply being by yourself, but being in spiritual solitude. It is the soul stillness of the Psalmist when he said, "Be still and know that I am God." It is worship, or in its more extreme dimension, mysticism.

Worship should not be confused with worship service. All organized religions have forms and rituals that are called "worship," but our concern is not with forms and rituals but with human experience: an experience of rapt and even enraptured, attention in which the worshipper feels himself to be in intimate personal relations with Divine Being. The worship service may foster this experience, and even religious ecstasy, but it does not constitute the experience. Worship is not stylized performance, but a personal engagement. The worshipper is involved not simply with his physical behavior, but with his mental and emotional life as well. He feels "caught up" in a heightened awareness of religious values. He senses the reality of something mysterious and awesome, which is, at the same time, congenial, sustaining, and concerned. He feels enlivened and enlightened and joyous, even to the point of tears. Worship is not something easily defined, nor does it occur in all people, or at different times, with the same intensity or significance. Indeed, at times it seems to be little more than a religious kick, evoked by the sight of a crucifix, or a church steeple, or the sound of

a stirring hymn, or even a cheap, popular song of religious senti-
ment, effecting little more than a brief, sentimental exhilaration.
But, at other times, it can be an atunement to mystical consciousness which becomes sheer religious ecstasy.

Religious Mysticism   To understand worship as more than "religious kicks," it might be helpful to look at it in one of its extreme
forms—in the form called mysticism. This degree of religious experience is not common. Not everyone truly experiences it. But it is
universal; that is, it is an experience that has been reported in all
ages and in all religions, and the reports have always added up to
the same kind of experience. Christians may describe it in Christian
terms, Hindus in Hindu terms, Buddhists in Buddhist terms, but no
matter what terms are used, they all describe the same basic experience: one in which the mystic becomes lost in Ultimate Being, in
God, and enjoys an indescribable bliss. The mystical experience
itself is (1) an experience in which the consciousness is flooded with
an awareness of the interrelatedness and unity among all things: a
spiritual ecology which gives all things, including the mystic and
God, a common identity, and (2) an experience of bliss and con-
tentment which passes all human understanding. In the words of
the Hindu *Mandukya Upanishad,* it is an experience "beyond the
senses, beyond all understanding, beyond all expression . . . it is
pure unitary consciousness, wherein awareness of the world and of
multiplicity is completely obliterated. It is ineffable peace. It is the
Supreme Good."[11]

TWO FORMS OF MYSTICISM: EXTROVERTIVE AND INTROVERTIVE   If
the unity and ecstasy of mysticism are accomplished by turning outward to the world, to mankind, and to the cosmos, according to
Walter T. Stace in his *The Teachings of the Mystics,* mysticism is
extrovertive in form. If it is accomplished by turning inward and,
through meditative discipline, penetrating to the deepest level of
human consciousness, it is, according to Stace, introvertive in form.

The extrovertive mystic continues to perceive the world of
people and trees and skies and houses and butterflies, but he sees
them transfigured in such a way that not only physical and biologi-

[11] Quoted by Walter T. Stace, *The Teachings of the Mystics* (New York:
New American Library, Mentor Books, 1960), p. 20.

cal unity is apparent but a spiritual ecology as well. Of this experience Meister Eckhart wrote: "Here all blades of grass, wood, and stone, all things are One." And another mystic, Jacob Böhme, wrote: "In this light my spirit saw through all things and into all creatures and I recognized God in grass and plants." A modern mystic, Sokei-an Sasaki, gave the following account of his experience:

> One day I wiped out all the notions from my mind. I gave up all desire. I discarded all the words with which I thought and stayed in quietude. I felt a little queer—as if I were being carried into something, or as if I were touching some power unknown to me . . . and Ztt! I entered. I lost the boundary of my physical body. I had my skin, of course, but I felt I was standing in the center of the cosmos. I spoke, but my words had lost their meaning. I saw people coming toward me, but all were the same man. All were myself! . . . no individual Mr. Sasaki existed.[12]

This extrovertive form of mysticism is, apparently, a consciousness in which the world is transfigured and unified in one ultimate being.

Introvertive mysticism is much more extreme than extrovertive mysticism in that in this form the ego of the mystic is completely suspended. The experience of unity and ecstasy occurs, but, apparently, the mystic *does not know that he* is experiencing it. He is not experiencing unity and ecstasy; he *is* unity and ecstasy. He is not experiencing God; *he* is God. By arduous techniques (self-mastery) the mystic has systematically shut off all of his normal sensory-intellectual experiences. He does not feel anything, see anything, hear anything, think anything, experience anything. When this state has been truly accomplished, his emptied consciousness is abruptly flooded with pure, nonobjectified experience. He enters perfection, beauty, joy, love, ecstasy, God, and is completely lost to himself. Out of this kind of mystical experience, afterwards when he had returned to the "unreal" real world of normal mortals, the Flemish mystic Jan Van Ruysbroeck wrote:

> In the abyss of this darkness, in which the loving spirit has died to itself, there begin the manifestations of God and eternal life. For in this darkness there shines and is born an incomprehensible Light, which is the Son of God, in whom we behold eternal life. And in

[12] "The Transcendental World," *Zen Notes*, Vol. I, No. 9, p. 5, First Zen Institute of America, New York, 1954.

this Light one becomes seeing; and this Divine Light is given to the simple sight of the spirit, where the spirit receives the brightness which is God Himself, above all gifts and every creaturely activity, in the idle emptiness in which the spirit has lost itself through fruitive love, and where it receives without means the brightness of God, and is changed without interruption into the brightness which it receives . . . this brightness is so great that the loving contemplative, in the ground wherein he rests, sees and feels nothing but an incomprehensible Light; and through the Simple Nudity which enfolds all things, he finds himself and feels himself, to be that same light by which he sees, and nothing else.[13]

Extrovertive mysticism can happen quite spontaneously. One is walking along or sitting or standing quietly, and suddenly it happens. As Mr. Sasaki says it: Ztt! and it happens. But this is not the case with introvertive mysticism. Introvertive mystical experience is accomplished only with disciplined preparation and effort. By arduous effort the Yogis of India become proficient in turning off their thoughts and feelings, and entering samhadi. Christian mystics in Catholic monasteries have their own techniques. They usually call their techniques "prayers," but they are not prayers in the crude sense of asking God for something. They are more like the meditations of the Indian mystics. It does not come easily. It is not easy to stop thinking, seeing, hearing, feeling, remembering. It is not easy to empty the consciousness of all sensory-intellectual contents, thus few of us are mystics of this more arduous type.

Mysticism and Religion   It is generally assumed that mysticism is a form of religious experience, but some authorities think this may not be true. They argue that mysticism may be a nonreligious fact, and that its connection with religion is after the fact. In other words, an autonomous mystical experience may be so loaded with religious significance that it is appropriated and used to support and explain religion. It can be argued that when the mystical experience is stripped of all religious interpretations (such as those that identify it with Nirvana, or God, or the Absolute), what is left is simply the experience of undifferentiated unity. The world of things is transfigured so that unity shines through. This is an important

[13] "The Adornment of the Spiritual Marriage," trans. C. A. Wynachenck (New York: Dutton, 1916).

metaphysical fact, but it is not, perhaps, necessarily a religious fact. It becomes a prime religious fact only when the unity is interpreted as being God or some mode of the divine order. For our purpose here, however, it is probably enough simply to recognize that, at least, religion has taken mysticism unto itself, and that mysticism speaks relevantly to religion in a number of important ways. First, religion is concerned to repivot human life from self-centeredness to God-centeredness, and mysticism is a process in which the self falls away into fusion with an infinite and absolute One (often called God). Again, religion is concerned with the "eternal verities," and mysticism is an experience in which space and time are transcended in what Meister Eckhart calls "The Eternal Now." Again, as we have observed, religion is concerned to overcome basic human frustrations, and according to all mystics, the mystical experience is always, an experience of peace, blessedness, and joy. In such things, and many more, it seems obvious that mysticism relates naturally to religion, if not necessarily to it.

There is, however, a problem that should not be passed over without some examination, for there is a crucial point at which mysticism is not in perfect accord, especially with the religions of the Western world. In fact, to Judaism, Christianity, and Islam, mysticism at times almost approaches a heresy. This is so because mystics often insist that in the mystical experience they become one with God. This is acceptable to certain Asian religions where it is believed that in the end (in salvation) this is exactly what happens to men. They are merged with the beatitude of infinity. They enter Nirvana and become indistinguishable from Brahman. But among Jews, Christians, and Muslims there has always been an I-Thou relationship between man and God; a distance of difference between man and God; and indeed it is something of a scandal to think otherwise. The great Western religions have always proclaimed unequivocally that God is always and only God, and that men are his creatures. When Sasaki says that he must now recognize that he was "never created," he may be explaining something congenial to the Zen Buddhist religion, and of metaphysical importance, but it certainly smacks of heresy to Jew, Christian, and Muslim. There is a dualism in Western religion which is not comfortable with the mystical experience of absolute unity. St. Paul may say, "I live, yet not I but Christ liveth in me," but this is not the usual way that Christians think of themselves or of Paul. Not even in Heaven do men become God. In fact, to aspire to such grandeur was in some way the guilt of both Lucifer and Adam. The Jews say, "Hear, O Israel, the Lord our God is one."—and they mean it; and so do the Christians. And with equal obstinacy the Muslims declare: "There is but one God, Allah." To proclaim a unity of man and God is congenial to pantheism, where everything is somehow a projection of God, but only uneasily so to theism, where God is a person separate and alone. In the West, mysticism takes some additional explaining. The fact is that although Christian mysticism has always been acknowledged by Christians, the Christian mystic has usually lived under some suspicion of heresy.

Whether or not mysticism is a unique experience or simply another form of religious experience, it is crucially involved in the religious experience and demands consideration in any definition of religion.

Worship   There are only a few mystics in the world, even in all history. Few people ever really lose themselves completely in an ecstasy of union with the infinite ground of ultimate and mysterious being (with God), but there are many people who lose themselves at least a little bit in a similar experience. They worship.

> Far off the noises of the world retreat;
> The loud vociferations of the street
> Become an indistinguishable roar.
> So, as I enter here from day to day,
> And leave my burden at this minster gate,
> Kneeling in prayer, and not ashamed to pray,
> The tumult of the time disconsolate
> To inarticulate murmurs dies away,
> While the eternal ages watch and wait.
>
> "Divina Commedia"
> H. W. Longfellow

Many people turn aside from the hurry and confusion of every day and in a quiet moment, while ages wait, feel themselves as "I" to "Thou" with God. In this experience (as in the experience reported by the mystics) there is a fading of self-centeredness, but seldom (as in mysticism) is there a suspension of self-awareness. Jones is always Jones, and God is God. There is continued polarity: worshipper *and* divine object, I *and* Thou; there is no suspension of the ego. There is a feeling of community with God, but no loss of the feeling of multiplicity in life. The object/subject relationship remains. All things do not become one, although they may become intimately, even exquisitely related.

Early in this book we said that man was the religion-doing animal, and we examined why he does religion, and what he does when he does it, and we observed some of the practical benefits he receives in doing it. But in these last two chapters, we have been saying that religion is, for all this, something superbly more.

Even if, through some supertechnology, all of the practical values now available only through religion could be technologically produced for man, religion would yet be sought and treasured by those who had discovered its profounder dimensions. It would remain exciting and precious in the lives of those who waited on the Lord and mounted up with eagle wings, for those who found his footprint "just where one scarlet lily flamed,"[14] for those who took on love and charity and forgot themselves in fullness of living, and, perhaps most precious of all, for those who were still and knew God.

[14] Bliss Carmen, "Vestigia," verse 1, line 4.

Bibliography of
Selected Readings

CHAPTER ONE   ORIGINS OF RELIGION: PRIMITIVE

Campbell, Joseph. *The Masks of God: Primitive Mythology*. New York: Viking, 1959. On the nature and function of mythology and its significance for religion.

Campbell, Joseph. *The Hero with a Thousand Faces*. Princeton, N.J.: Princeton University Press, 1968; earlier publication, 1949. A comparative study of hero cults.

Codrington, R. H. *The Melanesians: Studies in Their Anthropology and Folk-Lore*. New York: Dover, 1972; first publication, 1891. A report on the preanimistic character of primitive religion.

Eliade, Mircea. *The Sacred and the Profane: The Nature of Religion*, trans. W. Trask. New York: Harcourt Brace Jovanovich, 1968. A well-known historian of religion explores religion as a manifestation of the sacred.

James, Edwin O. *Prehistoric Religion: A Study in Prehistoric Archaeology*. New York: Barnes & Noble, 1961. A picture of prehistoric religions by a renowned historian of religion.

Jensen, Adolf E. *Myth and Cult Among Primitive People*. Chicago: University of Chicago Press, 1963; earlier publication, 1951. An ethnological interpretation of primitive cultures.

Lessa, W. A., and Yogt, E. Z., eds. *Reader in Comparative Religion: An Anthropological Approach*, 3rd ed. New York: Harper & Row, 1972. Essays by ten social scientists on the origins of religion.

Norbeck, Edward. *Religion in Primitive Society*. New York: Harper & Row, 1961. An anthropological statement on the place of religion in primitive society.

Tylor, Edward B. *Religion in Primitive Culture*. New York: Harper & Row, 1958; first publication, 1871. A pioneer figure in the field of primitive religions identifies the origins of religion with animism.

CHAPTER TWO   OTHER ORIGINS

Bettis, Joseph Dabney, ed. *Phenomenology of Religion*. New York: Harper & Row, 1969. A collection of essays by modern thinkers who represent several ways of employing phenomenological methods in religion. See especially "An Introduction to Phenomenology," by the editor, and "What is Phenomenology," by Maurice Merleau-Ponty.

Durkheim, Émile. *The Elementary Forms of Religious Life,* trans. J. W. Swain. Atlantic Highlands, N.J.: Humanities, 1964; first publication, 1915. A pioneer student in the field of sociology identifies religion as a natural product of socialization. See especially chapter 7 and conclusions.

Feaver, J. Clayton, and Horosz, William, eds. *Religion in Philosophical and Cultural Perspective.* New York: Van Nostrand Reinhold, 1967. Especially Peter Kostenbaum's chapter "Religion in the Tradition of Phenomenology," a definition of phenomenology, and several examples of phenomenological method in religion.

Freud, Sigmund. *The Future of an Illusion.* Garden City, N.Y.: Doubleday, Anchor, 1961; first publication, 1927. Freud's insightful proposal that religion is an unhealthy neurosis, and God a surrogate father.

James, William. *Varieties of Religious Experience.* New York: Modern Library, 1961. The Gifford Lectures on Natural Religion, given in Edinburgh, 1901–1902. A pioneer study and classic in the psychology of religion.

Lang, Andrew. *The Making of Religion.* New York: AMS Press, 1968; first publication, 1898. Especially chapters IX and X, on the origin of the idea of God in primitive religions.

Otto, Rudolph. *The Idea of the Holy,* trans. J.W. Harvey. London: Oxford University Press, 1958; first publication, 1924. A classical statement of religion as the feeling of numinous reality: God, an inner experience from an outside source.

Schmidt, Wilhelm. *High Gods in North America.* Oxford, Eng.: Clarendon Press, 1933. The Upton Lectures in religion given at Manchester College, Oxford.

Schmidt, Wilhelm. *The Origin and Growth of Religion,* trans. H. J. Rose. London: Methuen, 1931. Argues that the earliest peoples believed in a supreme being in a monotheistic sense.

CHAPTER THREE   THE RELIGIOUS ANIMAL

Bernhardt, William H. *A Functional Philosophy of Religion.* Denver: Criterion Press, first publication, 1958. Copies available through the Iliff School of Theology, 2201 S. University Boulevard, Denver, Colorado, 80210. A functional definition of religion. See especially chapter 14.

Doniger, Simon, ed. *The Nature of Man in Theological and Psychological Perspective.* New York: Harper & Row, 1972; earlier publication, 1962. Essays by theologians and psychologists on the nature of man.

Du Noüy, Pierre Lecomte. *Human Destiny.* New York: Longmans, Green, 1947. A biologist sees evolution as now transferred from the physical realm to the spiritual realm.

Feifel, Herman, ed. *The Meaning of Death.* New York: McGraw-Hill, 1959. Essays by scientists, philosophers, and theologians discussing the problem of death.

Frazier, A. M. *Issues in Religion,* 2nd ed. New York: Van Nostrand Reinhold, 1975. See especially R. M. Rilke, "Chamberlain Brigge's Death," and F. Dostoevsky, "Underground Man."

Fromm, Erich. *Man for Himself.* New York: Fawcett World Library, 1973; first publication, 1947. A study of humanistic ethics which also contains a psychological analysis of modern man. See especially chapter III.

Fromm, Erich. *Psychoanalysis and Religion.* New Haven, Conn.: Yale University Press, 1950. On the nature and function of religion.

Kaufman, Walter. *Existentialism from Dostoevsky to Sartre.* Cleveland, O.: World, Meridian Books, 1965. Especially Albert Camus, "The Myth of Sisyphus," a beautiful and brief commentary on human emptiness and the moment of salvation.

Mead, George H. *Mind, Self and Society.* Chicago: University of Chicago Press, 1947; earlier publication, 1934. A classical statement on the nature of mind and self as emergents from social intercourse, by one of the most seminal thinkers of modern times.

Stace, Walter T. *Time and Eternity.* Princeton, N.J.: Princeton University Press, 1952. On "What Religion Is," pp. 3–8.

Tillich, Paul. *Theology of Culture.* New York: Oxford University Press, 1964. Especially chapter 1, identifying religion with the metaphor "depth"—religion is that which concerns man deeply, it is his ultimate concern.

Tillich, Paul. *The Courage To Be.* New Haven, Conn.: Yale University Press, 1962; earlier publication, 1952. A statement on the nonmanipulable aspects of religion and on the courage of religion—courage inspite-of, pp. 32–63.

Tremmel, William C. "The Converting Choice," *Journal for the Scientific Study of Religion.* Los Angeles: University of California Press, Vol. 10, No. 1, Spring 1971. On the nature of conversion.

Weiss, Paul. *Nature and Man.* New York: Holt, Rinehart and Winston, 1947. Man and his problems are one with the rest of nature.

Whitehead, Alfred N. *Religion in the Making.* New York: Macmillan, 1960; earlier publication, 1926. A fine statement by one of the finest minds of the twentieth century.

CHAPTER FOUR   METATECHNOLOGY AND
METAPSYCHOLOGY

Evans-Pritchard, E. E. *Witchcraft, Oracles and Magic Among the Azende.* Oxford, Eng.: Oxford University Press, 1968. A study based on three expeditions among the Azende people from 1926 to 1930. See especially part IV, on magic, sorcery and magicians, pp. 387–423.

Frazer, James G. *New Golden Bough,* ed. T. H. Gaster. New York: Macmillan, 1959. This is an abridgment of Frazer's extensive pioneering work, in which, among other things, he presented his theory of magic as the genesis of religion.

Hill, Douglas. *Magic and Superstition.* London: Hamlyn, 1968. A readable, extensively illustrated publication on magical practices and superstitions.

Lewis, C. S. *Miracles: A Preliminary Study.* New York: Macmillan, 1963, first publication, 1947. A persuasive statement in support of metatechnological (miraculous) intervention into the natural processes of human life.

Malinowski, Bronislaw. *Magic, Science and Religion and Other Essays.* Garden City, N.Y.: Doubleday, 1954; first publication, 1948. On the character and interrelationships of magic, technology, and religion in a primitive culture. See especially the title essay.

Mouss, Marcell. *A General Theory of Magic,* trans. R. Bain. London: Routledge & Kegan Paul, 1972; first publication in French, 1950.

Noss, John B. *Man's Religions,* 5th ed. New York: Macmillan, 1974; first publication, 1949. See especially the statement on magic in chapter one, "Primitive and Bygone Religions."

Roszak, Theodore. *The Making of a Counterculture.* Garden City, N.Y.: Doubleday, 1969. In the last chapter of his analysis and in his interpretation of the modern counterculture movement, Roszak presents an insightful apologetic for shamanism; the maker of magic does more than just perform metatechnological feats.

CHAPTER FIVE   THEOLOGY: EMPIRICAL AND
RATIONAL, WITNESSING AND STORY

Brown, Robert McAfee. "Story and Theology," *Philosophy of Religion and Theology, 1974,* ed. J. W. McClendon, Jr. Tallahassee, Fla.: Florida State University Press, 1974. On theology as autobiographical witnessing.

Castaneda, Carlos. *The Teachings of Don Juan: A Yaqui Way of Knowledge.* Berkeley, Calif.: University of California Press, 1968. How a

Yaqui Indian teacher, a spiritual master, works with a pupil to trans-
mit religious knowledge. Especially pp. 14–34.

Descartes, René. *Meditations on First Philosophy*, trans. Laurence J.
Lafleur. Indianapolis: Bobbs-Merrill, 1960; first publication in Latin,
1641. Meditation number three, on the existence of God, proved by
the innateness of the idea of perfect being in the mind of man. Meditation number five, on the existence of God, proved by a reformula-
tion of Anselm's ontological argument.

Frazier, A. M. *Issues in Religion*, 2nd ed. New York: Van Nostrand Reinhold, 1975. Chapter 12, "Anselm: The Ontological Argument,"
"Aquinas: The Five Ways," "Kant: The Moral Argument."

Hick, John, and McGill, Arthur, eds. *A Proof of God's Existence: Recent
Essays on the Ontological Argument*. New York: Macmillan, 1965.
Essays defending and criticizing the ontological argument.

Hick, John. *Faith and Knowledge*, 2nd ed. Ithaca, N.Y.: Cornell University Press; revised 1966. Some of the problems of religious knowledge.

Hume, David. *Dialogue Concerning Natural Religion*, ed. H. D. Aiken.
New York: Hafner, 1948. A brilliant critique of the proofs of God's
existence.

Miller, David I. *Gods and Games*. New York: Harper & Row, 1972.
Especially p. 183 on Campbell's function of mythology; and chapters 3 and 4 on the theology of play; pp. 99–108, on the origins of
religion; and pp. 80–91 on theology.

Otto, Max. *The Human Enterprise*. New York: Appleton-Century-Crofts,
1940. In chapter 11, Otto argues for the good human effects of not
believing in God; i.e., a Western personalistic God.

Ramsey, Ian T. *Religious Language*. New York: Macmillan, 1963; earlier
publication, 1957. An effort to show the use of contemporary language analysis in theology.

Wiesel, Elie. *Night*. New York: Avon, 1972; *Souls on Fire*. New York:
Random House, 1973; *Ani Maamin*. New York: Random House,
1974. In these three stories (and half a dozen others which are all
thinly-veiled autobiography), a Jew, whose baccalaureate was from
Auschwitz and Buchenwald, tells stories that are superb, and something more: they are theology, which, in agony, move from a God
of divine indifference to a God who, however hidden, suffers in and
with his creation.

CHAPTER SIX   *SALVATION THEOLOGY*

Brightman, Edgar S. *Philosophy of Religion*. Englewood Cliffs, N.J.: Prentice-Hall, 1940. Especially pp. 395–404 on arguments for and against immortality.

Epicurus. "Epicurus to Menoeceus," *Ethics*, ed. Oliver A. Johnson. New York: Holt, Rinehart and Winston, 1974. On death without fear.

Head, Joseph, and Cranston, S. L., eds. *Reincarnation in World Thought*. New York: Julian Press, 1967. An extensive survey of reincarnation in the thought and practices of mankind.

Lamont, Corliss. *The Illusion of Immortality*, 4th ed. New York: G. P. Ungar, 1965; earlier publication, 1935.

Langley, Noel. *Edgar Cayce on Reincarnation*, ed. Hugh L. Cayce, New York: Paperback Library, 1967. Accounts of people who have lived more than once, from the files of a noted American clairvoyant.

Larson, Martin A. *The Religion of the Occident*. Paterson, N.J.: Littlefield, Adams, 1961. Chapter 1, on the original savior God—Osiris.

Pope, Marvin H. *Job*. Garden City, N.Y.: Doubleday, 1973; earlier publication, 1965. A scholarly examination of the thesis that Job is a theodicy of "reverent agnosticism"; see especially the Introduction, pp. XV-LXXXV.

Stendahl, Krister, ed. *Immortality and Resurrection*. New York: Macmillan, 1965. Especially Oscar Cullmann's "Immortality of the Soul and Resurrection of the Body," the Ingersoll Lectures of 1955, comparing Semitic reincarnation with Greek immortality.

Wood, Ernest E. *Patanjali, Practical Yoga Ancient and Modern*. Hollywood, Calif.: Wilshire Books, 1973; earlier publication, 1948. A new translation of Patanjali's yoga aphorisms.

CHAPTER SEVEN   *REVELATION AND SCRIPTURE*

Baillie, John. *The Idea of Revelation in Recent Thought*. New York: Columbia University Press, 1956. Lectures on contemporary Protestant views of revelation.

Bultmann, Rudolph. *Jesus Christ and Mythology*. New York: Scribner, 1958. In this little book a major biblical scholar explains what he means by "mythology" and "demythologizing."

Carnell, Edward J. *The Case for Orthodox Theology*. Philadelphia: Westminster Press, 1959. Especially pp. 97–102 and 110–111, a discussion of biblical revelation from a conservative Christian perspective.

Champion, Selwyn, C., and Short, Dorothy, eds. *Readings from World Religions*. Greenwich, Conn.: Fawcett, 1963; first publication, 1951. Selections from the scriptures of twelve consummate religions.

Fosdick, Harry E. *The Modern Use of the Bible*. New York: Macmillan, 1925. A classic statement of the nature and use of the Bible as seen in Liberal/Modernist Protestantism.

Frost, S. E., Jr., ed., *The Sacred Writings of the World's Great Religions*. New York: McGraw-Hill, 1972. Selections from the sacred writings of thirteen living religions.

Selby, Donald J., and West, James King. *Introduction to the Bible*. New York: Macmillan, 1971. A solid general introduction to the Old and New Testament.

CHAPTER EIGHT   RITUAL

Campbell, Joseph. *The Masks of God: Occidental Mythology*. New York: Viking, 1964. Especially pp. 518–23, on the fourfold function of myth.

Cutler, Donald R., ed. *The Religious Situation in 1968*. Boston: Beacon Press, 1968. Chapter 8, "Civil Religion in America," by R. Bellah; chapter 16, "Secularization and the Sacred," by Huston Smith; chapter 17, "The Secularization of the Sacred," by Joseph Campbell; chapter 19, essays on ritual by K. Z. Lorenz, Julian Huxley, Erik H. Erikson, Edward Shils, William F. Lynch.

Eliade, Mircea. *Rites and Symbols of Initiation*, trans. W. R. Trask. New York: Harper & Row, Torchbooks, 1965; earlier publication, 1958. A survey of the rites of passage in religions, both primitive and consummate.

Eliade, Mircea. *Myth and Reality*, trans. W. R. Trask. New York: Harper & Row, Torchbooks, 1963. Especially chapter 1, "Structure of Myths."

Hamilton, Edith. *Mythology*. New York: New American Library, A Mentor Book, 1971. A compact, readable account of classical mythology.

Lessa, William A., and Yogt, E. Z., eds. *Reader in Comparative Religion: An Anthropological Approach*, 3rd ed. New York: Harper & Row, 1972. Especially Section III, "Myth and Ritual."

Sebeok, Thomas, ed. *Myth: A Symposium*. Bloomington, Ind.: University of Indiana Press, 1965; first publication, 1955. Essays by nine modern scholars.

Watts, Alan. *Myth and Ritual in Christianity*. Boston: Beacon Press, 1968; earlier publication, 1953. A description of the Christian year as seen in its symbolic/ritual forms.

CHAPTER NINE   MORALITY

Buber, Martin. *I and Thou*, trans. R. G. Smith. New York: Scribner, 1965; first publication, 1936. The relationship of God to man, man to God, and man to man must be one not of person to thing, but of person to person, according to this great Jewish, Hasidic-inclined, existentialist philosopher. See especially pp. 8, 75–83.

Fletcher, Joseph. *Situation Ethics*. Philadelphia: Westminster Press, 1956. A new way to conceive and practice religious ethics.

Heschel, Abraham J. *God in Search of Man*. New York: Meridian Books, 1961. A Jewish philosophy on three ways to God: the world, the Bible, and sacred deeds (*mitzvat*).

Hospers, Joseph. *Human Conduct: Problems of Ethics*. New York: Harcourt Brace Jovanovich, 1972; earlier publication, 1961. Especially chapter 6, "Kant's Ethics of Duty," pp. 264–296.

James, William. *Essays in Pragmatism*. New York: Hafner, 1951. Especially the essays on "The Moral Philosopher and the Moral Life," and "The Will to Believe."

Marty, Martin E., and Peerman, Dean G., eds. *New Theology No. 3*. New York: Macmillan, 1966. Especially James M. Gustafson's article "Context Versus Principles: A Misplaced Debate in Christian Ethics," an examination of the modern debate in Christian ethics; a debate which, on the one hand, rests ethical decisions in the existential ethical situation, and, on the other hand, in the objective moral principles given in the tradition.

Ramsey, Paul. *Nine Modern Moralists*. Englewood Cliffs, N.J.: Prentice-Hall, 1962. Especially chapter 5, "Reinhold Niebuhr: Christian Love and Natural Law."

CHAPTER TEN   GETTING IT IN SHAPE

Altizer, Thomas, and Hamilton, William. *Radical Theology and the Death of God*. Indianapolis: Bobbs-Merrill, 1966. Independent but concurring statements by two Christian theologians on the need for a new kind of theology.

Bedell, George, et al. *Religion in America*. New York: Macmillan, 1975. An excellent examination of religion in America, with pertinent documents included.

Cox, Harvey. *The Secular City*. New York: Macmillan, 1965. This author celebrates the rise of urban civilization and the collapse of traditional religion, exulting in a new freedom of secularization.

Ellwood, Robert S., Jr. *Religions and Spiritual Groups in Modern America*.

Englewood Cliffs, N.J.: Prentice-Hall, 1972. Brief, readable statements on the many new religious and spiritual groups in America.

Herberg, Will. *Protestant Catholic Jew.* Garden City, N.Y.: Doubleday, Anchor, 1960. A survey of the place of religious immigrants in American culture.

King, Martin Luther, Jr. "Letter from Birmingham Jail—April 16, 1963," *Why We Can't Wait.* New York: Harper & Row, 1974. Rev. Martin Luther King's letter of protest to his fellow clergyman of the South.

Kraemer, Hendrik. *World Culture and World Religions: The Coming Dialogue.* Philadelphia: Westminster Press, 1960. The impact of Eastern and Western religions upon each other.

Littell, Franklin H. *From State Church to Pluralism.* Garden City, N.Y.: Doubleday, Anchor, 1962. An examination of the movement of religion in America from state establishment to voluntaristic pluralism.

Needleman, Jacob. *The New Religions.* New York: Pocketbook, 1972; earlier publication, Garden City, N.Y.: Doubleday, 1970.

Newman, Joseph, ed. *The Religious Reawakening in America.* Washington, D.C.: U.S. News and World Reports, 1972. A survey of attitudes and actions in contemporary American religious life.

Raschke, Carl. "New Gnosticism?" *Philosophy of Religion and Theology, 1973,* ed. David Griffin. Tallahassee, Fla.: American Academy of Religion, 1973. Some critical comments concerning recent Asian invasions.

Rubenstein, Richard. *After Auschwitz.* Indianapolis: Bobbs-Merrill, 1966. A Radical/Death of God theologian of the Jewish Tradition.

CHAPTER ELEVEN   GOD

Bertocci, Peter. *Introduction to the Philosophy of Religion.* New York: Prentice-Hall, 1951. A personalistic statement of God and religion. See especially chapter 18, "How Then Shall We Think of God?"

Brightman, Edgar Sheffield. *The Problem of God.* New York: Abingdon, 1930. A statement about God being both transcendent to the world and immanent in it; God who is not a supremely peaceful being, but one who must struggle with a "given" element in his own nature.

Hartshorne, Charles. *The Divine Reality.* New Haven, Conn.: Yale University Press, 1964; first published, 1948. God conceived of as immanent, temporal, changing, and related to the world intimately. See especially pp. 22–34.

Hartshorne, Charles, and Reese, William L. *Philosophers Speak of God.* Chicago: University of Chicago Press, 1963; earlier publication, 1953. A monumental work on the idea of God. See especially the

"Introduction," pp. 1–25. See also the sections on E. Brightman, M. Buber, M. Iqubal, W. James, A. Schweitzer, S. Radhakrishna, A. Watts, A. Whitehead, H. Wieman.

James, William. *Essays on Faith and Morals*. New York: Longmans, Green, 1943. James talks about God from a pragmatist's point of view, pp. 82–84, 103–141.

James, William. *A Pluralistic Universe*. New York: Longmans, Green, 1909. Pages 181, 268–319.

Kaufmann, Walter. *God, Ambiguity, and Religion*. New York: Harper & Row, 1958. God's existence cannot be proved. The idea of God is essentially ambiguous. Religion is a matter of loyalty and tradition.

Maringer, J. *The Gods of Prehistoric Man*, trans. M. Ilford, New York: Knopf, 1960; earlier publication, 1952. An account of what is known of the Gods of preliterate man.

Plantinga, Alvin, ed. *The Ontological Argument*. Garden City, N.Y.: Doubleday, Anchor, 1965. An examination of Anselm's argument by philosophers from the eleventh to the twentieth centuries.

Sartre, Jean-Paul. *Existentialism and Humanism*, trans. P. Mairet. London: Methuen, 1957; first publication, 1948. See especially comments on Atheistic Humanism.

Teilhard de Chardin, Pierre. *The Phenomenon of Man*, trans. B. Wall. New York: Harper & Row, 1965; first publication in French, *Le Phenomene Humain*, 1955. An important work which identifies the emergence of man in evolutionary process, and God, or God action, as the complexification, direction, and Omega Point of the evolutionary process.

Whitehead, Alfred N. *Adventure of Ideas*. New York: Macmillan, 1933. Especially pp. 356–357.

Whitehead, Alfred N. *Process and Reality*. New York: Macmillan, 1929. Especially pp. 517–533.

Whitehead, Alfred N. *Science and the Modern World*. New York: Free Press, 1967; first publication, 1929. Especially chapter XI, "God," and chapter XII, "Religions and Science."

Wieman, Henry Nelson. *The Source of Human Good*. Carbondale, Ill.: Southern Illinois University Press, 1964; earlier publication, 1946. Wieman speaks of the processes of creation and the production of good from living events. This process, Wieman is willing to call, God: God is creative event.

CHAPTER TWELVE   *GOD COMING OF AGE*
IN THE WEST

CHAPTER THIRTEEN   *GOD COMING OF AGE*
IN THE EAST

Burtt, Edwin A. *Man Seeks the Divine.* New York: Harper & Row, 1957. An insightful examination of the religions of the world.

Campbell, Joseph. *The Masks of God: Oriental Mythology.* New York: Viking, 1962. Development of mythology in India, in China, and in Japan. The myth of "Eternal Return" vs. the myth of "Cosmic Restoration."

Campbell, Joseph. *The Masks of God: Occidental Mythology.* New York: Viking, 1964. Especially the "Conclusion" of the volume on the four functions of mythology.

Comstock, W. Richard, ed. *Religion and Man: An Introduction.* New York: Harper & Row, 1971. A substantial survey of the religions of the world by six scholars: Robert Baird, Alfred Bloom, Janet K. and Thomas F. O'Dea, Charles C. Adams and W. R. Comstock.

Loew, Cornelius. *Myth, Sacred History and Philosophy.* New York: Harcourt Brace Jovanovich, 1967. A survey of the pre-Christian religions of the West.

Martin, Malachi. *The Encounter.* New York: Dell, A Delta Book, 1971. See especially Book I, pp. 3–166, "The Priceless Moments." A succinct statement of the kairotic episodes in Judaism, Christianity, and Islam.

Noss, John B. *Man's Religions,* 5th ed. New York: Macmillan, 1974. For details on world religions both East and West.

The World's Great Religions. New York: Time, 1957. The collection of articles appearing in *Life Magazine* in 1955: February 7, Hinduism; March 7, Buddhism; April 4, Chinese Faiths; May 9, Islam; June 3, Judaism; December 26, Christianity.

CHAPTER FOURTEEN   *THE DEVIL'S DUE*

Brother Francesco Maria Guazzo, *Compendium Maleficarum,* trans. E. A. Ashwin. New York: Barnes & Noble, 1970. A facsimile reprint of a 1608 document showing "the iniquitous and execrable operations of witches against the human race, and the divine remedies by which they are frustrated." Edited with notes by The Reverend Montague Summers.

Douglas, Mary, ed. *Witchcraft Confessions and Accusations.* London:

Tavistock, 1970. The article by Norman Cohn entitled "The Myth of Satan and His Human Servants"; an important statement on the origins of the Devil concept, and on the "fantasy of witchcraft."

Franklyn, Julian. *Death by Enchantment*. London: Hamish Hamilton, 1971. A balanced, readable statement of the phenomenon of witchcraft.

Guazzo. *See* Brother Francesco Maria Guazzo.

Kelly, Henry Ansaga. *The Devil, Demonology and Witchcraft*. Garden City, N.Y.: Doubleday, 1968. Chapters 1 and 2 on the development of the concept of the Devil in Western traditions; chapter 4 on demonic possession and exorcism.

Kluger, Rivkah Scharf. *Satan in the Old Testament*, trans. Hildegaard Nagel. Evanston, Ill.: Northwestern University Press, 1967. A scholarly and penetrating examination of the idea of Satan, first published in German in 1948.

Littell, Franklin H. *The Crucifixion of the Jews*. New York: Harper & Row, 1975. How can Christendom claim credibility in the face of the deafening silence of church leaders before the brutality of the Holocaust?

Milton, John. "Paradise Lost". The presentation of this great poem in volume 4 of the Harvard Classics is especially recommended because it introduces each of the 12 books of the poem with a summary of the action taking place in that book.

Murray, Margaret Alice. "Witchcraft." *Encyclopaedia Britannica*, fourteenth edition. A statement on the nature of witchcraft, including Murray's theory on the origins of witchcraft.

Rudwin, Maximilian. *The Devil in Legend and Literature*. New York: AMS Press, 1970. Chapter 1 on the legend of Lucifer.

CHAPTER FIFTEEN　　RELIGION: EXOTERIC EXPERIENCE

Lewis, C. S. *The Four Loves*. New York: Harcourt Brace Jovanovich, 1960. A beautifully written and insightful study of love: as affection, friendship, eros, and charity/agape.

Lewis, I. M. *Ecstatic Religion*. Harmondsworth, Middlesex, Eng.: Penguin, 1971. An examination of the emotional states of religious people.

Marty, Martin E., and Peerman, Dean G., eds. *New Theology No. 3*. New York: Macmillan, 1966. Tom F. Driver's article on the "Sexuality of Jesus", an examination of the Christian tradition of disassociating Jesus from sexuality.

Streng, Frederick. *Understanding Religious Man*. Belmont, Calif.: Dickenson, 1969. See especially religion and art forms, pp. 84–91.

Suzuki, D. T. "Zen Buddhism," *Selected Writings of D. T. Suzuki*, ed. W. Barrett. Garden City, N.Y.: Doubleday, 1956. Chapter 10, on painting, swordsmanship, and the tea ceremony.

van der Leeuw, G. *Sacred and Profane Beauty: The Holy in Art*, trans. D. E. Green. New York: Holt, Rinehart and Winston, 1963; first publication 1932. The religious significance of dance, drama, architecture, pictorial arts, music; art as a sacred act.

Wach, Joacheim. *The Comparative Study of Religion*. New York: Columbia University Press, 1958. See especially chapters ii, iii, and iv, on the nature of religious experience.

CHAPTER SIXTEEN   RELIGION: ESOTERIC EXPERIENCE

Bassuk, Daniel. *The Secularization of Mysticism: An Analysis and Critique of the Mystical in Rufus Jones and Martin Buber*. Doctoral dissertation, Drew University, 1974; available from the University of Michigan Microfilms, No. 74–27, 897.

Buttrick, George A. *So We Believe, So We Pray*. Nashville, Tenn.: Abingdon, 1951. A study of prayer.

Huxley, Aldous. *The Perennial Philosophy*. New York: Harper & Row, 1945. A statement of "the metaphysics that recognizes a divine reality substantial to the world."

Johnson, William, S.J., *The Still Point: Reflections on Zen and Christian Mysticism*. New York: Fordham University Press, 1970. Especially chapter 8, "Defining Mysticism."

Jones, Rufus. *Pathways to the Reality of God*. New York: Macmillan, 1931. A Quaker mystic discusses the many ways that men have come to God.

Koestler, Arthur. *The Invisible Writing*. New York: Macmillan, 1970; earlier publication, 1954. The autobiography of a modern contemporary mystic.

Otto, Rudolf. *Mysticism East and West*, trans. B. Bracey. New York: Collier Books, 1962; earlier publication, 1932. A comparative analysis of the nature of mysticism East and West.

Stace, Walter T. *Mysticism and Philosophy*. Philadelphia: Lippincott, 1960. Especially the section on mysticism.

Stace, Walter T. *Teachings of the Mystics*. New York: Mentor, 1960. Especially chapter 1, "What Is Mysticism? "

Watts, Alan W. *Behold the Spirit: A Study in the Necessity of Mystical*

Religion. New York: Random House, 1972. Watts argues that the dimension of feeling, so prevalent in Eastern theology, must be included in Western theology, which is overly intellectual and dualistic, pp. 132–173.

Watts, Alan W. *Psychotherapy East and West.* New York: Pantheon Books, 1961. Watts study shows how Eastern philosophers long ago faced the problem of man's existence in a hostile world; an understanding yet to be achieved in the West.

WRITINGS OF SEVERAL MYSTICS

The Complete Works of St. Teresa, ed. and trans. E. Allison Peers. New York: Sheed & Ward, 1946. Spanish mystic, 1515–1582.

The Essential Plotinus, trans. Elmer O'Brien, S.J. New York: Mentor, 1964. The writings of a great mystic of antiquity.

Meister Eckhart, A Modern Translation, trans. Raymond Bernard Blakney. New York: Harper & Row, 1957. German mystic, 1260–1328.

San Juan la Cruz, trans. Bernard Gicovate. New York: Twayne, 1971. St. John of the Cross, 1542–1591.

Zohar, The Book of Splendor, ed. Gershom G. Scholem. New York: Schocken, 1949. Basic readings from the Kabbalah, a book of Jewish mysticism.

Index